W9-AXR-838

Becoming a Visible Man

Becoming a Visible Man

Jamison Green

Vanderbilt University Press
NASHVILLE

Library of Congress Cataloging-in-Publication
Data

Green, Jamison, 1948–
Becoming a visible man / Jamison Green.-1st ed.
p. cm.
Includes bibliographical references and index.
ISBN: 0-8265-1456-1 (cloth)
ISBN 13: 978-0-8265-1457-8 (pbk.)
    1. Green, Jamison, 1948–   2. Transsexuals-United States-
Biography. 3. Sex roles-United States. 4. Gender identity-
United States. I. Title.
HQ77.8.G35G74 2004
306.76'8'092-dc22

2004001006

This book is dedicated to Francis Michael Thomas Graham (1944–2000), King of Cups and Gypsies, Fast Frankie from Philly, my pal who always believed in me. It is made in memory of Alice K. and W. Ray Green, two strangers who took me in and gave me life after the fact, with more integrity than many biological parents; much of my success is owed to them. This book is also for my wife, Heidi, my true companion, and for my dear children. May the lives of all children be safe and rewarding; and may they have the opportunity to know and be who they are.

Contents

Foreword

I first met Jamison Green in 1990 while I was doing research for my second book, *FTM: Female-to-Male Transsexuals in Society*. James had only been living as a man for a few years at that time. Lou Sullivan was still alive and had not yet asked James to step into his shoes at the helm of what was later to become FTM International. Even then, James was an articulate and compelling ambassador and educator for trans people. Over the intervening years, our friendship has grown and it has been my pleasure to observe as James has matured into an international leader in the field of advocacy for the human rights of trans people. As I have watched, I have come to admire the incredibly valuable and tireless work that Jamison has done on behalf of transmen in the U.S. and internationally. He is without peer in this regard.

One of the special skills that James has honed over the years is his ability to reach out and to connect with people in all walks of life. From students to CEOs to factory workers, from medical professionals to government officials, James has been uniquely able to tap into the concerns that create barriers to understanding gender and sex diversity. Because of misinformation and stereotyping, it is all too easy to turn trans people into cardboard cutouts, to see trans people as alien. When others are not real, it is a simple, short step to hostility, fear, anger, and abuse. However, when we can bridge that gap, when stereotypes and cardboard cutouts give way to real people, fear and anger are more likely to become understanding and friendship. James inspires confidence and touches people with his compassion. In his myriad speeches, publications, and media appearances James's ability to communicate effectively has enabled him to render trans people real and understandable for all who have had the privilege to be exposed to him.

Becoming a Visible Man is a continuation of this work. In this book, James brings to bear his special talent for striking just the right balance of stories about his own personal struggles to grow into his manhood and the placement of those challenges within larger social and political contexts. He gently brings the reader into his world, allowing and inviting the reader to see how the struggles that he has confronted as a transman are at their core *human* struggles which we all share, trans and non-trans alike. Throughout the book, James skillfully weaves back and forth in a comfortable and subtle rhythm. He entices the reader to identify with him, using his personal stories to build empathy and connection, carefully stretching the reader's limits to extend that empathy to a much larger constituency than simply himself. In so doing he erodes some of the foundations of fear of difference upon which prejudices are built.

This is both a profoundly personal and a powerfully political book, and *Becoming a Visible Man* is a book that you can give to anyone to read. It's an easy read; one is drawn into the stories. One does not feel harangued by the politics; it feels more like gentle persuasion. This is a book that brings trans experience to life and brings it home without sacrificing advocacy and analysis. Yet it is a book that remains accessible to anyone who cares to know more about what it feels like to be trans. Jamison Green has once again seen a need and stepped forward to offer himself up to the task. We were in need of a vehicle to bring the reality of trans lives to the hearts and minds of a larger swath of the public. *Becoming a Visible Man* will do just that.

Aaron H. Devor, Ph.D.
Professor of Sociology
University of Victoria

Acknowledgments

Acknowledgments are due to all the transsexual men and women who have provided shelter in my travels around the world, and encouraged me along the way—they are many strong, amazing people with rich stories of their own, especially Aaron, Adam, Alejandro, Alex, Alison, Andrew, Andy, Armand, Ben, Blake, Brynn, Camille, Cliff, Chris, Dan, Daniel, David, Denis, Dion, Dylan, Ernie, Francis, Garuth, George, Gitte, Gwen, Hap, Jack, Jason, Jay, Jed, Jeremiah, Jesper, Joel, John, Jordy, Jude, Julie, Kaspar, Lyle, Masae, Matt, Michael C., Michael H., Nick, Patrick, Rikki, Riley, Sam, Sara, Sarah, Sean, Sharon, Sky, Stafford, Stephen, Taylor, Thalia, Thomas, and Tony.

I want also to acknowledge the partners of transpeople, particularly these present or former partners of transmen: Aimee, Bianca, Courtney, Danielle, Diane, Francine, Greg, Hope, James, Jane, Jeanette, Jim, Katherine, Leigh, Lydia, Lynn, Mary, Meryl, Michael, Michiko, Petra, Rebecca, Sarah, Sheila, Stacey, Stella, Stephanie, Sue, Tova, and Vera, for their ability to love beyond conventional boundaries.

Thanks, also, to these non-trans friends and colleagues who have been especially supportive: my brother Eric and his family, Mariette Pathy Allen, Mary Boenke, Sandra Cole, Bestor Cram, Chris Daley, Milton Diamond, Lin Fraser, Karl Grimm, John Gunty, Felicity Haynes, Fran Jackler, Juli Johnson, Gordene MacKenzie, Andy Martin, Jill Randall, Candace Schermerhorn, Bruce Silverman, Rosa Von Praunheim, and Xiao-Yen Wang.

Special acknowledgment goes to my friends Marcus Arana, Simon Aronoff, Kate Bornstein, Larry Brinkin, Kylar Broadus, Loren Cameron,

Cheryl Chase, Jason Cromwell, Paisley Currah, Steve Dain, Dallas Denny, Booh Edouardo, Susan Falkenrath, Leslie Feinberg, Phyllis Frye, Sheryl Harris, David Harrison, Rachel Hollowgrass, Armand Hotimsky, Jaron Kanegson, Jennifer Levi, Nancy Nangeroni, Shannon Minter, Lisa Mottet, Kit Rachlin, Susan Stryker, Stephan Thorne, Max Valerio, Stephen Whittle, Riki Anne Wilchins, and Jessica Xavier, whose conversations and feedback have helped to shape my educational speaking, writing, and policy work. I extend gratitude and deep appreciation to P. B. Austin, Jeffrey Dickemann, and Marcy Sheiner for editorial consultation, and to Aaron H. Devor for contributing his foreword. Special thanks to Susan Stryker and C. L. Cole for referring me to my editor, Michael Ames, and to Michael himself.

———

Excerpts from the *FTM Newsletter* in Chapter 3 are reprinted by permission of FTM International, Inc. Portions of Chapter 4 appeared in the essay "Getting Real about FTM Surgery" in *Chrysalis: The Journal of Transgressive Gender Identities*, vol. 2, no. 2 (1995), 27–32; used by permission. Portions of Chapter 5 first appeared in the essay "On Being a Trans-Parent" in *TNT: Transsexual News Telegraph*, Issue 9, Autumn 2000. Portions of Chapter 6 first appeared in the essay "In the Body of a Man" in *Male Lust: Pleasure, Power, and Transformation*, ed. K. Kay, J. Nagle, and B. Gould, New York: The Haworth Press (2000). Portions of Chapter 7 first appeared in the essay "Look! No, Don't! The Visibility Dilemma for Transsexual Men" in *Reclaiming Genders: Transsexual Grammars at the Fin de Siècle*, ed. K. More and S. Whittle, London: Cassell (1999), and "The Art and Nature of Gender" in *Unseen Genders: Beyond the Binaries*, ed. F. Haynes and T. McKenna, New York: Peter Lang (2001). Earlier versions of these last two essays appeared in *Transgender Tapestry*, the magazine of the International Foundation for Gender Education. Reprinted portions are used with permission.

Becoming a Visible Man

1
How Do You Know?

"You all know what sex you are, right?" That's how I like to start. To most students I look like a professor, a psychologist, or a businessman. I am short, athletically built, with a full, trimmed beard, a balding head, and a deep voice. I seek out the students' eyes, as many as will meet my gaze. They are a mélange of ethnic backgrounds, ages, and life experiences, a generation or two different from the much more homogeneous group with whom I attended college in the late 1960s, and I think how much richer education can be today with so many diverse viewpoints close at hand. That is, provided we are not afraid to listen and give credence to different voices.

Most of the students look blankly at their papers or at the empty chalkboard behind me, but a few stare quizzically at me. Some look at me and look away. Are they afraid? Am I fearful of their judgment, or of their misunderstanding? Can I get through their preconceptions, their resistance, and their various cultural positions that I have no time to explore? I am not their instructor; I'm merely a guest lecturer the instructor wants them to meet. I only have an hour or so with them, and—like everything else—mine is a topic that can be explored in so many ways. I can only skim the surface with them. I can only hope to awaken them, to alert them to the possibilities.

"Come on," I encourage them. "You all know what sex you are, right?"

A few students nod in affirmation.

"So, how do you know? Without looking down . . . no cheating, now. . . . How do you know what sex you are?"

Now some of them start to laugh. "Your mother tells you," someone suggests.

"And you believed her?" I ask, smiling. "Seriously, how do you know?"

"By your chromosomes?" someone asks.

"Okay, I don't mean to embarrass anyone, so don't volunteer information you are not comfortable sharing, but how many people in this room have had their chromosomes checked?" I inquire. In over ten years of lectures like this, speaking to several thousand people, I've encountered only three individuals who confessed to having had their chromosomes checked, all for development-related anomalies. This time not one hand is raised. "Right," I explain. "It's rare that any of us knows what our sex chromosomes actually are. Did you know that 1 in 20,000 men have two X-chromosomes, rather than one X- and one Y-chromosome? They don't find this out until their female partner can't get pregnant and doctors eliminate her infertility as the reason. Sure, there are plenty of reasons for a man to be sterile, but one possibility is that he has two X-chromosomes. One in 20,000 men is a 46-chromosome, XX male; ten percent of those have no Y-chromosome material. That's a pretty high number for something we are led to believe is impossible. That statistic is from Chapter 41 in the 13th edition of *Smith's General Urology*, a standard urology textbook. And what does that tell us about the Y-chromosome? Not that you need a Y to be male, but that you may need a Y to make viable sperm. Maybe! Because there are two species of small rodent-type mammals, called mole voles, in which there is no Y chromosome, yet they are still reproducing both males and females, still procreating just as other mammals [Graves, 2001]. So if you can be a man with two X-chromosomes, and at least 1 in 20,000 men is, what makes you a man?" Some students, particularly males, are scowling now, confused, possibly getting angry. "That's right: it's all more complicated than we've been led to believe."

"We can identify the sex chromosomes in a developing fetus, but geneticists will tell you we have no idea what genes are firing. We especially don't know what genes are firing during embryogenesis, when the embryo is formed. Our science so far understands certain clusters of gene firing, like those that control the development of limbs or cause the webbing between the fingers to go away, but we do not understand the sequence of gene firings necessary to create an unambiguous male or female result, regardless of what the sex chromosomes are. The fact is, both the XX and XY karyotypes have bi-potential; that is, either karyotype can produce a male or a female result depending on which genes fire. There are gene expressions in each pair that can go down what we might call a male pathway or a female pathway. Those gene expressions, which trigger myriad events in the future, and which combine with myriad other expression events to form combinations we cannot anticipate, are the root of what we don't yet understand about the generalizations we've labeled 'female' and 'male.'

"According to the Intersex Society of North America, 1 in 100 people have bodies that differ from standard male or female. That means that one out of one hundred bodies has some quality that doctors would specify as an abnormality of sexual differentiation. Roughly 1 in 1,000 births involves what's called 'ambiguous genitalia,' in which the doctor can't tell by looking whether the infant is a boy or a girl. One in 1,000 births! That's a pretty high number. And what do you suppose they do in such a situation? Until recently, the standard has been that the doctors will decide what sex to assign the child, based on what kind of genital reconstruction surgery would be easiest or most effective from the doctor's point of view. But now this policy is hotly debated. Do you think they get it right every time? Do you think just because your genitals are a certain shape that this tells you what sex you are?" Horrified looks cross some students' faces. "So how do you know what sex you are?"

"By how you feel?" someone usually suggests. It seems to be the only avenue I've left open to them.

"Certainly that's a big part of it. Most people have feelings that correspond to the type of body they have. We sometimes think of feelings as something having to do with feeling attracted to another person, but certainly we all have feelings about ourselves, too. We have feelings about how we look, and how our personalities and interests correspond with those of other people with whom we identify. Now, what we're talking about today is not sexual orientation. I'm not talking about to whom you are attracted or what kind of sexual role you like to play. I'm talking about your relationship to your own body.

"Most people do feel connected to the type of body they have; that is, generally, the female type or the male type. And people may be attracted to people who have opposite-type bodies, or people who have similar-type bodies, or maybe they're not attracted to body types at all, but to individual people regardless of their bodies, but when we start connecting only feelings about bodies to sexual response and bringing in very complicated social ideas about sexual behavior it's easy to become confused about which idea or feeling or belief leads to what other specific idea, feeling or behavior. So let's not complicate matters just yet with too much talk about sexual attraction and relationship entanglements, though we certainly need to acknowledge that these are important aspects of our social lives that are strongly influenced by our relationship to our own body. What I want to focus on right now is the relationship one has with one's own sense of self, in their body, and the individual's sense of how that body fits or relates in the world. It can help us to understand this if we talk not just about sex, but about gender, too. Sex and gender are not the same things. Who can tell me the difference between sex and gender?"

The students are all watching me closely now, and several volunteer guesses; sometimes someone comes very close to the response I'm seeking. Still, it's likely that I'll need to explain: "Sex is a system of classification that divides body types based on presumed reproductive capacity as determined typically by visual examination of the external genitalia. There's a second meaning of the word 'sex,' which is that sex is also an activity we can engage in, and that activity has complex social meanings itself. We sometimes use the word 'love' as a euphemism for this second meaning of the word sex—having sex and making love. That second meaning leads us right back into sexual orientation, so for now we're going to discuss sex as just that system of classification of body types.

"The language we use to discuss sex as biology is derived from the study of plants. Our science about human sexuality is still very young. Plant biology? People have been studying plants for thousands of years, and we think we have them down pretty well. But we don't understand much about human sexuality. We've only been studying it seriously for a little over a century. It's not as simple as Xs and Ys or in-ies and out-ies. Science cannot tell us exactly what events must occur in the development of a human embryo that will give a completely male or completely female result. Remember, we don't know, in full scientific detail, what constitutes human maleness or femaleness. We're not plants that can be classified by the color of our petals or the shape of our leaves. We're much more complex than the color of our skin and hair or the shape of our genitals. We have social characteristics, too, like gender and sexual orientation, and maybe more characteristics that we don't yet know about. If we look closely enough at people we can see that none of these things—sex, gender, or sexual orientation—is the same, nor are they necessarily causal factors in relationship to each other, though they are certainly intertwined. But for now, to recap, sex is a system of classification of bodies that we call 'male' and 'female.'

"So, what's gender? Gender is another system of classification that describes characteristics and behaviors that we ascribe to bodies, and we call those characteristics and behaviors 'masculine' or 'feminine.' For example, we perceive a high-pitched voice as feminine, and a low-pitched voice as masculine; or we think of fine-motor skills—the ability to do small, dexterous work with the fingers—as feminine, and brute strength as masculine. And, as individuals, we can both express and perceive these qualities, these characteristics or behaviors, so it's an interactive system, this thing called gender. You may see a very beautiful woman, with long hair and a gorgeous body, and think of her as very feminine, but when all of a sudden she lifts up a park bench and says, 'not another step closer, or I'll shove this down your throat' in a deep, menacing growl, you may realize there's more to her than meets the eye. So if you had that experience, what would you think?"

"She's really a man," someone will suggest. After all, they may know I'm there to discuss transsexualism. They want me to get to the juicy part. But I haven't finished laying the foundation yet.

"What makes you think that?"

"Women don't do those things."

"Well, yes, generally, most women can't lift park benches, and most women don't have really low voices. But that doesn't mean this particular woman is not a woman. It could simply mean she's a woman who has a low voice and great strength. I notice you said, 'She's *really* a man.' I think it is interesting to consider why it's so tempting to conclude there is a deception going on. What makes us so confident that we know what's real? I see this as a cognitive process: we make assumptions based on what we observe, and when we find our observations were incorrect according to some arbitrary system of categorization, instead of recalibrating our categories we react with shock, horror, shame, anger, embarrassment, whatever, toward the person or object about which we were incorrect. It can't be our fault we were wrong in our categorization; it had to be that we were deceived, or we wouldn't have been wrong at all. I think it's fascinating that we perceive it this way, instead of saying to ourselves, 'Wow, she's strong, and beautiful, and what a sexy voice, and I guess I'd better back off because it seems she means business!'

"So we make assumptions about what is real or possible based on the gendered characteristics and behaviors that we learn in our culture. Another interesting thing about these gendered qualities is that the category they're assigned to can change between cultures, or change within a culture over time. What were decidedly masculine once, like the occupations of secretary, telephone operator, bank clerk, and tailor, went through a feminine phase and are now more gender-neutral. Another example of this kind of shift occurred in the 1960s and 1970s when some American men began to wear their hair long (again, after a few generations where short hair was the fashion), and people thought a man with long hair was trying to be a woman, or at least was expressing himself as a feminine man, whereas now men can have long or short hair and it's far less likely to be interpreted as a gender statement.

"Changing hairstyles often challenge gender norms. More than a few long-haired men in the 1960s were beaten up because they challenged gender norms. We experienced a culturally similar, though not as physically painful, shift when women began to wear jeans everywhere, not just in the barn. And a man with fine-motor dexterity will be praised for it if he applies his abilities to tying fishing flies, or building model railroads or ships in bottles, or playing a musical instrument, but he'll be ridiculed if he likes to crochet doilies. We tend to prefer our male-bodied people to have masculine gender characteristics and our female-bodied people to have feminine gender characteristics, and when they don't, particularly if the dichotomy is highly visible, it can make some people uncomfortable, even angry, when they feel they don't know how to classify the person they are observing, or when the other person's gender qualities threaten the observer's sense of confidence in her or his own gender. I find this level of response to gender variance fascinating. How is it that someone else's gender can throw a person's sense of confidence or solidarity out of balance? What cognitive mechanism is at work here, and what purpose does it serve? We learn as young children that behaving according to our assigned gender role means doing expected things based upon conformance to the sex we appear to be. If our sex and gender correspond, that's not too difficult for most of us, and we assume everyone feels about themselves the same way we do, and experiences similar difficulty or ease in adjusting behavior and appearance to conform to the gender norms of our culture. And if we travel to a new cultural environment, we quickly learn any new gender norms because we want people to perceive us as 'who we are.' If those new gender norms went against our ability to internalize or express them, we would experience tremendous discomfort.

"Like sex, gender is also more than one thing. It's more than the external presentation of gendered qualities. It's also one's deeply felt sense of self. That's what we call gender identity. Gender *could* be what we call male and female from a social standpoint, without regard to the need for reproduction, and it could be that there are more than two genders. Similarly, intersexed people potentially demonstrate that there are more than two discrete sexes, even though we tend to classify everything in these dichotomies of female and male, feminine and masculine.

"Perhaps this computer analogy will be helpful: think of sex as the hardware; gender as the software. In between there is an operating system that allows the software and hardware to give meaningful instructions to each other so they work together to accomplish tasks. It's easy to see how that works if a person's sex and gender are aligned, but what happens if your body doesn't match your sense of self? Think about that for a moment. Imagine you are exactly who you know yourself to be, you feel great about yourself, you have plans for your future, but when you look down your body is the opposite sex from who you know yourself to be. You know you're a woman, but you have to dress like a man, you have to behave like a man, because you have a male body. And you guys who know you're guys, you have all the feelings you know so well, but imagine your body is female. What's more valid: your feelings and your certain knowledge of yourself, or your body, the thing that other people see which signals to them what they can expect from you? Imagine what it would feel like to live with that discrepancy. That's something like what many transgendered people feel, what they have to deal with every day.

"For transgendered and transsexual people, their sense of self doesn't line up with their body in various ways, or they may be perceived as belonging to one sex or gender when they actually belong to the other, or they don't feel they belong at all. But people seem to be more closely connected to their gender than to their sex. That's hard to grasp if your sex and gender are aligned, but not so difficult if you are one of the millions of people who are to some extent in-between. All the evidence of the physical body doesn't mean much when a person has a gender identity that doesn't match that body. Gender identity—the sense of self—is stronger than the body, and will find a way to manifest itself.

"To return to the computer analogy, one of the things we really don't know about in people is the interface between the software and the hardware. Take that male person with masculine characteristics: he may actually feel feminine, no matter what he looks or acts like. Or you might see a male person with feminine characteristics and assume that he is gay, but he may very well be straight or bisexual. And he might think of himself as masculine, no matter what you might conclude from observing him. Or he could think of himself as androgynous, and still have a prideful sense of himself as male and as a man. You simply can't tell by looking at someone what his or her sexual orientation is, or what the person's gender identity is. You may see aspects of the person's gender, just as you may see aspects of the person's sex, as in secondary sex characteristics, but those may or may not be the aspects with which the person identifies or experiences affinity, and those may not be the aspects that define that individual as to their gender or their sex by any particular standard. For example, we think of thick body hair as a masculine trait because it is more common for males, but many women have significantly visible hair on their arms or faces. Hair on her arms won't make a woman feel she's a man, nor does it necessarily detract from her femininity. If a woman wears jeans it doesn't mean she has a masculine gender identity. And if a woman is attractive and seems feminine to you, sir, it doesn't mean she is attracted to men, or even that she thinks of herself as a woman.

"This is very complicated human behavior. We can reduce it to this: if you're a girl and you want to wear lipstick because you like the way it makes you look and feel about yourself, and you're not allowed to wear lipstick, you may be able to divert your desire to wear lipstick, but that desire to express that gender-related characteristic will surface somehow, whether by finding times and places where you can wear lipstick with impunity or by finding some other way to express the same motivation. If you're a girl in a male body, those feelings don't change just because you're in a male body. It's your gender identity that's in the driver's seat.

"If you think it's difficult for you to understand, think of how it feels to *be* someone like that. While it is true that such feelings *may* indicate a delusional or dissociative disorder, we tend to think *everyone* like that is crazy somehow, that the feeling that your body doesn't match your sense of self is always some kind of delusional state. Or we tend to blame the person whose gender characteristics don't match their physical sex as if it is that person's fault for making us feel confused. Wrong. It's our fault for not being secure and sensitive enough to allow that person a vehicle for honest self- expression. I challenge you to consider why it would ever be necessary, except to survive under coercion, to conform to someone else's notion of maleness or femaleness, either biologically or socially.

"I'd like you to think about both sex and gender difference as variations, not as deceit or defects, but as natural diversity that occurs with surprising frequency in human beings. We are not cookie-cutter men who all have penises that look exactly alike, who all feel the same way about ourselves or about women, and we are not all cookie-cutter women who like exactly the same clothes or want to wear the same hairstyle, and none of us focus on our gender or sex all the time . . . there are other things to think about in life. Yet if we don't find a point of comfort or balance between our gender identity and our social interactions, no matter who we are, we won't be able to find peace in any aspect of our lives."

Then I tell them: "I learned about this because I was born with a female body." If they weren't paying full attention before, they are now.

Students seem to like the shock factor. Sometimes the instructor will tell the class in advance that they will have a transsexual speaker at their next session, and students are disappointed when they see me because they think the transsexual couldn't come after all. They think they know what transsexual people look like, and I don't fit the picture. But rather than confronting them with the nutshell version of my life story, I like to provide a frame of reference, some context for relating to experience that differs from the presupposed, to encourage people to think in new ways about something most of us take for granted, but that some of us struggle with our entire lives.

After all the years I've spent thinking and talking about this, I still wonder about the connection between the hardware and the software that I live with, that is the condition of my life, too. It is often difficult for me when students ask, ""How did you know you were transsexual?" or, in the parlance of queer culture, "How did you come out as trans?" I always pause in the face of this question and acknowledge that it was complicated.

Coming Out

For me, the process of coming out as trans was less like opening a closet door and more like slowly lighting a series of candles in a dark cave. Each of us, every transperson, has his or her own unique story; there may be some elements that overlap or ring true for some and not for others. Some transpeople say they knew from their earliest consciousness; others say they realized it later in life, in their 30s or 40s or even later. Yes, there are people who begin transition in their 50s and 60s. Because I was born in 1948, my experience will be different from that of people who are coming of age now, when a language of transgender or transsexual experience has developed and made certain concepts more accessible. Still, I suspect there are aspects of my own experience of increasing awareness that are somewhat common for many of us, including for some people who do not identify as transsexual or transgender. The search for identity, community, and self is common to us all.

Older family members tell me that I began to refuse to wear dresses before I was two years old. Like many female-bodied children, I struggled all through my childhood against wearing clothing that designated me as female. I did not have a say in the matter. There were times when I was simply required to dress "properly." The tenets of the northern European heritage I received from my reserved, socially and politically conservative parents included "proper" (read: sex- and gender-role–specific) attire and behavior as a sign of respect for my elders and society. But to me, wearing a dress was a form of subjugation that concretely symbolized my lack of power to assert myself, just as wearing a suit and tie might feel to a feminine, male-bodied child. And when, even though "properly" dressed, my behavior, bearing, or demeanor seemed inappropriate to the gender role designated by my attire, or when strangers registered confusion as to whether I was a boy or a girl, the blame for their confusion rested squarely on me as though I had a choice in the matter—if only I were more conscientious, I would not so willfully disrupt the social order. To me, on the other hand, the easier course would have been for them to acknowledge the boy they were trying to suppress and let me wear the clothing in which I felt right. Instinctively, I knew the discrepancy would not be so glaring. But although I could resist (often, but not always, successfully) "proper" attire, I could not find the words to say that I felt like a boy.

My parents, who in spite of their conservative bent were gentle, loving people, also believed children should be free to enjoy their childhood. They struggled to allow me to be myself while trying to indoctrinate me with "a good upbringing." I learned housework and cooking and how to serve guests, and I learned to sit and stand with my legs together (though it always felt awkward), not to roughhouse or climb trees in a dress (though I frequently did anyway). And when we came home from the Presbyterian church we attended on Sunday, or when I came home from school every weekday, I got to change into my "play clothes"—pants and a shirt that felt infinitely more comfortable—and I could just be myself, but I had no words to say who that self was. I had no words to tell them that I was trying hard to be who they wanted me to be, but it just didn't feel right.

In spite of my own discomfort with the dissonance between my innate gender identification and society's gender-related expectations of me, I was lucky. Even though my gender expression was more often aligned with my identification than with my apparent sex, and this often caused frustration or irritation in my family, I have been relatively unscathed by the aberrations of family life. There was no alcoholism, no adultery or infidelity in my family, no divorce, no criminal behavior, no sexual abuse, and no mental illness—all of which have been proposed as causes of transsexualism. Sex role stereotyping and corporal punishment, though present, were not enforced as harshly in my family as in many others I've seen or heard about. The neighborhood I grew up in was safe throughout my childhood, and nearly all our neighbors were kind and generous with all the local children. My intellectual development and my physical freedom were both encouraged (though periodically constrained by social convention), and I was always given the message that I was valued and loved, even if I was also sometimes misunderstood. The drama of coming to terms with my difference has been a subtle one, punctuated by occasional moments of stark absurdity and lucid clarity.

The NBC network's live telecast of *Peter Pan* starring Mary Martin in March of 1955, when I was six years old, was one of those lucid moments. I clearly remember thinking, during Peter's first scene in the bedroom as he tries to retrieve his shadow, "If she can be a boy, then so can I." And as I watched the performance progress through flying and sword fights and pirates and Indians, I remember watching closely, thinking, "And I'll be a much better boy than she is!" Certainly I would not have been so cavalier with Wendy's affections, or fearful of taking on the father role. The closest I could come to talking about how I felt, though, was to ask my mother to make a Peter Pan outfit for me. She did. I put my rubber dagger in my Roy Rodgers cap gun holster and flew around the back yard for most of the following summer, saving Wendy and Tiger Lily from evil and leading packs of wild boys on harrowing adventures.

My parents gave dinner parties for their friends every few months, and once, when I was about eight or ten years old, a visiting couple was invited who had moved out of the area when I was an infant. The woman saw me standing next to my father and she said to him, "Oh, Ray, your son is the spitting image of you." My father, in a moment of absurd humor only he and I shared, clapped me affectionately on the shoulder and replied proudly, "That's my boy." Then he gently said to me, "Go to your room." It was a Saturday and I was wearing "play clothes," jeans and a T-shirt, nothing particularly gender-specific by today's standards. Yet this incident typifies my particular transgender experience: people often perceived me as a boy, sometimes even when I was wearing a dress. Though some people might find it absurd that others would see me as male, for me the absurdity occurred when people interpreted me as female, yet I understood I was absurdly expected to act in ways that would support their beliefs, not my own. Some parents might have told the woman about her "mistake" after I had left the room; perhaps she would laugh with embarrassment and apologize, and they would commiserate over the difficulties of ill-mannered children. I don't think my father would have done that, though. I think his goal was to avoid making a guest uncomfortable. That left me hidden, invisible, perhaps due to his fear about how my gender variance might be interpreted by others.

Terminology

It is easy to read a transgender childhood as a lesbian childhood (or a gay one, as the case may be), but there is an important difference. First, I use the term transgender to mean "breaking or going across gender boundaries," and I define a transgender childhood as one in which the child unconsciously (at first, and perhaps consciously later) expresses gender characteristics or behaviors that are typically associated with those of the opposite sex to the point of making other people uncomfortable or otherwise acutely aware of the dissonance. It is important to note, too, that some children may have these feelings acutely, without manifesting them in any way. Just because transness is invisible in some people, that does not mean it doesn't exist or that their experience of it is any less valid.

Transpeople, in my experience, consistently report, to varying degrees, a sense of separation from their bodies that gay and lesbian people who are not transgendered do not seem to experience or report. Certainly many gay and lesbian people—adults and children—struggle with gender variance. These are the men or boys who've been labeled "effeminate," "sissy," or "queens" for their feminine characteristics, and the women or girls labeled "tomboys" or "butch" for their masculine characteristics. I oppose the demeaning of any gender—regardless what kind of body is expressing it—but I would propose that individuals targeted by such remarks are having transgender experience, whether or not they so label it. Some people clearly enjoy their degree of variance. Others who may be troubled by their difference as children may be able as adults to reconcile those feelings and achieve a sense of comfort through identifying with their physical body. Social validation is extremely important for all human beings, and many gender-variant people do find validation in the gay or lesbian community. They are able to feel like they belong somewhere. Their variance is understood in a social context and they are able to find some measure of acceptance or love. Then, of course, not all transpeople are erotically attracted to people of their same natal genital configuration, which is one reason why it is confusing for transgendered kids when other people react to transgender expression with homophobic violence. It's also why many transgendered kids are, like I was, tempted to take on those homophobic projections and identify as gay or lesbian. I don't think there is anything wrong with experiencing and acknowledging erotic or romantic emotional attraction to other people regardless of their sex or gender. To me, the qualities of a healthy sexual relationship—attraction, caring, mutual respect and pleasure—are not exclusive to particular combinations of sexes or genders. The problem that sends most transgendered kids on long, torturous inner and outer journeys lies in the social invisibility of transgender experience, which I believe is a contemporary complication of our institutionalized hatred and fear of homosexuality. Nor does our collective lack of understanding about sex and gender in general help.

Usually when parents or other adults identify a child as being transgendered (using the technical term of "gender dysphoric" or the phrase "unhappy with the assigned gender") and refer the child for psychiatric intervention, it is because the adults fear that the child exhibits "pre-homosexual" behavior, and their intention is to prevent the child from developing homosexual attachments. This may not be what the child is experiencing at all, and the reaction pattern only emphasizes the confusion our culture has about gender and sex. If we had a better understanding of how gender and sex are different and how they interact, if we had a greater tolerance for variation in gender presentation, we might be less likely to torture ourselves or our children about imaginary inadequacies, or to treat problems that don't exist, which only creates other problems. But giving more latitude to transgendered children wouldn't necessarily make transsexual adults disappear.

"Transsexual" is a term that the medical profession has applied to that subset of transgendered people who seek hormonal and surgical assistance to change the sexual characteristics of their body to bring their gender and their body into alignment, people for whom that physical change is the only possible satisfactory accommodation to their transgender status, and who usually wish to be accorded full legal and social status in their congruent gendered sex. However, not all people who identify as transsexual actually seek medical assistance, and not all who experience a medical sex transition identify as transsexual, which are two reasons why there are no accurate statistics to tell us how many U.S. citizens are transsexual.

"Transgender" is a grassroots term, not a diagnosis like "transvestite" (a psychological condition) or "transsexual" (a medical condition). "Transgender" is a self-identity label for some and a useful political term for others. Many people who are either transsexual or gender-variant despise the term "transgender." "Transgender" does *not* mean people who want to change their sex. It is *not* a euphemism for "transsexual," the way gender is often a euphemism for sex. Because the category is so new, broad, and subjective, we have no way of counting the number of transgendered people in the world, either. To use "transgender" and "transsexual" interchangeably is to erase both individual experience and the very different social needs of these diverse categories. For example, when health insurance administrators refer to "transgender care," do they mean access to hormonal and surgical sex reassignment, or do they mean the ability of all gender-variant people to obtain basic, general health care that acknowledges their gender identity without prejudice or adversity?

Incidentally, I do not claim that my definitions are the last word in these matters: I believe we are still learning, still defining, and we may have a long way to go before we clearly understand these conditions. I will use the term "trans" from time to time to encompass both transsexual and transgender experience in general, but I do not—*ever*—claim to be describing all transgender or transsexual experience at any time. Transpeople are far too diverse for that. I also do not believe that there is any one way, or any better way, to be transgendered or transsexual, or that one expression is more real or valid than any other.

Early Dialogues

Sex, gender, sexual orientation, gender identity, gender role, the perceptions of others, the expectations that some project onto others, and self-awareness, all interact in complex, non-binary, non-dyadic ways to inform every one of us about our lives. For instance, my early attraction to girls, stimulated by my experience of myself as different from them, while largely unexpressed, was subsumed within my sense of my body as male, which came both from within me and from other people's perception of me as a boy. I was incapable of verbalizing this clearly, but I do remember two incidents in which I tried to convey my limited understanding of myself to others. Both took place during my early adolescence. I think the first was at twelve or thirteen (this would have been 1961 or 1962) when I told a slightly younger neighborhood boy that I thought I would not start menstruating like other girls (and his older sisters), but that I would grow up to be a boy after all. His response was to nod thoughtfully and say, "Yeah, I can see that." We then rode our skateboards over to the UC Berkeley campus, and inside the student union building my friend showed me how to use the men's restroom, because if I was going to grow up to be a boy he thought I would need to know these things.

My second attempt to communicate was when I was fourteen. I remember talking to my mother, lying on her bed, watching while she put away freshly laundered clothing in my father's dresser and her own.

"Mom, how come I'm not like the other girls?"

"What do you mean?" she asked.

"I'm different, and everybody knows it. Maybe if I had a dress like Vicky's* dress, then maybe I'd be like the other girls. Maybe if I had a purse I'd really be a girl."

"What kind of dress does Vicky have?"

"Oh, I mean this one dress she has that's like a skirt and a vest together."

"You mean a jumper?"

"Yeah, I guess. It's plain enough, and she looks like a girl when she wears it. Maybe I could have one like that?"

"Well, sure you can, honey. But don't you worry. You're perfectly normal. You're just a late-bloomer. I'm sure you'll grow up to be a very handsome woman." Did she say handsome because she knew I'd rather be handsome than pretty? That did appeal to me, it was true, but there was something about the late-bloomer phrase that hurt me. She seemed to be saying there really was something wrong with me. Late-bloomer didn't seem very positive.

I know she meant well, but what she offered didn't do much to alleviate my daily awkwardness among my peers, who only gently ridiculed my masculinity but were positively assaulting whenever I attempted a feminine appearance. When I arrived at school in a pale blue jumper and soft blouse (instead of my typical gray pleated skirt and white oxford button-down-collar shirt), with a modest clutch purse atop my stack of books, my friends laughed and pointed and teased me mercilessly, accusing me of trying to pretend to be someone else. I abandoned the purse after a few days (it was a lot of trouble anyway), and the next time I wore the jumper I also wore my usual button-down shirt, to much better effect and a greater sense of comfort on my part as well. I found myself wishing I'd gotten a dark colored jumper instead of the pale blue, but I was trying to be feminine and I thought the blue was softer somehow. I could never wear the kind of shoes most girls wore, preferring tennis shoes and socks to flats and nylons, so I always looked silly anyway in the skirts and dresses that were required of girls every day. Apparently trying to be like everyone else was to be a fruitless enterprise.

As I matured physically, the difference between my body and my

*All given names used alone are pseudonyms unless otherwise noted or associated with a surname.

gender created problems for me with nearly everyone. Once I was in college, after I'd turned eighteen, I had my first sexual relationship with a heterosexually-identified young woman who knew I had a female body, but was able to acknowledge her attraction to my masculinity. It took her several months of persuasion before I kissed her for the first time, but I found I liked it and it wasn't long before we were sleeping together. While she and I were together for three years and are still very good friends to this day, I have to acknowledge that it is possible we might not have stayed together if her mother had not discovered us making love in her bedroom one afternoon and thrown me out of the house. We were compelled to take care of each other from that point forward. After we'd been together for one year, she suggested that I might "enjoy having a sex change operation." I told her: "Oh, no. No! Only crazy people do that. If I got a sex change I'd probably never get a job, I'd lose all my friends, and my family would disown me. Nope. No way. And I don't ever want to talk about it again." I was terrified. The truth was I didn't even know whether it was possible to change from female to male. But I did understand, somehow, that being a transsexual was not exactly regarded as wholesome.

During roughly the same time period, a drunken fraternity boy punched me in the stomach on the street, calling me a "dirty pink-o hippie" because my hair was long—for a boy. It was actually short for a girl. And a waitress in a restaurant asked my lover and me whether I was male or female, "because all the help in the kitchen has been placing bets, so we just have to know. Hope you don't mind."

By the time I finished graduate school in 1972, I had determined that since I had a female body and I was attracted to female-bodied people, I must be a lesbian, so I left the university town to try to make a life in a city where there was a vibrant lesbian community. There I found that lesbian women were attracted to me, and I didn't have any problem meeting potential partners, but there always seemed to be a problem with regard to my degree of masculinity. In those days, it was becoming less fashionable for lesbians to appear to mimic traditional gender roles, so while most of the women I grew close to were at first drawn to me by something I can think of only as gendered attraction, after a time they would begin to chafe against what felt to them like being with a man, or at least another of the boyfriends (or husbands) they were trying to leave behind.

Several failed lesbian relationships later, at age twenty-six in 1975, I met Samantha, who appreciated my masculinity. We often talked about what I then called my "cross-gender" state, my maleness in a female package, my perception of myself as male, but I was adamant that I had no intention of changing my body. I interpreted her acceptance as another one of those messages from outside myself that was like a match struck in the darkness of my fears. My own feelings said I was male; other people's did, too. Candles in a cave.

In 1976, a friend of mine, Meg, who had gone off to New York with her girlfriend to promote the girlfriend's career as an actress, wrote me a letter telling me she was beginning the transition from female to male. She had found doctors there who were prescribing testosterone, she was passing as a young man, had changed her name to Michael, and she would be coming back to the West Coast to have surgery in a few months. She wrote something to the effect that I ought to try it, too. She knew I'd really like it. I seriously doubted that.

Before long, Meg/Michael returned to the city where Samantha and I were living because the university hospital there was one of the few places where female-to-male (FTM) sex reassignment surgery was performed at that time. I saw how happy Michael was, being perceived socially as a young man. Even Samantha noted, while riding in a car, seated between Michael and me, that she felt I was male, too, which made me feel seen and acknowledged. I began to wonder whether he had been right that I would like it, too. But I put it firmly out of my mind when he told me that while he wasn't doing it for social privilege or economic gain, he did feel nevertheless that now the world was showing him "the respect that he deserved." The thought that only men, and not masculine women, deserved respect was abhorrent to me. My reaction to this was to reflect through my own feminism that Meg had not been strong enough to make it as a "different kind of woman" and had had to choose sex reassignment as a survival strategy. No matter how much I might "enjoy" a sex change, it was not what I would resort to for respect. I viewed Michael as taking the easy way out. I was adamant that I was fine the way I was.

I think it was the summer of 1977 when I saw Steve Dain on television, and I was newly inspired and newly threatened. Steve had been a girls' physical education teacher in a Northern California high school, and had been selected as California's Teacher-of-the-Year, but then he transitioned from female to male and was engaged in a legal battle to retain his profession as an educator. His story made all the major papers, TV news, and most of the nation's talk shows (such as they were in those days). Steve was handsome, articulate, and poised. And he was not ashamed of his transition. He did not do it because being a man was somehow better than being a woman, but because it was the only thing he could do to be himself. It was about the truth, not about hiding. He was the kind of man with whom I could identify. This event brought me face to face with my fear again. I was drawn to the idea of becoming a man, but I didn't yet have the courage to live as a transsexual man. I still thought I understood what was involved, and the idea of taking hormone injections for the rest of my life, which I thought might cause cancer, and the fear of being judged incompetent or insane were serious impediments. I still couldn't admit to Samantha or to myself the intensity of the appeal that changing sex held for me, like the distant point of light that I crept toward as I felt my way along dark rock walls. I didn't know enough yet. I didn't know enough about the biological facts of transition, nor about the nature of my own fears, yet I could only keep moving.

I continued to struggle with the separation between my gender and my body as I watched Michael go through surgery, marry his girlfriend, Jane, arrange for donor insemination for her so they could have a child, and experience the birth of their first child, a boy. There were times when I felt that Michael didn't want to be seen with me because I suspected he felt my own androgynous appearance called his masculinity into question. He did not have much facial hair or a very deep voice, and I knew he fretted about those features. When we were out in public together, feeling very much like brothers, I could sense the familiar questioning, particularly from other men, wondering whether I was male or female. Then I could see their scrutiny passing from me to Michael, and I realized he had transitioned to avoid that scrutiny, that judgment, that sense of being found wanting, of not being "man enough." I would sense his back stiffening. To avoid being outed or challenged in his maleness, he would become dismissive of me in the presence of other men, and afterwards he would be distant and sad. I think this was painful for both of us, though we never spoke of it. Eventually Michael and his family moved away, and our contact diminished over the years.

Interconnections

Meanwhile, Samantha also wanted to have babies, and by the early 1980s I felt secure enough in my career that I could afford to provide for a family. We went to a sperm bank and selected a donor that resembled me as much as possible, and after eleven frustrating months of multiple attempts, Samantha conceived. When our daughter Morgan was born in 1985, my life was changed forever. My heart was opened in a phenomenal way, and I really grasped what it means to be willing to die for someone you love. When it came time for Samantha to fill out the birth certificate form, there was space for information about the mother and the father. Samantha and I talked about the fact that there was no box to check for "other parent" and wondered what we should do. She knew that I felt like Morgan's father, but her feelings in the matter were more ambivalent. She saw us as being outside of both conventional lesbian and heterosexual contexts. I was not interested in pretending to be a legal father, but we finally decided to put my name in the "father" space because it was closest to the truth of our family situation. The attending physician had told us if that was the way we felt, then she would sign it, and Samantha thought my name—Jamison—was masculine enough to escape the scrutiny of the Registrar of Births. When the official document was available weeks later, I was thrilled to see myself listed as Morgan's father. It was the way I felt, all right. I was a father.

But outside and inside our home I became "the other mother," a label I couldn't accept. That label fixed me in the female body that I had spent a lifetime ignoring because it did not express me. I felt like a father, not an "other mother." And then, when Morgan began to attend nursery school with children of heterosexual parents, she identified me as Daddy, though we had never used that word. So Samantha and I explained to her that even though I looked like a daddy, even though I acted like a daddy and did all the things that a daddy does, most people think only men can be daddies, and she shouldn't call me daddy because other people would be confused, since I was not a man. Morgan looked at us as if we were both being ridiculous, and I knew we were. I was her daddy, and I knew it in my heart and soul. I was her daddy as truly as her mommy was herself and Morgan was our baby. I was her daddy as truly as my own father was mine. It was all I could do to live day-to-day in my androgynous state, holding onto the belief that I was just fine the way I was, when what I really felt like was a man and what I really wanted was for others to see me as one.

Over the next few years, as we enjoyed our daughter and planned for (and worked at conceiving) a second child, I struggled with the conflict I had internalized. No matter how comfortable I felt with myself, the fact remained that I never knew when people around me would threaten or challenge me because they didn't think I was acceptable. Riding on BART, the Bay Area's version of the subway, a man stared at me from across the aisle and then began yelling, "What is that? That's a woman! Christ, it's a fucking woman!" Terrified, I got off at the next stop. If I had been a woman, I might have reacted differently. I began to struggle consciously with what I called the lie in my existence: if people perceived me as male, I had to worry about whether they might find out that I had a female body, and then would feel betrayed or deceived and entitled to punish me for it. But if people perceived me as female and treated me the way they treated women in general (even if this was polite, respectful, or deferential), I felt invisible, as if I didn't exist. It was hard enough living with this myself and with my partner, but to inflict this on children, to ask them to carry the burden of the dichotomy that was my physical being, was asking too much. I wanted an acknowledged father relationship with my children: how could I ask them to treat me like a woman and a father simultaneously while outsiders were calling me their "other mother," something I could never be? It was more than I could handle.

I had already been working on a novel about two transgendered people, one who ended up getting a sex change and one who did not; I worked on this manuscript for six years, from 1982 to 1988, producing nearly 600,000 words, but I was still unable to acknowledge that I was considering sex reassignment for myself. Not because I believed I needed to know for myself, but (I told myself) only out of necessity to make my manuscript accurate, I had begun doing serious research about the female-to-male transsexual process, and through a circuitous route I came into contact in 1987 with Lou Sullivan, an FTM transsexual man in his mid-thirties who had dedicated himself to providing information to others. Sullivan had started a small support group in San Francisco just months earlier, and he had started to publish a small newsletter for FTMs. The next scheduled meeting—they happened four times a year—promised a presentation by Steve Dain. I had to be there.

I was scared. I invited a friend along, another masculine-appearing woman who had also expressed a desire to change sex. We went to the restaurant where the meeting was to be held, and I was sure we were in the wrong place, there were so many men there. I had expected a lot of androgynous people like myself, not real men. But soon Steve Dain appeared, as real and as manly as could be, and I gradually realized all the men in the room had once had female bodies. It was eerie and encouraging all at once. When the presentation was over, I went up to introduce myself to Steve, and he asked me how long I had been taking hormones. He was surprised when I told him I hadn't been. He introduced me to his wife Vera, and she asked me how long ago I had had my chest reconstruction surgery. She was surprised when I told her I'd had no surgery. I arranged to have a private consultation with Steve to discuss the realities of hormonal and surgical sex reassignment. He said it was okay to bring Samantha so she could have her questions answered, too.

When I got home from this momentous first support group meeting, Samantha asked me, "Well, are you really a boy now?" She seemed to be laughing at me, just a little, partly humoring me, and partly ridiculing. I thought about how my own preconceptions had been shattered that afternoon, and I felt certain that she would come to understand as we learned more together; she had always been supportive and understanding before. She later told me that the attitude she was trying to express was that she thought I was fine the way I was and that I didn't need those people in Sullivan's group, or sex reassignment. She still believed that I was only doing research for my novel, and I didn't know how to tell her anything different. But I was entering another world, finding another sense of myself that felt more solid, more real, more possible than ever before. Was I really a boy now? "Yes," I answered. "Yes, I am."

In the process of my long self-investigation, it finally dawned on me that I had not been able to grow up fully because I was never going to be an adult woman. I knew that the only way I could grow up—really be an adult—was to become a man. I needed to go through a puberty to which I could relate. I needed to move beyond the restrictions that I had placed on myself—and that others had placed on me—because of the opposition between my gender identity and my physical body. I needed to balance my body and my psyche so I could leave that struggle and that lie behind and move forward in my own life.

My conversations with Steve and Vera, with Sullivan and the dozen or so other transsexual men I had met by then, and with many of my friends (both those with trans experience and those who were normatively gendered), enabled me to realize that I could indeed make the transition. As I talked it over with Samantha, she said she wanted me to be happy and that she would try to stay with me, which I experienced as a great relief. I found that I did have the courage to risk the unknown and learn how to actualize myself. I felt confident she would continue to appreciate me. I believed that as I had seen Michael become happier with himself, surely Samantha would see the same kind of improvement in me. By making this ultimate investment in myself, I knew I could finally grow up. I felt supported and ready to embark on a miraculous journey. Some of us do this entirely alone, without social support or dialogue with anyone. Sometimes other people are more of a hindrance than a help. When I look back and consider my feelings about myself throughout my life, I surmise that I would have transitioned somehow, at some point, no matter what other people said, no matter whether I was aloof and uncomfortable socially, or whether I was gregarious and interconnected with others. Transsexual people's lives are all different, so our processes for reaching that place of determination and resolve necessarily vary.

For me, even after I outwardly acknowledged my transsexualism, there were a few additional layers of illumination that had to come from within before I could complete my process. I needed to combat the lesbian-feminist doctrine of male evil—that all men are bad—which I knew was wrong because I had always had close friends who were male and good relationships with my father and brother. I saw that doctrine as hypocritical, too, because many lesbians approved of masculine traits in women, but despised them in men. While I was trying to be accepted by the lesbian community I hid my discomfort with what I viewed as blatant anti-male bias but was afraid to confront for fear of being rejected. I also needed to balance what I thought of as negative overreaction toward men against what I recognized as the very real inequalities between the sexes that feminists were rightly fighting. I had to understand my part in that system of inequity, whether I occupied a female place and a masculine role or a male place and a masculine role. I needed to understand what it would mean—really *mean*—to change places: what responsibility would I have for maintaining or deconstructing traditional gender roles once I transitioned?

Would it be any different from what I viewed as my responsibility when I was perceived as an androgynous lesbian? As I became more conversant about transsexualism, I began to notice the times I would cringe and try to distance myself from it. I realized I needed to strip away my own shame of transsexualism if I was to be able to accept myself, and others, fully.

Like everyone else, I have groped around in my own psychic darkness until I found the tools, the candles and the spark, to light my way. One may worry he is going through the wrong tunnel, misleading himself into treacherous territory where he could run into hideous difficulty, complications, maybe lose himself, lose his life.* The whole process has not been easy, and yet in many ways it was not terribly complicated for me. And the actual bio-chemical and surgical transition is in some ways its own distinct story. But although I can express it casually now, coming out as transsexual was still arduous, soul-wrenching. While I know this is not true for all transpeople, for me it seemed that everyone knew before I did, everyone could see that there was something going on reflecting my sex, gender, and/or sexuality, but none of us had the words for it until I was almost twenty. And still there were not enough words then, in the 1960s and 1970s, to really understand what it was, what I was, what changing sex would mean to me and how it would impact my life and all my relationships.

My father died unexpectedly before I was able to be clear with him about my identity. Sometimes I think his death eight months before I resolved to metamorphose was part of what freed me to take the risk, since I could no longer lose his love. Or perhaps his death signaled my own mortality, and caused me to feel I had no more time to waste. I began my transition in October 1988, just a month before my fortieth birthday. My mother was furious and Samantha was highly ambivalent, though she still tried to be supportive. There is no denying that there can be a sense of betrayal that loved ones feel when someone close changes as dramatically as one does when changing sex. Parents often hope and dream particular

---

*I realize consistent use of masculine pronouns is often difficult for progressive readers; in fact, it is difficult for me, too, because I don't mean to marginalize or diminish female experience. But because the masculine identity of FTM transpeople is my primary focus, and trans masculinity or maleness is often marginalized even in transsexual literature, I feel this emphasis is necessary. Where concepts are more universal to both male- and female-identified people, I use feminine pronouns, too.

futures for their children that their children cannot or will not realize, and adjusting to that reality is often painful for them. But by the time she died, in 1995, my mother knew who I was and had reluctantly come to accept me as her oldest son. Samantha accepted my transition much more thoroughly. She acknowledged and then consummately rejected my maleness. She did not want to be with a man.

In the summer of 1991, nearly three years after I had begun the process of changing my body from female to male, I was still working at the same company where I started working just a few weeks before initiating my transition. I had been an engineering group manager in the operating system software division. When I joined the company in 1988, there had been some 7,000 employees; in 1991 there were over 12,000, so the environment was one in which people were forced to learn to handle or at least tolerate certain kinds of change. I was in conversation that summer with one of the women in the editorial department, and she said to me, apropos of nothing: "It's quite amazing, really."

"What?" I asked.

"Watching you go through the change. To look at you now, it's like it never happened."

I smiled, grateful for my masculine traits that testosterone now emphasized, but I was trying to forget about that change, too, since at that time I still believed that the mark of success for any transsexual person is when he or she is able magically to make his or her transsexualism disappear.

"Every once in a while," she continued, "a rumor circulates that one of the engineering managers is a transsexual, and the people who know you only smile and watch the people who don't know you staring nervously at all the managers trying to figure out which one used to be a man or which one is going to start wearing a dress. Then after a few weeks, when they can't figure it out, they forget about it. They never think it could be you."

I laughed and nodded. "Yeah, I'm lucky, I guess."

Lucky.

I had a secret, an unlucky secret, the kind that can eat people alive.

2
Initiation

Through the decade of the 1990s I directed a great deal of energy toward improving the quality of life for transsexual people around the world. Much of that effort has been very basic: convincing people that female-to-male transgendered and transsexual people actually exist. I've also tried to show that our stories and issues are not exactly parallel to those of our male-to-female (MTF) counterparts. Society still has a long way to go to destroy the stereotypes that cause some people to revile and ridicule transsexual and transgendered people, still a long way to go to ensure social safety and equal access to basic human services for all transpeople, and to constructively address the racial and class issues that plague transpeople—and society at large.

My own experience as a transsexual man gives me hope that if society can learn to incorporate and value transpeople in all their variation, most if not all of the other social problems that arise from intolerance and misinformation may be manageable. I think we can address multiple prejudices and fears in the process of dealing with one primal concept upon which many of our assumptions about the human world are based: the norms attached to sex and gender and the conjunction between them. So much faulty logic emanates from this locus of assumption: e.g., women are inferior to men; heterosexuality is the only proper or legitimate orientation; external genital appearance is indicative of reproductive function; you cannot change someone's sex; transsexual people are always obvious; a person who is different from me has less value than I have; women are women and men are men and there is nothing in between, but if "something" should appear as a freak of nature, "it" must be destroyed. Because

27

it is so easy to agree with this "logic" many people actually fear utter chaos in the face of change. The paradigm shift that will accompany what I call "trans inclusion" is equivalent to the flat world becoming round, but it is just as real, just as necessary.

Coming of Age

The year 1991 was a turning point for me. That year I experienced an initiation into manhood, through both completion of surgery and the reissuance of my corrected birth certificate, and through acceptance into a community of men. I also took on a new responsibility that contributed to the initiation of another, very different community: the newly forming transgender community.

In March 1991, Lou Sullivan died from complications of HIV, just one week after securing my promise to keep his quarterly *FTM Newsletter* alive. I had thought producing his typically four- to eight-page collection of news, information, and letters to the editor would be a small task for an experienced writer and publications manager such as myself, but it turned out to demand much more from me—and to give back much more than I expected, too. At the time, though, my perspective was limited by my own inhibitions. I didn't consciously know it then, but there was some significant internal work I had to do before I could fully appreciate the significance of my developing role in this new community. At that juncture, I had no intention of doing anything to alter the status quo for myself or anyone else. My only goal was to get through the process of transition that I had laid out for myself, and to ride out whatever repercussions would arise from it.

That February I had filed a petition in Superior Court for a change of name and sex. I was born in California, and under California law it has been possible since the 1970s for transsexual people to have their reassigned sex legally recognized. The process requires public notice of the proposed change for four weeks, and various forms of proof of publication, which take time to accumulate, so it was April before this activity was completed. I had a brief hearing at which the judge accepted my petition, including an affidavit from my surgeon, Donald R. Laub, M.D., confirming, under penalty of perjury, that my medical records showed "extensive medical, psychological and psychiatric evaluations were performed . . . relative to [my] true gender," and that I had "undergone hormonal and surgical therapies which have irreversibly altered genital anatomy from female to male. Surgery was performed on July 24, 1990. [I] accomplished total psychological reorientation as well. Therefore, [my] gender should now be considered by one and all to be male [and I] should be accorded a change of all legal documents to reflect the male gender as the correct one." I thought the legal language conflating sex and gender was, at this point, probably convenient, since it was technically permitting my gender to override my originally assigned sex as the determinant of my social reality, which was what I needed.

The judge, who was probably not much older than I was, said, "You look like a fine young man to me. You're not doing this to deceive your creditors, are you?" "No, Your Honor," I replied. He then declared me male in the eyes of the law, and issued an order that entitled me to a new birth certificate and would permanently seal the old one in the state's records at the capitol. I walked out of the courthouse feeling both elation and an ironic sense of anti-climax. It had been so simple, almost like nothing at all had happened, and yet my entire life had been dramatically, irreversibly altered. I was legally male, and yet the social construction of my maleness—*not* my masculinity, about which there was no doubt from any social quarter— was still incomplete. I still needed to learn how to respond to all the social expectations that go along with having a male body.

But in June I attended another courtroom session in which another judge removed my name as father from the birth certificate of Samantha's and my son, Mitchell, at Samantha's request. She had ended our relationship in 1989 immediately following the first stage of my sex reassignment surgery, when Mitchell was just over two months old. I had no legal standing because Samantha and I had not been married and because Mitchell was conceived using sperm from an anonymous donor. There was nothing I could do except offer my ongoing commitment to the child we had brought into being together, which the judge noted as he accepted the petition before him. There was no legal reason for him to deny her request. Samantha left my paternity in the case of our daughter unchallenged because, she said, Morgan was already bonded to me and was old enough to suffer were we to lose contact. Samantha did not regard me as Mitchell's parent, and she severely restricted my time with him. Because of what she had said about Morgan's bonding, I believed that Samantha wanted to ensure Mitchell would not bond emotionally with me. Whether or not Mitchell was bonded to me, though, I had already bonded to him. I was wounded beyond words, yet helpless to change it. All I could do was remain present for him through his sister, and hope that one day he would understand who I was—who I might still be—to him and how much I loved him.

In July I received a copy of my new birth certificate from the California Department of Vital Statistics confirming my male name and sex, along with an unexpected congratulatory letter from the Secretary of State. In August my position was eliminated at the computer system development and manufacturing company where I had worked as an engineering group manager, publications operations manager, and senior editorial specialist. This turn of events had nothing to do with my transsexualism, fortunately, or it might have been more devastating than it was. Instead, I actually welcomed this change, too. With a lump-sum severance payment, I embarked on a much-needed year of reflection and re-evaluation. I spent time developing basic informational materials to facilitate responding to the increasing number of inquiries that I was receiving from around the world because of the FTM group. I did plenty of socializing with friends. I also thought about what I might do for work when the money ran out. On the surface, life was good.

One evening at dinner with a group of non-trans friends, a man I'd considered one of my closest friends for over a decade recounted how he had revealed to someone else that I was transsexual, explaining, "I didn't want him to be left out of the joke."

I said, "The joke?"

"Well, you know; that you're a transsexual," he tried to explain, seeing he had hurt my feelings. Everyone at the table was silent.

"The joke?" I said again. "I am not a joke."

Suddenly I was uncertain of the loyalty of my friends. It really was time to take stock. I was cut off from my nearly-three-year-old son, and had only rigidly scheduled access to my now-seven-year-old daughter every other weekend, plus a few hours one afternoon each week. I was cut off from my career, too, and wondered what I wanted to do with my life as I adjusted to a world that now perceived me as an adult man and therefore projected upon me all the assumptions that correspond to that category. Intellectually, I had known that changing my sex was going to be a challenge, that it would force me to re-examine every relationship I had. I had thought that my own continuity would count for something, that the people who related to me as friends would be able to see me through it, but perhaps that would not be possible for everyone.

I was reminded of a time when I was seven or eight years old and I had been helping my father clean out the basement when we found a trunk full of his World War II memorabilia and started going through it. He told me about how he got the Nazi flag, the German officer's sword, his sergeant stripes, his Purple Heart. Then he gave me a spare cap to play with, a cap that had sergeant stripes on it. The next day I took the cap to school and had put it on at recess and was playing alone, crouched down drawing in the soft dirt that collected in one corner of the playground, when a group of kids started throwing rocks at me. I stood up to face them, about six of them, and I shouted at them to stop, but they didn't. They kept throwing rocks at me and I stepped back against the chain-link fence and started shaking it, yelling, "Hey, stop it! Cut it out." At last the fourth-grade teacher came over and told them to stop it.

"What's going on here?" she demanded.

"She's wearing that hat," one boy exclaimed. "She can't wear a hat like that."

"I can so," I retorted. "My dad gave it to me."

"Girls can't wear hats like that," the boy complained loudly. The other boys and girls reinforced his protest.

"Well, you shouldn't wear hats like that if you don't want to get in trouble," the teacher said to me. "All you kids run along now." She never told them it was wrong to throw rocks at someone else. It was just a cap, something my father had given me; I wasn't hurting anyone by wearing it. Why did people think I was wrong for being me, even now when I felt I had done everything I could to realize my authentic self?

I now felt faced with rebuilding my relationship with the entire world. I had no one to guide me through what was turning out to be a new adolescence composed of the physical changes and social adjustments necessitated by becoming a visible man. My father had been dead for four years already, and my mother was refusing to acknowledge my transition. My relationship with a new lover, Marcy, did not help me feel less alone. We argued too frequently, made up in bed, and started over again. The sexual dynamic of masculine and feminine worked so well between us that it was easy for us to deny the problematic difference between my chronological age (mid-forties) and my biochemical age as I recreated myself (late teens). There weren't many other transmen I could talk with, since "community" didn't really exist then. All I could do was bounce my experiences, ideas, and feelings off a few close friends who were no more sophisticated than I about how to manage transsexual experience in an ignorant, hostile world.

I had been seeing a compassionate psychotherapist to help me deal with the depression carved into me by the dissolution of my family, but a therapy relationship isn't the same as getting out there and walking in the world. I realized that much of the psychic burden I was carrying had to do with my judgment of myself as a failed child (I couldn't be what my parents had wanted), a failed parent (because I wasn't present in my children's lives), a failed partner in relationship to Samantha (because she didn't want to be with me any more), and as a transsexual man, a member of a social group with pariah status at best. I knew I hadn't done anything wrong, but being transsexual was something our physicians, therapists, and precursors counseled us to keep under wraps. As I struggled with the ramifications of my failures and inadequacies, I knew I needed some kind of connection to other people in which to find reflected the qualities in me that were of value. Ironically enough, it was the Men's Movement that gave me the context for finding that reflection.

The World of Men

In May, I attended my first meeting and rehearsal session for the Sons of Orpheus (the Sons), a men's group that I had wanted to join because it was also a performing percussion group. I didn't know anything about the Men's Movement. I had not heard of Robert Bly's *Iron John*. I didn't know that Shepherd Bliss, one of the men I met through the Sons, was responsible for adopting the philosophical term "mythopoetic" and applying it to contemporary men's pursuits (Kupers, 1993). I was not seeking refuge from women, or trying to reconnect with the deep masculine, whatever that is. I really did join the Sons because I wanted to play music in an ensemble. I wanted to play drums and other percussion instruments because I had always been told I couldn't. When I was about twelve, my parents had told me drums were not for girls; besides, they couldn't bear listening to me practice, as if my drums would be any worse than my little brother's squeaky clarinet! Later, when I was in my thirties, Samantha, a very talented musician herself, also discouraged me from taking up percussion because it would be too noisy. But now I was on my own, and no one could tell me what to do. The fact that the Sons was an all-male troupe was a bonus, a chance to see how a group of other men with no knowledge of my past would relate to me, and how I would relate to them.

I wasn't inordinately apprehensive when I walked into the studio the first evening; it wasn't the first time I'd entered male-only space. After all, I'd always been the captain of my neighborhood baseball and football teams, I'd been the first "girl" to take wood and metal shop classes at my junior high school, the first "girl" to climb the ropes in the boys' gym, first "girl" on my high school ski team, the only "woman" in my graduate school creative writing program, the first female-bodied person to work as a construction cable splicer for the Bell System in the Pacific Northwest (1973–1976). In spite of my female body, I'd been relating to other men as a boy or as a man, from my perspective, in many contexts for most of my life, though usually, from their perspective, as an acknowledged interloper. Transitioning on the job in a predominantly male, but highly codified white-collar environment where I had started out in a position of authority was not the same as being the new man in a small room with men from all walks of life. Now I would have to participate on their terms, no longer as a special case.

There were about thirty men in the room that first night when the group's founder and leader, Bruce Silverman, asked us to form a circle and quietly look around and notice the other men in the room. I looked, and saw the rest of them looking, too, taking in the presence of other men: mostly white men, but a few black, several Chicano, some mixed race, most with a kind of openness in their faces that seemed unusual for men. I realized they were all happy to be in that room. I also noticed that three or four of the men were close to my size, while the rest ran the gamut from a little bigger to a whole hell of a lot bigger. So when Bruce announced that there were two new men in the room that night and it was time for their initiation, I felt a momentary panic at the thought of what that initiation might entail.

Bruce called for one of us to step into the center of the circle of men, and while I hesitated a huge, balding man stepped forward and stood there apprehensively. "Say your name, please," Bruce said. "Karl Grimm," the big man said. All the men stared at Karl in silence for a second, and then, in unison, a chorus of thirty strong voices said Karl's whole name back to him three times. Karl gave a quick smile. Bruce thanked him, and Karl stepped back to his place in the circle.

I thought, "That's a relief—no scary hazing or rough play—I can handle this." Then Bruce asked for the other new man to step into the center, and I stepped into the unexpectedly magical zone of that circle. Bruce asked me to say my name, and my voice came out choked and nervous. But the voices that came back to me were clear, deep, resonant, and as they looked at me and said Jamison Green three times, I was surprised by the power of the moment. I felt seen and accepted and supported unconditionally by other men. It was strange, because all they had really done was allow me to be in the room, look straight at me, and say my name. No one had ever said my name that way before, let alone a chorus of unfamiliar men. Bruce thanked me, and I returned to my place in the circle. Then, after a few beats of silence, Bruce began to drum a soft, syncopated, story-telling rhythm on the skin of a big mahogany-colored tumba.

One by one, to the sound of that single low drum, men stepped forward to give brief messages about the state of their souls, and each one was received and acknowledged. In just a few minutes tears were streaming down my face as I listened to man after man say something that I also felt. I looked again at these men: some were handsome, some were average, some seemed rigid or awkward while others seemed graceful, a few were recognizably gay and others appeared to be cut from the most terrifying mold of conservative straight man. Some were lean, or muscular, some were softer; some were assertive and confident, others shy or less intensely energetic. If it was the music that brought these men together, I thought, then there was nothing for me to fear. I knew that in that room I did not have to be anything other than the full human being that I was.

Later, as we moved into the larger rehearsal space, one of the men walked alongside me and said, "It's okay; I couldn't stop crying on my first night, either." I joined my section, the tamborims, and we began to play samba. The lessons of paying attention, listening, acknowledging, and of learning how each instrument's part works to form the whole ensemble's sound were not lost on me that night.

But I kept my secret. I kept my secret through other men's revelations about their frustration concerning the expectations implicit in gender roles, or their concerns about (or pleasure in) their sexuality. I kept my secret while other men talked about their inability to communicate with women and their sincere desire to connect with that communication—something I also felt. I kept my secret while other men talked about their frustration over being non-custodial parents engaged in disputes with ex-wives who refused to see them as human beings—man, could I relate to that! While other men talked about wanting validation as men from their fathers or other role models, I listened to my inner self, recognizing the validation I had received over the years, the connectedness I had always felt with other men, recognizing that my masculinity was natural and real, as natural and real as that of any other man in the room, and that if I had stayed in a female body my masculinity would still have been natural and real, because that masculinity did not depend on the possession of a male body.

Now that I had a male body, however, I realized it was that very body that was placing new constraints on me. In some quarters, masculinity is characterized as the defining trait that confers privilege on a man; this same masculinity is often the target of ridicule and parody meant to devalue or disempower men. So many men worry about their masculinity as defining the quality of their manhood: with the right amount of masculinity, they expect to be accepted by others, but if they feel their masculinity is deficient, then they expect not to be treated well in the world. I was beginning to learn concretely that my own masculinity was not in question, that my masculinity (in this case, a quality of perceived maleness) preceded my male body.

Masculinity in a female body caused one set of reactions and expectations; having a male body, however, brought on new challenges, some of which surprised me. Strangers spoke to me more often: in line for anything in a public space, people seemed perfectly willing to turn and speak to me—something that would rarely happen before. People didn't notice me as much, either; they didn't stare at me or lean away from me as they had done when they couldn't tell what sex I was. I had to learn how to be at ease with the interactions of strangers. I had to learn not to be instantly defensive, as if I were expecting to be teased, criticized, or attacked whenever a stranger spoke to me or called for my attention. At the same time, I became acutely aware of women's fear of men in general, something that I had never understood until it was directed at me as a man when I inadvertently surprised a woman by running up behind her as we were both entering a subway station. I didn't mean to startle her, and I did apologize, but the fear in her eyes when she looked at me, apparently thinking I was about to accost her, was a painful thing for both of us. It was my male body that she saw, not my masculinity or my character. It is the male body that distinguishes a man from a woman and makes him a target for random violence from men who would not hit a woman, not even a masculine woman. It is the male body that is used as a sexual weapon against women, and some people equate those expressions of anger or powerlessness lashing out from within male bodies with masculinity. Bad behavior is not the province of only one type of body, but bodies—*gendered* bodies—are a location of responsibility for social interactions. Bodies carry out those interactions. As I spent time each week in that studio with men who were willing to look at their behavior and their interactions while affirming themselves as men, I reflected on all the years I had thought my masculinity was the problem for my female body, and came to understand, more concretely than before, that it was my female body that had been the problem for my masculinity. I realized consciously that it isn't that one sex or one gender is better or more civilized or moral than the other, but that a person's relationship with her or his own body is what counts, because being true to oneself creates the integrity and self-respect we need to have if we are to extend that respect to others.

People who have bodies that match their gender identity take their bodies for granted in their process of identity formation. Transgendered and transsexual people don't have that luxury. We have to approach identity from another angle. We come to understand and accept (to one degree or another) our masculinity or femininity and its relation to our femaleness or maleness, but it's the body that gives us problems—it's the body that we have to deal with (whether we dress it up or alter it hormonally and/ or surgically) in order to express our deepest sense of self. The rest of the world has this reversed: while taking their bodies for granted, they assume their problem (if they have one) is masculinity or femininity, and this reflects on their self-concept as men or women. A gender-normative man, for example, one whose gender identity and sex are aligned the way observers expect, who is somehow targeted as "unmasculine"—as a wimp, a coward, a faggot, etc.—can respond by either ignoring the "insult" or by taking some action that would be judged masculine or manly in order to prove the instigator wrong. One of the worst insults a man can receive is to be called a woman, implying that he is a failure as a man. This distinction defines maleness only by its degree of difference from the female, a twisted logic that has developed into sexism. When confronted with someone whose body can't be taken for granted—someone who could be called transgendered because they are breaking gender boundaries in some way—those who rely only on bodies for data about individuals don't know what to do with what appears to be an overabundance of masculinity or femininity. When one's gender messages conflict with the visible body so that the messages of body and gender become confused or obscured, the result in the observer is sometimes indifference or mere curiosity, but in some people confusion can evoke loathing or anger that can lead to violence.

Observing the men in the Sons, most of whom seemed comfortable in their bodies, at a time when I was realizing how my own new body "worked" with respect to how it reflected me in the world, was instructive. I experienced a shift from the defensive posture I'd been forced to adopt by my previous gender variance (and then pretend I didn't have so I could get along with others), to solidity, balance, and groundedness. That change made me aware that the suffering visited upon gender-variant people, to which I had become accustomed in my previous life, was not a necessary condition.

I did not indoctrinate myself to believe that gender conformance was the ideal; in spite of the fact that I was now gender-conforming, I brought with me, into the world of men, the notion that gender variance was valid and deserving of its own integrity. I realized that men who did not devalue or ridicule whatever qualities or characteristics might be called feminine, in either women or men, were far more at ease with themselves and others. The point is not that people need to be gender-conforming to meet others' expectations, but that people need to have confidence in themselves, to know who they are, and to be able to appreciate others—and their otherness. We should each be entitled to have our own relationship with our body in the way that serves us best, whether or not our body and psyche "match," whether or not we want them to "match," and, if we want or need that congruity, whether or not we have the ability to make them "match."

For some transgendered people, sex/gender incongruity is exactly right, whether that incongruity is innate or cultivated. For some transsexual people, incongruity as perceived by others occurs when they transition, though they may feel themselves much more congruous within. That is, some people appear normatively gendered with respect to their bodies, and their transness is not apparent to others until they begin a physical transition that makes them appear unusual, as if their sex and gender are not aligned, which is the opposite of my experience. Just as I learned that strangers had an easier time with me once I was sex/gender aligned, transsexual people who leave congruent appearances for incongruent ones have to learn how to manage the discomfort of others, and that discomfort should not be condoned. Regardless of their appearance, transsexual people who are seeking their own balanced relationship with their bodies are no less real, no less human, no less entitled to basic respect or dignity, and no more responsible for the state of gender dynamics or wars between sexes than are those for whom congruity has always been the norm.

Through my first year in the men's group, I struggled with my need to acknowledge all of my experience, with my need to be accepted as a man, and with my fear of being excluded from the group of men if my history in a female body became known. One of the traditions of the Sons is that once a year each man has ten minutes to tell his story to the other men, to reveal something deep and informative about who he is. I wasn't sure I could do this. I struggled against the notion that the only good transsexual is a silent, secret transsexual, and the proposition that if people knew that I was born with female genitals, that knowledge would erase their personal experience of me as a man.

As I grappled with these ideas and psychological constraints, I was also taking over producing the quarterly *FTM Newsletter* and thus increasing my contact with other transsexual men around the world who were looking for emotional and informational support in their lives. Through this contact I continually heard stories of men who were afraid to go to the doctor, men who were lonely but afraid of intimate relationships, men whose careers were stagnant but who were afraid of changing jobs, all for fear of revealing their transsexual status. I felt the level of fear and shame that so many transpeople lived with was unacceptable, and I wondered if I was harboring those fearful, shameful feelings myself. Though the gender/body dichotomy had been erased for me in routine social contexts by my transition, the dichotomy, once again, between my experience of myself and other people's assumptions about me—though now these were clearly different assumptions than they had been before—still tormented me and made my self-imposed silence about my unique experience of manhood and my still different body increasingly painful. I felt my integrity was compromised by silence, and yet I did not want to be known as anything other than the man I was.

I kept my secret for five months, at which point Bruce invited me to help facilitate a second men's group he wanted to start. There was a waiting list for the Sons because the group could not accommodate more than forty without diminishing the collective experience; a second group could serve the dozen or so men who were on the waiting list. I felt that if I were to take on a leadership role, I would have to come out as a transsexual man. I didn't want to take a chance that someone would find out through seeing me in one of the two documentaries in which I had already appeared (though I used different pseudonyms in each one). I was concerned that someone might feel betrayed by the fact that I had withheld this information from him. I told Bruce that there was something I needed to discuss with him, and I refused to discuss it with him over the phone, so we arranged to meet a little early at the studio before the next group session.

Bruce showed up late for our appointment, dropped his keys as he tried to unlock the building, and spilled his papers on the sidewalk. He apologized; I said it was fine, but I was concerned that we were running out of time. He had a lot going on in his life that had nothing to do with me, but in my own self-conscious self-interest I imagined that Bruce's behavior was all about me, that perhaps he thought I was planning to tell him I was gay, or maybe that I was in love with him, and he didn't want to hear it, which in retrospect was a ridiculous assumption: Bruce was secure in himself, had no problem with gay men, and since he was also a therapist in private practice he knew how to handle misplaced emotions. But I was thinking only of myself, and by the time we got upstairs into the studio there were only fifteen minutes left before men would begin to arrive. I decided I needed to show him that I did not intend to violate his personal space, so I went to lean against the wall a good ten feet from where Bruce had planted himself.

"Well, there isn't much time now," I began, "so I guess I'll just cut to the chase. I am very interested in the leadership opportunity you're offering me, but I feel that I should tell you something about myself before you invest any effort in training me. You need to know that I am almost forty-three years old, and I have only been perceived completely as a man for the past two and a half years. I spent my first forty years in a female body. I am a transsexual man. You may not think I am the right man to lead other men, and I want you to know this about me before you make that decision."

Bruce was visibly confused, then visibly relieved. I thought it was because he realized it wasn't about him, but he later told me that he had imagined I had a terminal illness. Relieved to know I was not dying, he looked confused again as what I had told him sunk in. He said, "What? What does this mean?" He had the responsibility of protecting the integrity and mission of the group, against which he had to balance the needs of its members, and he still recognized me as one of them.

"It means I've had gender confirmation surgery, I take testosterone to support my system because I don't have testicles that produce testosterone like you do. My experience of being a man is different in some ways from that of other men. There are a lot of common experiences guys share that I have not experienced, like boy's locker rooms in junior high, registering for the draft, pissing contests. It's like I came here from another country. My experience is different. But I assure you, I am a man." Just then we heard familiar voices outside, men arriving for the meeting.

Bruce stared at me. "I have so many questions," he said. "I wish we had more time."

It was two weeks before he said anything more to me. I had stayed to help put things away after the rehearsal, and Bruce said, "If you are still interested in that leadership role, I still want to offer it to you."

"Really?"

"Yes. I've been thinking about this and watching you. I think I've taken apart everything I knew about gender and sex and what it means to be a man, and put it all back together again. When I look at you, I see a man with musical ability who is responsible, capable, reliable, who shows up and is willing to do his part in the group. I'm not sure I fully understand it yet, but I think you have something really powerful to teach us all, and I'd like to encourage you to tell your story to all the men in the group."

"Oh, I'm not ready for that. That's way too scary for me right now."

"Okay, fine, no pressure. It's your story. You make that decision. But I encourage you to tell the rest of the leadership team when you feel ready to do that."

Over the next few weeks, I was able to tell two more of the five men on the leadership team, and these men astounded me with their acceptance and their willingness to keep my secret with me until I was ready to give it away. One of them, John Gunty, summed up his reaction in a way that others since have confirmed as mirroring their own: "At first I thought it was strange. I knew him, but now there was this new piece. He was a man, but people had treated him as a woman, and that's very different. I wondered what makes him a man, what makes *me* a man? I wondered whether I would see him differently from that point on. It was like a cognitive dissociation. But eventually I just settled. I saw that the James I knew now was the same man as the James I knew before." He would articulate this sentiment in the 1997 film, *You Don't Know Dick*, but before that he expressed it through his friendship.

This acceptance was highly reassuring, but another eight months went by before I felt the time was right to present my truth to the entire group. All the intellectualizing I could manage wouldn't diminish my fear of being thrown out, of losing the music, the camaraderie, the sense of finally fitting in that I had found there.

Letting Go of Shame

Throughout that same eight-month period I was coming to realize that the only way for me to cast off the fear and shame that I kept hearing in the stories of other transsexual men was to find a way to live without it. To do that meant to reconcile my past and present, to internalize the belief that there is nothing wrong with being a transsexual person, and to recognize that we don't have to be ashamed of the conditions into which we were born or of the choices we made in dealing with our transgendered lives. I kept telling myself these things, kept questioning why people had so much fear and shame, and kept coming up with no reasonable answer beyond the fear itself, fear that was based in real violence, rejection, and discrimination. To face that fear, I needed to address what caused it.

I understood the common misperceptions: that transsexual people are mentally unbalanced; that they have a sexual perversion that forces them to want to mutilate their bodies; that their identity may be viewed as a delusion; that they are simply homosexuals who cannot accept their own homosexuality so they beg doctors to make them "normal." I knew that I didn't fit those stereotypes, and increasingly I was meeting transsexual people who were much more like me than like what we were "supposed" to be. I was also aware that not every transsexual person has access to the medical system, or to good information about the options available to him or her. When people are disadvantaged, economically, racially, physically, or even when it is only self-confidence that we lack—when the playing field is not level in all respects—we who are judged inferior often suffer disproportionate social abuse as a result of our inability or unwillingness to "play the game" to get what we need. I thought there should be no reason why some people should have their gender identity validated and others shouldn't just because they couldn't afford surgery to bring themselves into alignment, or because they couldn't be aligned the way other people were for whatever reason. I began to practice letting go of the vicious judgments that we unconsciously adopt when we don't know what to think about gender variance. I realized that if people like me did not tell the truth about us, how would anyone learn about the reality of transgendered and transsexual people's lives? How else would those causes of fear and shame be eliminated? Once I had successfully internalized these concepts I knew it was time to come out to the men in the Sons.

I was very nervous that night in June of 1992 when I was slated to tell my story. I had been in the group for thirteen months; my story was overdue, and the men were curious. There was an air of excitement in the candle-lit room as everyone settled in on the floor, facing me, and Bruce began to tap the soft story-telling rhythm on his large hoop drum that brought the men to calm attention. I wanted to run away as I stared into each of their faces. But I stood up before them and told them from my heart that once upon a time there was a little boy named James. I told them what his life was like as a boy who was generally happy and healthy and loved, but who had problems now and then because his body was different from other boys' bodies, because he wasn't allowed to do things other boys or men were expected to do. James had problems now and then when people told him he had to wear a dress because he had a female body. James had to learn to accept people for who they are no matter what they look like, no matter what his own expectations for others might be, and to learn how to be himself in the most productive way, regardless of the limitations his body might impose, regardless of scars, or infertility, or having a small penis, or a penis that doesn't function the way others might expect it to function. Because James knew it's not a penis that makes someone a man. Being a man is a gestalt, a wholeness of mind and body in which one part may have to be stronger than another in order to make the whole complete; it's being a human being who happens to be some combination of masculine and male, and maybe with some feminine thrown in. And it all has to be okay because that's just part of being alive. I told them. And at the end Bruce's drumming stopped, but my heart pounded louder than it ever had before. I waited for the men's response.

There was a long moment of silence, and then one of the most admired and respected men in the group, a rugged, deep-feeling sixty-year-old Mexican man, spoke slowly and deliberately: "Never in my life have I had more respect for any man than I have for you now, and I am proud to call you my brother." He set the tone and the others heard it, and there was a thunder of applause and appreciation so like a hero's welcome that I bathed in the glory of it like an infant relaxing in a warm bath after the trauma of birth.

Over the next several weeks many other men told me how much they appreciated my story. One man my own age confessed to me that my words had given him the key to letting go of some shame that he had long held about himself, that he realized had been holding him back. Over the next several years I was affirmed over and over by these men who revealed to me how my own masculinity and my ease and comfort in my body was an inspiration for many of them, both before they knew my secret, and long afterward. In large part because of their affirmation, as well as the thinking I had been doing, in 1993 I began to use my real name in films and interviews about transsexualism.

My life is still filled with little comings-out, though they have never again been so charged since that June night with the Sons, and since I finally let go of my own shame and of the need for approval from others. Being a transsexual man has become an integrated part of me like being adopted or having food allergies or a particular ethnic or religious background, or a preference for broccoli over kale, or an interest in photography, or the ability to teach someone else to ski. I don't discuss it all the time, or when it is inappropriate. It important to who I am, but it is not the most important thing about me. When I come out now it is to note that my experience is different from that of other men because I spent forty years in a female body; not that I used to be a woman, but that I have a bit more knowledge about what a woman experiences than do other men.

In the case of impending physical intimacy I will choose to come out, to inform my partner that my genitalia may not be what she or he expects to find, and to assure her or him that I have skills that will overcome any anticipated deficiency because I love my body now and am fully present in committing it to pleasure with a partner. And people who are able to shed their own preconceptions in the face of this knowledge about me will find that being a transman does not make me less of a man in any way. Without excessive compromise to my personal and private life, I do educational work now as broadly and as publicly as possible because I don't want people to have to suffer the internalized shame that kept me from dealing openly with my own transgenderedness for so many years. And I don't want non-transgendered or non-transsexual people to continue ridiculing, stigmatizing, persecuting, and punishing us because we are different. In fact, I believe my own—and other transpeople's—coming out (when it is safe to do so!) has the capacity to enrich everyone's experience of their own gender and the ability to accept diversity in others.

I cannot and will not blame transpeople who choose not to reveal their histories at particular times. Should every person be required to tell everything about himself to everyone? I don't think so. And if I don't tell someone that I am a transsexual man, does it mean I haven't told them that I am "really" a "woman"? Perhaps my being transsexual has no bearing on the relationship in question. Being transsexual is not a disease. I don't expose anyone to any personal risk by withholding that information about myself. Will you think something vile about me because I didn't tell you my "secret" at some particular time—say, before you felt attracted to me? If so, why? What damage do you suffer? Is it only that you would have been saved the embarrassment of being attracted to someone whom you feel is too strange, too mutilated, or too perverted? Should you have known better than to allow yourself to be "fooled" by something so "unnatural"? An honest answer here will display one's level of prejudice against transsexual people. I believe that learning not to fear difference and to recognize and combat prejudice whenever it is affecting us is crucial to ending the terrible legacies of sexism, racism, classism, and hatred and fear of homosexual or transgendered people that have so brutally scarred our collective psyche.

As the intensity of my political work increased in the mid-1990s, an energetic shift was also occurring within the Sons. The group began spending less time on performance-oriented percussion work in favor of processing their feelings. While this must have been necessary for the men involved, it felt to me like old business that I had put behind me. I needed more time for my writing, travel, and political networking, so I retired from active participation in Bruce's original group on July 13, 1994.

Meanwhile, John Gunty and I together led Bruce's second soul-making group for men from November 1991 through June 1995. I liked to call the group "Son of Sons." We taught the men basic drumming techniques and rhythms, and we encouraged each other to be honest with ourselves and to practice speaking to other men from our hearts. John is one of the most gifted listeners and creators of "safe containers" in which men can explore their feelings whom I've been honored to know. And the men who shared that work with us over those years were all brave explorers themselves. Several of them remain close friends. To borrow from John Lennon, "Some are dead and some are living; in my life, I've loved them all."

Taking Responsible Action

Initiation, whether independent or within a group, does not propel us fully formed, or fully informed, into some bright future; it only starts us down a path. When Lou Sullivan died in March of 1991, the FTM group of San Francisco took a quantum leap into the present and began to gather the strength it would need to help propel the nascent transgender community into a forward-thinking political and social movement. It was almost as if, in the year or two preceding Sullivan's death, everyone was being respectful of him, knowing he was ill, not wanting to make demands on him to which he couldn't respond. Approximately forty people (about double the usual attendance) showed up at the quarterly meeting following his memorial service, and a quick poll showed the majority wanted meetings to occur monthly instead of quarterly. Over the ensuing months and years, our visibility increased and even more people looked to the group for connection, information, and support. Tension developed between FTMs who wanted the group to be politically active, progressively accelerating social change, and those who just wanted to drop in for a while, get information, and go their own way—or preserve the status quo. I had not asked for leadership, but the group conferred leadership upon me, and it was up to me to rise to the occasion.

I tried to walk a middle line, developing a group that could accommodate divergent motivations or goals without invalidating anyone who either investigated or walked our transitional path. I made no requirements of anyone beyond showing up and giving each other respect. I felt the most important thing FTM transsexual and transgendered people needed at that time was to realize that we were not alone. We needed to be able to make contact with people like ourselves. We all needed to be able to network with each other to find reliable information about negotiating our lives out on the gender frontier. The older generation had to pass their knowledge on to the younger generation, and the lore of transition and/or successful androgyny had to be preserved.

When I took it over in 1991, the *FTM Newsletter* mailing list had 235 names—not many, really, but they were scattered around the world and each name represented many more people who belonged to support groups that shared a subscription or who were unwilling to have their name on a list because they didn't want to be found out to be transsexual. Back then, the internet didn't exist as a household appliance, and Sullivan had only had a computer for a short while before he died. His records were all handwritten. I knew carrying on Sullivan's work of bringing together the disparate elements of our collective experience would be a huge effort and a challenge for everyone who entered the sphere of our group, whether they attended meetings or simply read the *FTM Newsletter*.

The psychological model for an FTM transsexual has long been an independent tomboy-type who is sexually attracted to women and uncomfortable relating to women as another woman (R. Green, 1974; Fagan, Schmidt & Wise, 1994). It was common knowledge among people seeking surgical assistance for self-actualization that the doctor wanted to hear certain "facts" about your motivation before he'd treat you, so you told the doctor what he or she wanted to hear (Stone, 1991). Many doctors have, therefore, assumed that all FTM transsexual people were attracted to women, and that they were afraid to be homosexual—that is, they were homophobic and couldn't accept themselves as lesbians. As long as we were kept separate from each other, many of us felt that fitting the psychological model was the only way to get medical treatment. As recently as 1999 I heard a physician declare, "All *my* FTMs want tattoos," as if this proved "his" FTMs were typical men, or that FTMs who didn't want tattoos were somehow less authentic than "his" FTMs. An additional consequence of this monolithic analysis is that we ourselves labor under the mistaken assumption that we are all alike.

This monolithic model attempted to reinforce another aspect of stereotypical gender behavior—that men are uncommunicative. Since the 1970s, gender clinics and peer support groups alike sponsored rap sessions for transsexuals that were attended mostly by MTF-transitioning people. Because FTM people were not interested in hearing about female hormones and female grooming tips, they stayed away from these groups, prompting professionals to assume that, in order to be like "other" men, transsexual men cultivate independence and don't need or want support groups. I find it ironic that the rise of the mythopoetic men's movement (and other branches of the men's consciousness raising movement) in the 1990s coincided with the start of increased visibility for transsexual men. While "men's work" like that undertaken by the Sons of Orpheus has been widely ridiculed (as has transsexualism), it nonetheless has had an indelibly positive effect in the lives of countless men. As the stereotype of the strong, silent male is broken down in our society, transsexual men, the medical model adherents, and men everywhere are learning that communication among men does not threaten their independence. Transsexual men—just like other men—will come together to communicate when they realize that they are not alone and do not have to be afraid. For too long, individual transsexual men have gone to clinics or support groups only to become further isolated. Being told "We find the men like to go it alone" has reinforced the culturally required separateness between men and, paradoxically, decreased their autonomy by discouraging contact and information exchange with others like themselves.

In conforming to the early psychological-medical model, transsexual men have lived largely invisible lives. Although we may have found work and lovers or marriage partners, and lived in relatively stable situations, we have often kept our history secret from our partner's family, our communities, our children, and in some cases, even from our partners. This is how many wish to live, and some have been troubled by the increasing visibility of other transsexual men. Many do not want to be known as transsexual; many feel their past is not relevant, that it's no one's business but their own. Their goal is to live as men, and they're doing that, thank you very much; now, will you activists and attention-seekers please just go away? Well, probably not. There will always be people who seek attention, and they will come and go. Activists interested in social change may burn out or drop out, but collectively they won't stop. Not if the state of FTM surgery is to be improved. Not if the level of understanding is to increase, among psychiatrists, psychologists, doctors, lawyers, judges, law enforcement officers, employers, and society at large, about who we are and that we deserve respect and equality. Not so long as we are discontent with the lies that are perpetuated about us. Not if we want to obliterate the condition of shame that forces so many of us to avoid treatment or to deny our histories. Not if we want to be treated as human beings. There is too much suffering, and those of us who respond to human need will not give up easily.

Thus, my second initiation in 1991 was into non-profit organizational leadership, learning (and encouraging others) to take on responsibility for the group, and learning to apply what I knew about customer service from my business experience to providing service to others in a volunteer context. I felt it was necessary to learn to speak the truth about our collective situation so that we could make better life choices, obtain better medical and psychological treatment, have more surgical options, increase our self-esteem, and find a way to acknowledge our differences. I remain convinced that speaking the truth is the best way to ensure that we can live in safety and with dignity.

I experienced yet another initiation, this time into the world of political action to influence governmental policy, when I was invited to speak before an advisory committee to the San Francisco Human Rights Commission in 1992. The Lesbian, Gay, Bisexual Advisory Committee was being asked to learn about transgendered and transsexual people because Commission staff member Larry Brinkin noted that some of the worst discrimination and violence he'd ever seen was being perpetrated against transsexual people and crossdressers in San Francisco, and there was nothing in the city's administrative code that allowed him to address it.

There was considerable resistance from some members of the committee who felt there was no synergy between issues of sexual orientation and transsexual or crossdressing behavior. But meeting after meeting, for eighteen months, I and a few other transsexual people, a few crossdressers, and some local psychotherapists worked to educate the committee about the hatred that underlies violence against transgendered and transsexual people. We told about the history of transgendered people within the gay community and posed the possibility that same-sex relationships break the same gender boundaries that transgendered people are crossing. We brought in speakers from the transsexual and crossdressing communities who represented every race, multiple cultures, varied classes, and every sexual orientation. In 1993 the committee voted to ask the Human Rights Commission to add transgender to the advisory committee's name and also to recommend that the commission hold a public hearing to investigate discrimination against transgendered people in San Francisco. The commission granted these requests, and the committee formed a Transgender Task Force to organize the public hearing. A transsexual woman, Kiki Whitlock, was named the chairperson of the task force. I was the conduit to the FTM population. Psychotherapist Luanna Rodgers was also one of the primary organizers of speakers, along with Larry Brinkin, who helped us structure the events of the hearing.

The public hearing was held in the Board of Supervisors' Chambers in San Francisco City Hall on May 12, 1994. I was nervous about speaking in such an official atmosphere, to people who had power and authority. I didn't want to make any mistakes. Roughly one hundred citizens attended and, in addition to the forty-four scheduled speakers, twenty-eight private individuals turned in cards asking for an opportunity to speak for two minutes each during the public testimony phase. Many of those involved, including myself, had never been inside the City Hall before, and we were excited about the fact that we would be heard, yet we were skeptical that it would matter much in the long run. After a lifetime of being told you don't matter, or that you are so "wrong" you deserve whatever horrid things happen to you, it can be difficult to muster much faith in the system.

It was a complete coincidence that only a few days before the hearing, FTM group member and San Francisco Police Sergeant Stephanie Thorne announced publicly that he was a female-to-male transsexual and would be transitioning on the job with the support of his Captain and of the Chief. He was that day declaring that thenceforth he would be known publicly as Stephan Thorne (as we in the FTM support group already knew him), and that masculine pronouns would be appropriate in reference to him. Naturally, this made the evening TV news, the local papers (with headlines like "S.F. Cop Plans Sex Change Surgery" in the *San Francisco Chronicle*, May 6, 1994) and national magazines (Gorney, 1994). Loren Cameron would be mounting his first public exhibit of photographs of transsexual people in a local gallery the following week, where actress/playwright and performance artist Kate Bornstein and I would read from our works on opening night (a record-setting 260 people attended the event). And emerging actor/playwright David Harrison, another FTM group member, would debut his one-man play *FTM* later that same month (and take it on international tours in ensuing years). The climate couldn't have been better for getting the word out that this long-disenfranchised group was no longer content to live underground.

The term "transgender" had been around since the 1970s, conceived of independently by a number of people including Jude Patton (an FTM pioneer), but usually attributed to Virginia Prince, the "grand dame" of crossdressers, who started support groups in the 1950s, published numerous books on crossdressing, and eventually came to live full-time as a woman, though the term was just starting to come into common usage in the 1990s. Prince had used the term "transgender" in her many publications of the 1970s and 1980s to distinguish herself from transsexual people (whom she understood as desirous of sex reassignment surgery) and transvestites (whom she understood to be episodically expressing a psychosexual pathology), motivations she did not share. The term was being newly popularized by socialist writer Leslie Feinberg in the 1992 pamphlet "Trans Gender Liberation: a movement whose time has come" and promoted by Kate Bornstein, whose brilliant play *Hidden: A Gender* was first performed in San Francisco in 1989, and who would later publish several books. There was—and still is—a lot of dissension around the term "transgender," particularly among transsexual people who were—and are—afraid it would obfuscate their specific concerns and further marginalize those who undergo surgical sex reassignment. My opinion at the time was that although I didn't care for it personally, "transgender" was a politically useful term that could potentially help a vast number of people, and that we who were transsexual should take responsibility for making sure that our unique issues did not get lost. The concept of transgender seemed to allow discussion of the civil rights issues faced by gender-variant people without limiting the discussion to transsexual people, or conflating sexuality—and popular misconceptions about the role of sex and morality in transsexual identity—with gender-based social issues. And while I think many of the nay-sayers' prognostications of difficulties arising from the term were correct, the gains made from widespread adoption of the term "transgender" are difficult to dismiss.

Yes, it's a problem that people think "transgender" means someone who wants to change their sex; yes, it's a problem that "transgender health care" is used to mean hormones and surgery. We continue to latch onto "gender" as a euphemism for "sex." But the inclusion of transgendered and transsexual people in the civil rights efforts of all the national gay and lesbian groups in only a few years, and the willingness of these groups to realize that the discrimination against them extends beyond the bedroom and beyond their sexual object choice is a significant evolutionary achievement that will continue to transform the way society on the whole thinks about sexuality and about difference.

The San Francisco public hearing in May 1994 was to be documented in a report, and the Human Rights Commission sought a contractor to write it. Their project budget was significantly below my customary fee for technical or business writing, but I bid on the job knowing the report would be an opportunity to make a difference far beyond San Francisco. I won the contract despite some opposition on the basis that I was a white male. Once the transcript of the hearing was completed, I analyzed the testimony, summarized the proceedings, and developed the "Findings and Recommendations" that the San Francisco Human Rights Commission would later adopt in its *Report on Discrimination Against Transgendered People* (J. Green, 1994). Those findings and recommendations are a succinct summary of the issues transpeople face, and what should be done about them from a municipal perspective. That report continues to be one of the most requested public documents the city has ever published, and it has influenced public policy in many other jurisdictions.

The first recommendation was that protective legislation be created and passed to deliver the message that discrimination against transgendered people was not tolerated in San Francisco. I was invited to serve on the small committee that would assist the City Attorney's office in drafting the ordinance, and it was passed by the Board of Supervisors in December 1994, and signed into law by Mayor Frank Jordan, taking effect in January 1995. It sounds simple, but it was not an easy process. It took years of testimony, argument, persuasion, negotiation, cooperation, and tenacity. Many people were involved in the effort, and some powerful people opposed us, yet we won. I emerged with greater confidence, greater tolerance for the political process, and greater sophistication to guide me in the struggle that lay ahead. Though we had achieved a significant victory, everyone involved knew that one civic ordinance would not ensure social safety or equality for transgendered people the world over; transpeople would have to work very hard to raise consciousness and earn acceptance everywhere. I knew there was still a tremendous amount of very basic work to be done among our own members if the transgender and transsexual population was to develop any kind of cohesion and broader community consciousness.

3
A Vision of Community

My first foray into what might be called a community of transsexual men and their loved ones in 1988 introduced me to a paraculture of people who were decidedly apolitical, which was just fine by me. In those days, the few people I met who wanted to transition from female to male were concerned primarily with their own personal access to medical technology and social acceptance as men. Most were serious about keeping their transition a secret, leaving transsexualism behind, and getting on with their lives.

I was like that then, too. I was somewhat shy and did not consider myself a "joiner." In 1988 I was not interested in being part of any club or organization, and the fact that Sullivan's group met only four times a year seemed about right. After all, one doesn't want his whole life to be about his transition, which I believed should be a temporary condition, to be dealt with as expeditiously as possible, like an embarrassing flaw. Not a big deal; certainly nothing to discuss with strangers. I anticipated getting some information, getting a sex change, and going home to mow my lawn.

I connected with Sullivan through a little quarterly publication out of Atlanta, Georgia, called *The Transsexual Voice*. It contained mostly articles about male-to-female experience, but it was the only transsexual-specific ongoing publication I had found. I don't remember how I learned about it, but I had begun doing tentative research into transsexual experience and potential resources earlier in the 1980s. But in 1987 I noticed a tiny advertisement that read: "Information for the female-to-male crossdresser and transsexual. Send $6.00 to L. Sullivan . . ." at a San Francisco address. I did so immediately, marveling that I should have to subscribe to an obscure publication from Atlanta to locate something within a few miles of my home. Before long, the postal service delivered a little self-published booklet filled with information about expressing masculine social cues, advice about clothing and hairstyles, vignettes concerning women in the past who had lived convincingly as men (until they either got in trouble with the law and their female bodies were discovered while they were incarcerated, or they died and their female bodies were discovered after death), and the basics of male hormones and FTM sex reassignment surgery. It was also accompanied by a neatly penciled note on a yellow Post-it® square, saying: "Let me know if you wish to be on our mailing list and I will send you an invitation to our next Get-Together."

Lou Sullivan and the FTM Group

Louis Grayson Sullivan was a slender, affable man in his mid-thirties, about three years younger than I was. He had a warm handshake as he welcomed me into the "Get-Together," and I watched him with others as he spoke with them, observing that he treated everyone with the same level of courtesy. He would look in your eyes as he spoke to you, remembering the contact he'd had with you previously, either by mail or telephone, and like a genial host he would ask if you had met the fellow nearest you. Eventually, he would step up to the front of the room to call the session to order, make announcements and introductions, and get things rolling, whether that afternoon's agenda was a presentation or an open, free-flowing discussion. But he seemed to prefer being in the background for the most part. He was quiet and unassuming, with a bookish quality. He was not charismatic or dynamic, but he was organized, intelligent, and caring. He also had a wicked sense of humor that could turn sarcastic and then acid in a snap. He loved history, and was one of the founding members of the Gay and Lesbian Historical Society of Northern California (now known as the GLBT Historical Society). He went out of his way to engage in dialogue with professionals who were contributing to the literature, like psychiatrist Ira Pauly, and psychologists Paul Walker and Walter Bockting, to try to expand clinical awareness of FTM issues. In particular he stressed the difference between sexual orientation and gender identity, and the fact that transsexual people could be gay or lesbian or bisexual after their transition—orientations as valid as heterosexuality. People respected Sullivan because he was honest, intelligent, principled, and co-operative. He wasn't the first to offer support groups for FTM people; Jeff S. in Southern California, Rupert Raj in Toronto, and Johnny A. and Mario Martino on the east coast were already doing it. Sullivan's success was that he had a sense of what information others needed, and he tried to offer it through his communication. He continually invited suggestions, other ideas, and leadership, but if no one else stepped up he was willing to do the work required to organize the local meetings and produce the *FTM Newsletter.*

That publication was one of the most important services Sullivan provided. Though it often was only a single eleven-inch by fourteen-inch sheet, half of which might be about some historical female-bodied person who had lived as a man, and the other half book reviews and a recap of a meeting three months prior, it was devoured by its readership. In those days, the content of the newsletter didn't seem to matter. What did matter was that there was finally something outside ourselves that we could look at and realize that, although we were different, we were not alone. That newsletter was a lifeline for people outside the San Francisco Bay Area who were isolated and could find no other contact with people like themselves. Those of us in the Bay Area also had the benefit of Sullivan's "Get-Togethers."

Over the next three years, through 1990, there were a few "regulars" who could be relied upon to attend Sullivan's meetings. There were always people who drifted in and out, or who came once or twice and then vanished, but the core group who would show up fluctuated between six and twenty people. In those days, Sullivan screened every attendee by mail or telephone, and some received an in-person interview, too, before they'd be given the meeting location. Confidentiality was extremely important to everyone then. The last thing any of us wanted was to be known as a transsexual person.

I didn't consider myself one of the "regulars," though I don't think I missed more than two meetings in those years. My own reservation about being considered a regular attendee was about perceiving myself as independent, someone who could take care of himself and didn't really need other people. I had my partner, Samantha, and a few close friends, and I had my work associates and my family—that was enough to deal with. I didn't need more people in my life. I told myself I just went to the meetings because they were there. Sometimes there were people at those meetings who were not really people I'd want to be friends with, people I thought were too angry or too depressed or too messed up somehow. But the truth was that even though everyone wasn't just like me, even though everyone wasn't someone I'd have chosen as a close friend, it was fascinating to meet and hear stories from people who shared my own feeling of knowing we were male people who had been born with female bodies. It was encouraging to meet others who were all in the process of trying to understand themselves and manage their lives.

Loren Cameron, photographer and author of *Body Alchemy* (1996), was one of several men I met at my first FTM meeting in March of 1988 and with whom I soon became friends. He recalled that he had been twelve years old and living in Arkansas when he first sent away to the Janus Information Facility to learn about transsexualism. Loren probably wrote to Janus's predecessor, the Erickson Educational Foundation (see Meyerowitz, 2002, chapter 6, for a concise history of transsexual-focused organizations in the 1960s and 1970s). For Loren the issue was one of great discomfort with the form of his body. In spite of his internal discomfort, his attraction to women led him to enter the lesbian community, where he lived for eleven years. "I had some separatist leanings," Loren told me, "mostly from frustration with the way men treat women culturally." But while he sensed his difference from the women around him, his feminist pride demanded that he bury his masculine feelings. At that March 27, 1988 "Get-Together," the second one he'd attended, he was seeking practical information about local medical resources for basic healthcare. I perceived him as intense and determined. He had been living as a man for almost a year, though to me, underneath his motorcycle jacket, jeans, and steel-toed boots, he still looked as androgynous as I did. I liked his quick intelligence and his independent streak.

At the opposite end of the experience and knowledge range were Steve Dain and John G., the guest speakers at that meeting. They seemed so mature and solid, wearing chinos or jeans and sport shirts, casual and self-assured, aware but not wary or guarded at all, open and willing to share themselves with everyone. Their stories of self-discovery and journeys toward self-acceptance closely paralleled my own. That was what I needed to see and hear in 1988. I was pushing my own limitations in managing my androgyny and figuring out how I fit into society. My personal comfort zone was shrinking. I wasn't sure I could go on much longer in a female body, living what was apparently a male social role, having a male self-image, and using a little-boy persona to convince people I was likable and not too threatening—the same little boy act I'd been using since childhood. I had responsibilities now, and it was time to grow up. I felt so different from the women I knew and loved and worked with, I was certain I could never grow up to be a woman; I was afraid that for me growing up really did mean becoming a man. After all the years of knowing that truth and still trying to avoid it, I was then starting to face a reality that was both exhilarating and terrifying. The men at that first meeting were living proof that I could make this transition. And the risks of social and economic loss, the health risks of hormonal changes, and the surgical risks of mutilation or even death, while daunting, no longer seemed as dangerous as a life unfulfilled. When the meeting ended, I watched those men, Steve, John, Lou, Loren, and the sixteen others who were there, walk out of the building and disappear into the fabric of society, as most FTMs can and do, and the reality of it took my breath away, filled me with anticipation and anxiety, and confirmed my resolve. It only took attending a couple more of Sullivan's "Get-Togethers" before I realized I cared about these people and looked forward to seeing them. For the most part, they were average-looking men; well, a little bit shorter than average for the most part, but they still presented your typical San Francisco cross-section of styles and backgrounds from working class to prep-boy yuppie, from professional to chronically unemployed.

We had three self-identified female-to-male crossdressers in the group, too, which was interesting considering that the psychological literature at the time said there was no such thing as a female crossdresser. These individuals were each very different from the other, while all three of them were different from those of us who were undergoing or hoping to undergo biomedical transformation culminating in a legal change of sex. Francis fit the classic description of a crossdresser: she was employed as a female, and she frequently wore feminine clothing. She was married to a man. She had a male persona that emerged when she dressed in a man's suit and tie, often with a fedora or other dapper masculine accessories. She'd drop her voice nearly an octave, and acquit herself in a masculine way that did not seem quite possible for her when she was dressed as a woman. She had fun going out at night in her male persona and flirting with straight women, and she fancied himself as a kind of gangster from the 1940s.

Sam and Tony were not like Francis at all. Both of them regularly wore men's suits to work, and neither of them tried to mask her female voice, female name, or female identity. But Sam was on a crusade to find others like herself (she dropped out of sight in 1993), and Tony was actively resisting, yet seriously considering, living as a man and transitioning to a male identity, which he did in the mid-1990s.

There were also two African-American men who were struggling in their different ways with the fact that anything having to do with sexual variance was taboo in their culture of origin. They were trying to get their family members to understand and accept their gender identity, trying to negotiate their changes of sex without losing their jobs, trying to adjust to being perceived as black men in a hostile, racist society. One of them, David, a tall, muscular, strikingly handsome man, with a deep sense of spiritual integrity, has remained my friend to this day. The other, Seth, who lived with his gracious wife in a lovely upper middle-class neighborhood home, was an educator. Neither David nor Seth discussed or claimed any connection to the lesbian community. Seth and his wife moved out of the area by the end of 1990, as I recall, and I haven't heard of them since.

There was also Kim, an Asian-American scientist who had been living as a man since 1979. He was glad he had gone through transition at age twenty-two, when he was younger and closer to his chronological puberty. He felt his early transition helped him grow up and learn his role as a man more gradually. He didn't feel as tied to the lesbian and feminist movements as many others did, but he was still conscious of women's issues and had become a vocal advocate for equality between the sexes. And there were several other transsexual-identified men, Latino, white, Hawaiian, black, immigrants from Europe, the Middle East, India, China, and Malaysia, who drifted in and out.

Sullivan, leader of the pack, really liked this kind of variety. His own identification was with the gay male community, but he didn't make a big deal about it, just referred to his particular experience in the same matter of fact way that everyone else spoke of their own. Most of the people attending the "Get-Togethers" expressed attraction to women. Whenever anyone expressed their position about anything in a way that implied superiority, the rest of the usually small group would gently convey the message that there was no superior way to be. We agreed that we all had different experiences, different perspectives, and that each of us was equally valid as a human being.

Sullivan himself was not advancing any agenda other than the notion that getting reliable information about the medical technology FTMs use and the social issues FTMs face should not be as difficult as it had been historically. He did have three pet peeves that he expressed directly and indirectly often enough that I cannot think of him without imagining a situation in which he's saying something about one or another of them. The first was that sexual orientation should not be a gating factor determining access to surgical transformation (which it definitely was at the time); another was that it wasn't right for anyone to judge whether someone else's expression of masculinity was "correct," no matter what kind of body was doing the expressing; and the last was that FTM people deserved as much attention, study, and recognition as MTFs. I couldn't agree more.

I also enjoyed reading the little *FTM Newsletter* that Sullivan produced with the help of his friend Kevin Horwitz. Issue #1 appeared in September 1987; the first issue Sullivan sent to me when I wrote to him was #2, December 1987. Sullivan would send out a flyer announcing the next meeting to his local mailing list, and you could come and pick up your newsletter, hang out for a few hours with some interesting people, and maybe listen to a guest speaker. If you couldn't make it to the meeting, Sullivan would send your newsletter immediately following the meeting, when he sent them out to the rest of his mailing list. The numbers were small enough that he could keep track of everyone. Since he had lost his job after being diagnosed with AIDS in 1987, all Sullivan wanted to do in his remaining days was to help make life better for FTM people. He spent hours responding to letters from lost, lonely transsexual people, trying to build the networks that he wished had been there for him, and that he hoped would sustain the rest of us after he was gone.

Although he was often irritated by the resources available to MTF people in contrast to the lack of awareness about FTMs, even among transsexual people, Sullivan felt a strong connection to the MTF crossdressing and transsexual community. He patterned our meetings after the ones held by ETVC (Educational TV Channel), primarily a social group for male crossdressers, their predominantly female partners, and a few MTF transsexual people. The group, now known as Transgender San Francisco (TGSF), even in the late 1980s boasted a membership of over 300 local people. They usually met in bars or restaurants that offered meeting spaces, and usually purchased enough liquor that the management appreciated their patronage regardless of what they were wearing. Through his connections to ETVC, Sullivan organized FTM meetings in one of the same restaurant locations, but the small number of people attending the FTM group didn't drink much, and didn't seem to have money to spend on restaurant meals, so before long we were forced to seek other venues. By 1990 we were meeting in a rented room at the Metropolitan Community Church in the Castro District, the heart of San Francisco's gay business district. Money for the rental fees came from donations at the door.

The lore of FTM transition was exchanged in the pages of the *FTM Newsletter* and in the various support group meetings that were occurring with greater frequency around the world. One of the great services that Sullivan's newsletter provided was disseminating some of the information he gathered from FTMs in other U.S. cities and abroad. He connected us with other publishing efforts by FTMs on the east coast, like the New York "irregular" *Rites of Passage* edited by Johnny A., and the sporadic output of Toronto-based Rupert Raj. Through the medium of the newsletter, as well as the face-to-face meetings at the "Get-Togethers," we began to see how the language we used to describe ourselves differed and overlapped. We also learned about the differences in treatments that transsexual people received in various countries. In the September 1989 issue (#9), Sullivan published these two letters that give voice to some of the differences, and the similarities of longing for both connection and information.

Dear Readers of FTM,
In this case I will tell you a bit about the situation in The Netherlands. We have here a "men's group" with 150 members. Every three months there is a meeting somewhere in the country. In these meetings 70 to 80 members get together, some with their wives, others alone or with their family. [These numbers were astounding to me!]

Twice or three times a year we have a theme, varying from hormonal treatments, side effects, social problems, or operation-technics [sic]. There are several speakers and one of them once was Walter Bockting [a Dutch psychologist working at the University of Minnesota]. So it was very amusing to read he had also spoken at your meeting in April [April 9, 1989, as documented in *FTM* #8, June 1989].

The most important reason for people to come to our meetings is the possibility to meet others, change [sic] information, hear the news about operations technics and be available to the new generation of transsexuals. They have a long road to go, and it's easy for the older ones to give some warnings and attention. We don't have a magazine especially for our members. Our meetings are based on charity, this means that I will send letters to our people. They who will come to the meeting pay me back for the stamps. If somebody wants something to eat or drink they will bring it with them.

There is no real difference in our group between transsexuals or transvestites. Most crossdressers are not sure enough about themselves. After some talking with others, they are sure about the life they want. If it is only crossdressing, they don't need our group anymore. It is for a woman easy to dress in men's clothes in this world. Some of them sometimes will return, just because they like it to meet friends.

There is also a special group here for transsexuals of both directions and transvestism. This group has 200 paying members and is named TenT (transvestism and transsexualism). I am also the chairman of this group. Not all people can stand transvestism. This group gives out a magazine named Transformation. Perhaps one of you would like to write a letter in this?

One of your members wrote in FTM about the difference between here and The States. His experience with hormone shots I have never heard before, although I have met around 150 FTMs during the last 10 years. [A contributor to #8 had written that European injections were "extremely sexually stimulating" and resulted in "speedy" feeling the next day and a painful lump at the injection site that remained for a week, while he got better hair growth and no negative side effects with American testosterone preparations.] The lump where the injection had been given is only painful if it has not been done well. It's an oil-based substance and it's very important to give the injection very slowly. It's true that there are many people here with just a little hair growth. The hormones which are used here are Andriol and Sustenon. Which are used in The States? Perhaps we can change [sic] information about this?

For so far my writing about our men's group. I'm waiting for your response. With kindly regards,
J. A., The Netherlands.

And this letter from the United Kingdom:

Dear FTM Members,
I am a 23-year-old FTM in London and I am writing to you on behalf of myself and members of the GDT (Gender Dysphoria Trust). The GDT is for MTF as well as FTM but the ladies greatly outnumber us.

In the GDT we don't meet as a group as you do. People are generally more secretive here in the U.K. I think generally we have more problems legally than you do. I believe that in the States you are allowed to get your birth certificate changed, which we can't do, so in the eyes of the law we are still females. It makes life difficult with regards to employment, marriage, etc. How long has it been allowed in the States to get the birth certificate changed and did it take a lot of lobbying? Our problem is a lack of people willing to stand up to the government and our laws. That's what it really needs, but obviously people want to try to be anonymous and live a normal life when they change over and have surgery. I have to admit that I don't want my name all over the papers as I'm training to be a doctor and don't want to be conspicuous.

I haven't actually begun my therapy yet, but will soon, and I have the full support of my medical school. At the moment I am investigating what surgery is available. We have a selected few people over here who do good mastectomies, but almost without exception none of us have any genital surgery done. I was hoping that in the States the state of surgery is better than here. That is one of the reasons I'm writing to you: to find out if you have more information than we do, or if any of your members have had phalloplasty done and would be willing to give us some details of exactly what they've had done. Also, do you have the names and addresses of any good surgeons in the States who do phalloplasty and how much it costs?

I and probably other members of our group would like to correspond with some FTMs in the States. Are any of you interested in setting up a link between FTM's [sic] in the U.K. and the U.S.A.? Also, do you know of other similar groups in the States?

Like I said, we don't meet as a group as we are spread out all over the U.K., but we write to each other and meet individually, although we're hoping to get together for a weekend in the near future. I myself don't feel nearly as alone now that I have other transsexual friends.

We'd also like to hear not only from the FTM's [sic] themselves, but their lovers and partners.

I hope to hear from you and hope you'd like to set up a link.
Best wishes,
V. C., London, England

I was intrigued by the differences in experience and outlook expressed in these two letters. I had always been interested in other cultures and foreign travel, and it was reassuring to me to know that people like me existed in other places, that people with different cultural experiences of gender were experiencing the same drive to change their sex, even if they rationalized or described it in different ways. The kind of information that we could obtain from each other was simply unavailable through medical professionals or journal articles because it was always filtered through someone else's interpretations of what we needed—or ought—to hear. It was a rare American professional in those days who would encourage a transsexual person to seek others for information or social support.

In 1990 Sullivan introduced me to Jason Cromwell and Jude Patton, both of whom had already been working long and hard to educate others about our experience, and still it seemed we FTMs had not made much progress at all. For people like Jude and Jason, members of a marginalized group with special needs and historical forces that opposed their very existence, trying to balance everyday family life and regular jobs with the daunting task of creating social change was difficult at best. Neither of them wanted to be seen as a "professional transsexual" either. We all wanted to be invisible as transsexuals once we found our footing and made our transition to being visible men. We wanted to move on, but where could we go? I was beginning to realize that there is a difference between wanting the fact that one is transsexual not to create an environment of prejudice and wanting to have one's transsexual status rendered permanently invisible. I was beginning to understand that it was not possible to leave a transsexual past completely behind.

I met Blake, an Afro-American Indian university student, early in 1991. He was just beginning his physical transition, and one of his doctors referred him to Sullivan's group because she thought he should meet other FTMs for support. He and I formed an instant connection and became close friends. Blake spent most of his childhood insisting that he was male: at age three he accused his parents of having stolen his penis, and he spent years looking for the boy's name that felt right to him as opposed to the female name his parents had bestowed on him. But he learned in high school that it was best not to try to rock the boat. His mom told him if he didn't shape up he would turn out to be a lesbian; his father didn't comment directly, but gave him a book with a case study of a female-bodied, male-identified person who didn't fare well in the eyes of the study author. Even though all Blake's early lovers were heterosexual-identified women and somewhat mystified by being involved with someone in a female body, he thought if he moved to the west coast and lost himself in the lesbian world he could blend in and leave the frustration of transsexualism behind.

He was never a separatist; like me, he always had male friends, both gay and straight.

"I actually felt misplaced most of my life," he told me. "I didn't relate emotionally or cognitively to women, but I could with men. I thought if I never talked about how I felt it would go away. I kept the psychological pressure to a dull roar by seeking male-identified work where my masculine qualities were an asset rather than a liability."

So long as he did nothing about the lack of congruity between his body and his psyche, he was a champion of feminism, rebelling against limiting social roles. As soon as he realized he had to be honest about his identity in order to integrate himself, he became "a traitor to my sisters, a sell-out. I was constantly being perceived as male, getting sir'd left and right, and my friends thought they were defending my honor by correcting people." The net effect of their action was to expose Blake to harassment and abuse. "I was sick of people on the street confronting me as a 'he-she' and flying into rages, saying things like, 'I thought you was a dude—god damn! What the fuck does your husband think when something like you climbs into bed with him?'"

It is so difficult to get people who don't know what this feels like to understand. It is so easy to dismiss what we know to be true about ourselves because the only words we have can so easily sound preposterous.

"I want people to understand that this is a matter of identity, not a matter of desire," Blake emphasized over and over. "We are not women who wanted to be men. We are men who are largely invisible because we were born into female bodies."

On February 23, 1991, Lou Sullivan asked me and another friend, Peter, to come to his apartment to talk about keeping *FTM*—both the newsletter and the "Get-Togethers"—alive. His health was failing rapidly. Peter lived just a few blocks from Sullivan, and by the time I arrived he had helped bathe him and rubbed lotion into the sores on his back. On that day, Sullivan was thinner and paler than I had ever seen him. He could barely move his body, but though he tired easily his mind and spirit were there, as fresh and as clear as ever. He lay in his bed and pointed out his files and explained his methodology to us. He said his journals and most of his papers would go to the Gay & Lesbian Historical Society, but the material necessary to create the *FTM Newsletter* and continue providing information to others would go to us. We went over some of the correspondence to *FTM*, and he told us how he would respond to a few of the letters. "Of course," he said, "you'll want to handle things your own way." We assured him we'd try to stay true to his intentions, to his guiding principles. When we had finished going over things he said, "Great! Now it's done. I feel like a huge weight is off me. I'm sure you guys will take care of everything. Now all I want to do is hang on until my fortieth birthday in June."

A week later I was attending the OUT/Write conference, an annual gathering of gay and lesbian writers that was beginning to incorporate transgendered writers, too. Sullivan was supposed to speak on a panel with playwright Kate Bornstein, and I was looking forward to attending that session. Kate and another panelist were there, ready, and the audience waiting, when someone rushed to the front of the room and whispered something to Kate. She looked shocked for a moment, then she nodded, and as the person moved to speak with the other panelist, Kate beckoned me to come to her.

"Lou died this morning," she said simply. "I'm sorry."

I nodded, feeling like the wind had been knocked out of me, yet strangely peaceful.

"You're in charge now," she added.

"Oh, my god," I whispered. I hadn't thought of it that way. "Oh, my god."

Sullivan died peacefully on March 2, 1991, at his home, in his sister's arms. It was his sister's birthday. He left me with a roll of stamps, a stack of index cards with names and addresses comprising the *FTM Newsletter* mailing list, and a few articles that he had accumulated for the next issue of the publication. A "Get-Together" had already been scheduled for the very next day, and an astounding forty people showed up, including Kate. Members of ETVC presented me with a check for $210 that they had collected in Sullivan's memory to support our group and help us continue. People in the room contributed nearly $200 more on the spot. I used the money to buy paper and postage for the *FTM Newsletter* and other correspondence, and to pay the rent for the mailbox and our meeting space. And I told people that I didn't want to be in charge, that it was not my group, but our group, and any contributions of ideas or leadership would be positively welcomed. That day people rallied around the idea of monthly rather than quarterly meetings, and others, notably Sky Renfro,

Mike Hernandez, Billy Lane, and Josh—four relatively new group members—stepped up to help with hosting the meetings, since it was obvious we could not afford to rent meeting space that frequently.

Sullivan had figured Peter would run the support group meetings and answer letters because he was a good host, the care-taking type, well organized and methodical. Peter was deeply intelligent in a scholarly way, educated, articulate, thoughtful about universal matters, and considerate of those close to him. But he was shy and reclusive, far more so than I. After Sullivan's death, Peter would retrieve the mail once a week or so from the box Sullivan had rented, and he responded to most of the letters for a few months, but he stopped attending the group meetings almost immediately. It wasn't long before he told me he just couldn't keep dealing with the details of all these other people's lives. He did serve as a sounding board for me for quite some time, as I tried to find my own methods of handling the influx of requests for information and support, but he wanted to put transsexualism behind him and get on with his life. So did I, even though I knew it was logically impossible; the conflict between that desire and reality mirrored another conflict I was trying to manage regarding my responsibility to the FTM group.

Sullivan had anticipated that I would do educational presentations outside the community, since he had already invited me to take over a number of his regular university classroom speaking engagements as his health had been failing. I had taken over some of Steve Dain's regular lectures, too, the previous year, since he and Sullivan had agreed that my relaxed, open style and masculine appearance helped me to be effective in helping dissipate people's fears about transsexualism. And Sullivan presumed I would handle the *FTM Newsletter* because I was a writer and had been accustomed to regularly producing technical publications for many years. In fact, my Master of Fine Arts degree in English (fiction writing), experience as an instructor of legal writing, three years as a medical writer, over a decade as a technical writer, and a stint nearly as long in corporate management, all served to prepare me to communicate the FTM population's complex legal, medical, and general social needs effectively in a variety of settings. Sullivan thought Peter would have more hands-on social contact representing and running the local group. I was less accessible because of my job and family-related stresses. I was not a good host: I would just as soon take care of myself and preferred others would take care of themselves.

Though I enjoyed public speaking, I was shy, even reticent, in groups; I did not share my feelings easily, and I was uncomfortable sharing food with others in social settings thanks to lifelong, life-threatening food allergies. I liked people and cared about them, but in the abstract, from a distance. Communication was the most important thing—information exchange. I was a writer; I was accustomed to working alone. Being part of the group was difficult enough; feeling responsible for it was even harder.

Peter went back to school, seeking a new career as part of his effort to carve out his new existence as a man and to come to terms with the pain he felt because he was cut off from most of his family, including the daughter he had given birth to six years earlier. I kept myself busy, piling on tasks as a way of protecting myself from the pain I was then experiencing in my own family life. I was holding down a management job in a fairly high-stress work environment. I had also recently completed my genital reconstruction and was finished with the aspect of transition that required direct medical assistance. I was in the process of the court petition for my change of name and sex and issuance of new birth certificate. My relationship with Marcy demanded my attention, and I felt under a virtual emotional siege when I received a summons as notice that Samantha was suing me for non-paternity with respect to two-year-old Mitchell. Meanwhile, I was trying to keep my relationship with six-year-old Morgan running smoothly and as stress-free as possible for her because I wanted so much for her to have a happy childhood. I felt guilt for contributing to any distress my daughter felt as a result of her parents' separation, compounded with feelings of helplessness because I didn't want to be apart from her. Taking on the responsibility of maintaining a support network for others at just the time when I could use one myself seemed like a ridiculous thing to do. What I really wanted to do most of the time was crawl under a blanket and sleep. However, I was one of the few people around who had actually been through genital reconstruction, who could actually answer questions about it, and I knew it was only through those of us who had engaged this process sharing our own experience that others would get information. I made myself available as a listener, and as an information conduit, by phone, through more and more college lectures, and through responding to mail from people looking for Sullivan's informational book or wishing to subscribe to the *FTM Newsletter*, and writing and editing the newsletter itself, thinking all the while about the feelings people expressed: elation over finding themselves, and finding themselves in good company, worry or frustration about accessing medical services, and the paradoxical fear and shame over being transsexual. It was directly because of that newsletter that I became an activist, which was not something I had expected to happen.

Unlike many of the technical manuals for which I've been responsible in my professional career, the *FTM Newsletter* was actually read. Subscribers all over the world anticipated receiving it because it was their only connection to others like themselves. In the abstract, I understood, but I didn't really appreciate the gravity of it until I started receiving letters and phone calls the first time I was late with an issue. People weren't angry; they were concerned that the lateness meant something was wrong, that something might have happened to me or to the people who were helping me, and they dreaded being cut adrift in a sea of fear and prejudice in which they didn't want to swim alone.

My already-broken heart was ripe for an infection of compassion. On the telephone, in those periodic calls from isolated FTMs, I kept hearing things like, "I'm so afraid I'm going to lose my job," or "I don't know how to tell my family about this, I'm so afraid they'll kill me." These are completely rational fears. The letters that came in began to work on me, too: holding those handwritten pages, reading the brave words of people who had worked hard to find a way to be themselves, yet had difficulty finding a physician to treat their basic needs since they had changed their bodies, or who recounted events in which people had treated them badly or dismissively or had blatantly denied them services upon finding out about their transsexualism, I would wince as they apologized for what had happened to them as if they deserved it. I realized that if I could live in a way that declared my own self-acceptance—that is, not to broadcast my history every minute of the day, but to speak up honestly when it was appropriate, not necessarily with anger or even impatience, but with the compassion that I was finding within myself, to dispel myths and stereotypes that people cling to about us—that it would show others they could do it, too. Together we could change the conditions that generated our fears.

I continued to meet kind, hopeful, frightened, tentative, strong, wonderful, intelligent and creative people who were coming forward in greater numbers each year seeking sex reassignment as an answer to the gender dissonance they experienced. Yes, I occasionally met disturbed people, too, but for the most part I met perfectly ordinary, uniquely extraordinary people, just like most anyone else.

Stephan Thorne, a tall, solid, Nordic-looking fellow who is a career law enforcement officer, began his physical transition in 1993, but he started living as a man privately about a year earlier. As far back as he can remember he consistently expressed his desire to be a boy. He had parental permission to undergo sex reassignment when he was seventeen, but then he discovered feminism, which led him to reconsider.

"I decided that maybe what I wanted was what men *had*, not really to *be* a man," says Stephan. "I thought that if I just took what I wanted of what men had, such as being lovers with women, such as the types of jobs men had, then I wouldn't have to be a transsexual. I could simply be a lesbian, and that was fine for twenty years."

Like me, Stephan felt pretty much at home in the burgeoning lesbian world of the early and mid-1970s. Certainly it was a better fit at the time than the mainstream alternative. But with each new relationship, after five years or so, when the routines of daily living were established and there was time again for introspection, the muffled theme of transsexualism was still playing its refrain beneath the women's rights anthem. Like me, because he was proud of himself as a strong woman, it was difficult for Stephan to know what his true feelings were. "It was so painful for me when people would be confused about what sex I was and then registered such deep disgust when they realized I had a female body, yet appeared so masculine. It threatened them, and it put me into isolation and pain. I couldn't take it anymore," he told me. These are the kinds of social pressures we often experience when we are gender-variant.

"The last straw was just a few months before I formally started transition," Stephan said. "I was just leaving a restaurant in Alameda and walked past a table where four pretty, young women were laughing together, joyously, with their heads thrown back. It was such a happy moment, and the sight of them made me feel good. I smiled at the two who were facing me, as if to say, 'I'm glad you're having such a good time,' and I watched their smiles melt and turn into absolute horror. I knew, from years of experience, that their horror was because one of those butch lesbians was looking at them, was maybe going to make a pass at them. I walked into the parking lot and I couldn't hold it in any longer. I felt myself disintegrating. I wept.

This was how my existence was reflected back to me. I couldn't live that way any longer."

Our monthly group meetings were dominated by discussions about what motivated us, the mechanics of our transitions, how to get access to medical care, and the effects of hormones and results of surgery. But the most compelling business was negotiating our families, our jobs, and our day-to-day existence—the now of it all. Jeff, a journalist who began his transition in 1994 at the age of forty-three, had put off his treatment at the request of relatives. He said that after settling into his transition he realized he had put himself to sleep at about age thirteen, and he felt now that he was waking up where he left off.

"Chris [another FTM group member] calls it the Rip Van Winkle effect," Jeff told us. "You wake up and look around for the feelings you had back when you fell asleep, and your forty-year-old psyche is having to do a real high-speed personality integration, as opposed to what most people get to do over the time of their adolescence."

Divorced several years previously, Jeff was the mother of a teenage child, and he was concerned about the discomfort and embarrassment his child felt about his changing.

"I tried hard to let the world define me and to be what other people said I should be, and it never worked," Jeff said. "Now I've got to look within my own heart and define myself. There is an incredible strength in coming from your own truth. I only hope my child will understand how hard it has been for me to wait all these years while other people told me to live a lie for my child's sake. I love my child very much, more than I love anyone else, but I have to live my life, too. At least I'm not running away."

Jeff, like most of us, was aware that there is a double standard with respect to cross-gender behavior in childhood exhibited by girls as opposed to that exhibited by boys. "Girls get subtle pressure to conform, mixed with disapproval as they get older. But boys get positively slammed if they act like sissies when they're young," Jeff offered at one meeting. We often told each other what we already knew, but the verbalization was important. Most of us had never had the opportunity to hear our theories, our feelings spoken out loud, to have our experience mirrored in a positive way. It seemed we always were isolated and made to feel that there was something wrong about us in some deep, intrinsic way that we should have been able to just change because we were told to conform. Yet the invisibility and lack of pathology ascribed to female-to-male crossdressing permits a broad range of cross-gender behaviors among female-bodied individuals, no matter what the person's gender identity or sexual orientation. At a panel discussion on gender issues at the May 1993 American Psychiatric Association convention held in San Francisco, Dr. Richard Green reported that a longitudinal study of "tomboy girls" was denied funding by the National Institute of Health (which funded Green's famous longitudinal study of "sissy boys"). A woman on the funding review committee had objected to the project on feminist principles, saying, "Calling a girl a tomboy is like calling a black a nigger." The result was nice for girls, but not so great for female-bodied children with masculine gender identities.

"If people spent as much time learning and processing about gender and identity and what transsexuality is all about as they spent expressing their concern for my child," says Jeff, "maybe the world would change such that it would be easier for transsexuals and the people who love them to exist." His daughter has turned out to be a self-confident, capable, loving, and happy young adult herself, who loves her mother and appreciates that her mother is also a happy, self-confident, capable, and loving adult man.

People often suggest that if society had a place for us, we would not need to take such dramatic steps as surgical sex reassignment. They seem to think that if just being a lesbian won't do it, perhaps if western society had something like the concept some Native Americans have of "two-spirit people," then transpeople would be better integrated without resorting to physical change. The popular idea of a "two-spirit person" is one of peaceful co-existence, but Blake describes the conflict that moves some people to change: "My frustration at trying to express my masculinity from within a female body was interpreted by my family as an internal battle between two spirits, a masculine one and a feminine one. Being viewed as a 'two-spirit person' by my nuclear and extended family was not sufficient to relieve the pressure for me. I couldn't change my psyche, but I could change my body to match it. I wanted to be anatomically correct. My family interpreted my transition as the masculine spirit winning out. I still experience my family's interpretation as a failure to grasp my essential maleness."

Blake scoffs at the notion of instant male privilege, too, that some people think FTMs attain with testosterone. He comes from a large family, and most of his siblings are male. He says, "Since my transition I have come to understand society's fear and hatred of black males. For me, gaining male privilege has meant the opportunity to be treated with the same fear, suspicion, and hatred as the rest of my brothers."

Kim feels that instant male privilege is something of a myth. "Male privilege is not automatic," he states. "There are so many aspects to an individual. I don't feel I've gained male privilege, that's too simplistic. I'm small, I don't take up a lot of space or make demands of other people. I certainly didn't change my body because I thought I'd get any special privilege. I changed because it was the only way I could be seen as myself."

I think when transmen fail to see how they benefit from male privilege simply by being seen as men, they are living with a kind of blindness that may—in Blake and Kim's case—be caused by racial sensitivities, which in the United States can be more demanding as a survival issue on a day-to-day basis than gender concerns. Other factors could be at play, too, for any transman, such as conditioning that keeps him from experiencing his maleness fully because he is always on guard against being discovered as a transsexual man. Any given transman may or may not remain aware of, and connected with, the social position of women. A kind of blindness also may be caused by a solid identification with the kind of maleness that polarizes men and women, so that the transman only sees himself as being at the mercy of women whom he perceives as having power over him. Any of these positions indicate a misapprehension of the meaning and effect of male privilege, which in U.S. society seems to be—in simple terms—the presumption of freedom, access, and authority. In this society, women may earn this privilege, but men have it automatically. Masculine women can experience male privilege, too. Transsexual men of color have different manifestations of male privilege within their own cultural groups, and they must learn to negotiate their racial differences in heterogeneous settings from the new position of being a man. All transsexual men have male privilege even if they aren't aware of it, and they have opportunities to manage it differently than do non-transsexual men. Their male privilege may be taken away from them along with their recognition as male (if their transsexualism is discovered by those people who refuse to acknowledge the veracity of their gender), but male privilege is not what most transsexual men are seeking. Most transsexual men with whom I have spoken are seeking nothing more than consolidation of their own identity: they want to be seen as themselves.

Dialogues on subjects like these happened constantly in groups like ours. Whenever I went to other cities and visited with local groups, I heard the same kinds of exchanges. We were listening, giving each other the permission to speak that had been denied us in so many other venues. It was okay to hear the same thing more than once from so many different people. I understood it was part of the process of building a foundation, establishing common ground. Yet, in those early days, the notion of community was something few of us imagined. The most common path for FTMs was to attend a few meetings, get the information they needed, and then disappear into ordinary lives. It was expected that someone who transitioned successfully would not stick around associating with other transsexual people, but some of us began to acknowledge that if some of the "elders" did not stick around to pass the collected wisdom on to—and endure the challenges of—the next generation, we would never progress beyond reinventing the classical transition to invisibility.

Unconventional Conventions

In the spring of 1992, I attended my first convention of the International Foundation for Gender Education (IFGE), held that year in Houston. I learned that similar conventions, sponsored by local groups in various cities, were held across the country at least seven times each year (give or take a couple), and that this phenomenon had been going on since the 1970s with occasional, though rare, FTM participation. That year there were fifteen FTMs in attendance, about ten percent of the total registrants. Most people there were MTF crossdressers (heterosexual men), some with their wives or girlfriends. Some of the people attending were transsexual women, and they tried to arrange some joint workshop sessions to include the transsexual men, but all the speakers and presenters were women, and their reflections of FTM experience were not helpful for us, even though all of those women had been born with male bodies, and one might think they would have something useful to impart. The majority of them seemed mired in gender stereotypes, though, and it was puzzling to me. When they would have trouble with their purses or other accessories, they would often say, "I'll bet you never had these problems when you were a woman." As if the only way to exist in a female body was to be equipped with a purse and clip-on earrings, and to have perfect mastery of them.

In Houston I had my first encounter with Virginia Prince, whom I recall being dressed for dinner like a 1950s prom queen, and who was accorded great respect by the other people in dresses. At that time, Virginia had a distinctly dismissive attitude toward FTMs. When the FTM contingent was gathered in the lobby one evening, she declared that she didn't believe it was possible for a woman to become a man. "In fact," she said, scrutinizing us each in turn, "I don't believe any of you." Then she stopped and stared at me. "Except you," she said, shaking her finger at me with a hint of a smile in her eyes. Everyone laughed, and I thanked her for sharing her opinion, and told her that we didn't believe her, either! She and I have since enjoyed many philosophical conversations when we meet at the conferences she is able to attend. She celebrated her ninety-first birthday in 2003.

Virginia had examined the appearance of a group of a dozen young-looking men, many of whom had been in transition less than three years, and judged them insufficiently masculine. It is possible that she was prejudiced by her awareness that these men had been born with female bodies. There were a number of things that were done or said in Houston that were painful for me and the other FTMs and their partners. One was that the three or four female partners of FTMs who had also registered for the conference were asked to leave a workshop offered for partners of transsexuals and crossdressers because the wives of the MTF people felt that female partners of FTMs must be lesbians and therefore would not be able to sympathize properly with the difficulties faced by heterosexual women whose partners were changing their gender expression to female. Another was hearing an MTF transsexual tell a room full of people that the realities of transsexualism meant that MTF people would have to "adjust to taking lower-paying jobs, while FTMs can look forward to better employment opportunities." I was stunned when I heard this. Most FTMs are just not prepared to become captains of industry. Also, many FTMs go through periods of unemployment and career redirection both during and after transition. If their transsexualism is known, FTMs are frequently subject to the same adverse treatment as MTFs. Jobs are gender-typed; this applies no less to pink-collar jobs and white-collar jobs than to blue-collar jobs. There are male and female management styles, as well as masculine and feminine communication styles, and taking hormones doesn't instantly change one's socialization. Male socialization is often more successful in corporations where people are expected to be aggressive and competitive; people who are not raised to play male hierarchy games often unconsciously put out the signal that says, "I'm number two." Often the very skills which made a pre-transition FTM successful in business—qualities like cooperativeness, enthusiasm, team-building, and listening skills—will work against him as others begin to relate to him as a man, interpreting him as weak and conciliatory, possibly lacking the aggressive leadership style some companies expect from male managers. There is also the education factor: men who received socialization as women in the 1960s, 1970s, and even 1980s were not uniformly steered toward occupations in which they could later find success as men, in spite of the progress of women's equality efforts and a general loosening of gender stereotype constraints in populations where education levels are above average. All of those ideas ran through my head in that Houston workshop, but I was too overwhelmed to say anything at the time.

We faced the additional impact of being regarded as somewhat exotic. Many of the MTF people there, crossdressers or transsexual people, had never seen a transsexual man before, let alone a small pack of them. When we showed up in our suits for the Saturday night banquet, the demand for photographs of us in groups, or of us with various crossdressers and transsexual women, was almost overwhelming. It was simultaneously heady, intimidating, and, depending on how their requests were delivered, even patronizing. Personally, I had never received so many compliments on my appearance in my life, and I found it both rewarding and unnerving. Here we were, a handful of mostly short men, surrounded by scores of comparatively tall women, all decked out in ball gowns and sequins, with big-hair wigs and glittery shoes and jewelry, some fawning over us as if we were movie stars. While the majority of them still ignored us, the outgoing ones who were kind and welcoming were bright, fun, gentle and encouraging. They were often quite beautiful, and even those who were awkward or not as well-put-together, or who knew they would never appear as attractive as a woman as they'd like to, were deserving of compliments for the effort they made to grapple with reconciling their various issues with masculinity and femininity, body and soul, even if their progress was slow and circuitous. Some of the MTF people I met at that convention are still some of my favorite people, remarkable for their kindness, integrity, and tenacity.

I met two dedicated Texas transmen at that meeting, Taylor and

Aaron. Taylor and his wife produced a small line of undergarments that assisted FTMs in enhancing their male appearance. Aaron was interested in computers, and was establishing the first FTM-focused bulletin board on the internet, something that, in 1992, was barely comprehensible to most people. We began to talk about community-building, about deliberately staying in touch with each other, no matter where we lived, and about starting to advocate for a model of transness that diverged from the man-in-a-dress cliché.

Jason Cromwell was there, and some of the IFGE leaders knew him already; they knew Jude Patton, too, because of his previous involvement with their group. It was good to spend time with these predecessors of mine, getting to know them better and strategizing about what efforts were needed to bolster the growing numbers of FTMs who were reaching out for contact all across the country. A handful of the IFGE old-timers knew Steve Dain and had known Lou Sullivan as well, and they would make use of these contacts as a way to connect with us. People like Yvonne Cook-Riley, an MTF whose partner Dan was an FTM-identified, female-bodied individual, were genuinely glad we were there, and tried very hard to make us feel welcome. Yvonne had used her influence on the IFGE board to advocate for FTM inclusion and had recruited Professor Holly Devor to the board to increase contact with the FTM population. Still, much of what went on in the general sessions at that convention made us feel left out. We were never included in any salutations—it was well into the late 1990s before we would hear anything other than "Welcome, ladies" spoken from the podium at most conferences of this sort—and for the most part our workshops were in isolated rooms, away from much of the conference goings-on. Further, the high cost of these events meant that few FTMs would be willing to make whatever personal sacrifice was necessary to attend when they could get more camaraderie from their local groups, or even just from the *FTM Newsletter*.

I learned a great deal from that first convention experience: different from a support group, a conference could be another kind of idea exchange, where people took much of the personal emotion out of the equation and focused on practicalities. Many people got to express their ideas, and attendees were exposed to a wider variety of experience and people than they would otherwise meet. If we FTMs were to hold a conference, we would have to work at real inclusion, but the opportunity to meet and network with other transsexual men who were looking for information or had access to resources of which others weren't aware was appealing. Roving conferences like IFGE's, going to different places and finding a different audience each time, also gave people the opportunity to travel to unfamiliar cities. I thought this was valuable; in our local support groups I felt we ran the risk of becoming too homogenized, of over-integrating each other into our own lives, possibly losing sight of the variety in people that is such an important factor in learning to adapt and relate to others that strengthens social and economic skills. I also saw that the MTF crossdressers, more so than MTF transsexuals on the whole, had the money to support this kind of event, while most transsexual people were suffering economically. There were some racial minority transwomen present, but for the most part the attendees at these meetings were middle-class, white, and heterosexual. I saw this as a problem with respect to the extensiveness of transgender experience and the number of people who needed networking, information, and support who would not be served with this model because of racial, class, economic, and social issues that were not being addressed. When I thought about the prospects of FTMs gathering like this for themselves in feasible numbers to underwrite such a conference, I thought it would be difficult, if not impossible, to accomplish. But I decided that networking with the people at these established MTF-oriented meetings could only help us by forging alliances and increasing our visibility. Maybe we could learn something about running organizations from them, too, since they'd been around awhile. Certainly we had something to offer them in the way of unlearning homophobia and moderating their stereotypes of both women and men.

Intolerance

Back in San Francisco, however, we had problems of our own with anti-gay attitudes. When I returned from Houston, I found out that a handful of men from our group had decided that there were too many gay-identified guys joining up, that too many people who looked like lesbians were coming to the meetings. Because I tolerated what they saw as a problem, they assumed I was gay, and therefore they decided the group wasn't supportive enough for guys who were straight. They began holding their own meetings in another city. Since I identified as heterosexual, and often talked about my relationship with my girlfriend, I was surprised by this turn of events. I couldn't understand why they didn't talk to me about their feelings, why they made an assumption about the group and then projected it onto me to justify their actions. I knew instinctively that there was nothing I could do other than continue to remain true to the underlying principles of providing quality information and support for all FTMs and their loved ones without judgment, and working to empower others to improve their lives. I thought it was sad that this group of people felt they had to break away, but perhaps that was their own form of self-empowerment, and that had to be fine with me. I only wished that they didn't have to view themselves in opposition to the rest of us, and that they didn't make assumptions about me and turn those assumptions into declarations. I've since learned that this dynamic happens all the time in groups, and while it is occasionally painful and could be avoided by adhering to an ethic of honesty, caring, and cooperation, it simply happens for various underlying reasons. Politics is the art of negotiation among divergent goals, and cooperation is difficult when people are unaware of their motives or goals, or unable or unwilling to reveal them. Understanding the emerging politics of the FTM population was to become a second full-time job for me over the next few years. I still felt strongly that there is no one way to be an FTM, no right way to do transsexualism, and no single, uniform characteristic that marks a person as transgendered. Others will always have their own ideas about who we are, who we ought to be, and who should be allowed into "the club."

At the same time, in the early to mid-1990s, I collaborated with a number of other people who were involved in working to advance the cause of civil and human rights for transgendered people. We felt a logical step was to seek the support of the Gay, Lesbian, and Bisexual (GLB) community, since so much of the oppression and violence experienced by transpeople was a result of the perceived links between transness and homosexuality, whether or not those links were real in any given instance, and also because transpeople who were also gay, lesbian, or bisexual felt excluded from those groups because of prejudice against their transness. There was a great deal of institutional and personal resistance from within the gay and lesbian communities to this kind of integration, but we found natural allies in bisexual people who had already fought a similar, though also very different, battle for inclusion. Many gay people wanted to avoid further stigmatization. They claimed not to understand how gender identity issues were related to sexual orientation issues. They felt their community was only about who they wanted to have sex with, and they apparently didn't think about the violation of gender norms that homosexual expression constitutes in the eyes of heterosexual people. They forgot that straight people often think that gay people want to be the opposite sex, or think that crossdressing, transsexualism, and homosexuality are all different words for the same thing. While this battle had traditionally been engaged by MTFs alone, the increasing presence of FTMs, especially gay or bisexual-identified FTMs, made a tremendous difference. When so many people think of transpeople as only men in dresses, exposure to transmen can jolt some into realizing that their prejudice against transwomen is a thoughtless reaction to projections of their own fears about sexuality or judgments about what a woman should look like. Those who find themselves attracted to transpeople can begin to examine their preconceptions about sex, gender, and attraction, which may be one of the biggest threats transpeople present: that they might make people question their assumptions about themselves. It was time for transmen to shoulder their share of the burden of misunderstanding that transwomen had been carrying all these years.

With Anne Ogborn, a devotee of the 1960s school of protest and agitation for social change, I participated in discussions of progressive viewpoints on actions that needed to happen to improve transsexual lives. Anne was one of the Transgender Nation protesters who were arrested in 1993 for defacing public property and disturbing the peace outside the convention of the American Psychiatric Association in San Francisco, while I was inside on the convention floor, working with members of IFGE and ETVC to educate psychiatrists one-on-one in a less confrontational approach. The two strategies worked together, because when the noisy, angry protesters provoked the psychiatrists they came over to our booth to ask us, perhaps rhetorically, what those obnoxious people outside thought they would accomplish. Every day of the conference we were asked if we were affiliated with the demonstrators outside the Moscone Center; we said we knew some of them and we thought they were raising valid points. People asked us, "Why are they protesting? What do they want?"

"We want control of our own lives," I replied. "We want the stamp of mental illness removed from our foreheads. We want humane, responsible, and reasonably priced medical care, and we want ordinary civil rights."

"It's a lot easier for me to understand your message here in the booth than it is when I feel bombarded by demonstrators," one psychiatrist said.

"But if there hadn't been demonstrators," I asked, "would you have bothered to think about us at all?"

One woman came up to me and asked me, "Where's your dress?" I told her I don't wear those anymore. She looked confused, saying, "Then, why are you here?" I told her, "Because I used to have a female body." She gasped, looked me up and down like a mannequin and praised my appearance; I felt misinterpreted, as though I had just been judged a successful illusionist. Many times I could tell that visitors to our booth chose to speak to me because they thought I was not transgendered, while the crossdressers and MTFs were, for the most part, obviously not natal females. I was "safer" to speak with, especially for some of the men. One male psychiatrist stopped and looked at some of the MTFs, then approached me to say, "I didn't think anyone was still doing the operations; after all, with a postoperative suicide rate of thirty percent, it seems that not many people are satisfied with the results." I shrugged and said, "I don't know. . . . It worked for me!"

"You mean . . . you . . . ?" he sputtered.

"Yes. I used to have a female body. It's true that there are fewer gender clinics providing surgery today than there were in the past, but many private practitioners now take up the slack between supply and demand. I think that thirty percent figure is exaggerated."

"Amazing," he said. "Perhaps I'll take one of these information packets after all."

Another doctor refused my offer of literature, saying he didn't need it because, "I don't believe God makes mistakes." "Neither do I," I replied. He smiled and said, "Good," as he walked off, but I don't think he knew to whom he was talking.

On May 28, 1993, following the conference, the *San Francisco Chronicle* reported, "The APA proposed that well-adjusted transsexuals [should] not automatically be considered to have a mental disorder." I wondered: who would determine whether we were well-adjusted?

It took a few years of delivering the message, of showing up for meetings and talking about the similarities of our life experiences that make gay, lesbian, bisexual, and transgender (GLB and T) people natural allies, but eventually trans-inclusion started to become a reality, at least in name. In the early 1990s, many gay and lesbian groups saw a distinct disadvantage to connecting themselves with gender-variant people, since they saw their issues as primarily having to do with sexual orientation. By the mid-1990s, though, prominent leaders like Kerry Lobel of the National Gay & Lesbian Task Force had realized that gender variance is also one of the innate characteristics we need to acknowledge if we are to strive for real social justice and create a truly free and equal society. Problems still persist within various organizations and institutions that don't know how to deliver services for transgendered people, or where the sensitivity to gender identity and expression as a unique aspect of each individual is not well understood or integrated, but on the whole there has been significant improvement in acceptance of transgendered people among gay, lesbian, and bisexual groups. Homosexual orientation does not automatically render a person able to understand transgender issues or experience. Nor does inclusion in GLB contexts mean that all transgendered or transsexual people welcome that inclusion or make use of it.

Identity has often been a powerful organizing tool, but it should not be mistaken for the ideal model of community. Identity is not a rigid, monolithic psychosocial box into which we can each place ourselves, where we will permanently remain. We are all becoming something, and we can strongly identify with different aspects of our lives at different times, or new elements may be introduced into our lives that we must integrate into our identity, such as parenthood, chronic illness or sudden disability, falling in love with a person we wouldn't have imagined being with, or finding a new career. These evolutionary events often draw us into new communities and new identities. The tendency to "fix" people's identities as encompassing only one aspect of themselves, or as being unchanging in their various aspects, is equivalent to expecting a person to only eat apples because he or she was eating an apple when you met.

The label of "transgender" in the early 1990s, as used by transsexual activists, was an attempt to get beyond identity politics by invoking a term so broad and inclusive as to make room for multiple identities and expressions, and still refer to the specific oppressions that transpeople faced. At the time, I knew the majority of transsexual people and crossdressers did not relate to the term, did not accept it as an identity label, or did not want to be associated with the gay and lesbian community any more than the gay and lesbian community wanted to take on our particular issues. To me it felt as though we were fighting battles on all sides, trying to convince transpeople that they'd benefit from open discussion of each others' issues and from alliance with the GLB movement, trying to convince GLB people that trans issues were connected to their own, trying to educate MTFs about FTMs and vice versa, trying to educate mainstream people about transsexual and transgendered people, and trying to combat homophobia everywhere, all at once. In addition, we were building alliances with the newly forming intersex movement initiated by activist Cheryl Chase in the form of the Intersex Society of North America (ISNA). Perhaps because all these different, yet related, issues mushroomed all at once, there was a great deal of confusion about the margins of each organization, each group's issues and goals, and the nature of each group's investment in gender categories because most people, even among the gay, lesbian, bisexual, transgender, and intersex (GLBTI) groups, didn't have a clear understanding of each other. Gender and our presumptions about gender and sex and sexual behavior affect everyone, but not everyone has the same ideas about sex, gender, or sexuality. For example, ISNA has never attempted to create an alternative sex called "intersex," nor have they advocated intersex as an identity, nor lobbied for the eradication of gender or sex assignment. ISNA's goal has always been to end unwanted genital surgeries, to help heal the trauma that many intersexed people have experienced, and erase the stigma of difference that, because of ignorance and fear, affects the lives of families into which intersexed children are born. Likewise, just as not all transgendered people want to change their sex, those who do, transsexual people, are not advocating that all people with gender-variant characteristics should change their sex, take on a transsexual identity, or conform to stereotypical notions of gender in their new sex if they do transition. Even within distinct groups of GLBTI constituents, these understandings and goals are not clearly defined, and I feel we must all resist the temptation to project our individual understandings onto others, in the same way that we who are minorities ask not to have the projections of arbitrary notions of normalcy forced upon us by some majority members. The links between the categories—not the identities—of GLBTI are stigma, violence, and denial of specific civil rights.

The limitations of language are something about which all people who are searching for understanding complain: their identities are invisible, incomprehensible, minimized, marginalized, and unacknowledged—and it hurts. Some people respond to this by developing new language, new identity terms, and fresh lexicons of slang to differentiate themselves through which they can bond with others who are "in" enough to know the code. There are many variations on the theme of gender freedom, and many different interpretations of transgender ideology. While acknowledging this normal process of self-assertion, I realized that there are times when groups must accept less-than-ideal terms, at least temporarily, so they can build a broader base of support, comprehension, and understanding.

"Transgender," "transsexual," and "FTM" are all terms that I don't particularly like, but they are expressive of particular aspects of specific experience of overlapping commonalities, like moving from a female body or feminine gender expression to a male body or masculine gender expression, or going across sex and gender boundaries, that allow outsiders to take initial steps toward understanding us. I realized that my commitment to education that would improve the quality of life for all transpeople would have to be a long-term one, because it would take a long time to achieve that goal, and that some measure of consistency in vocabulary over the length of this effort would be important. Not that evolution is bad or impossible, but ideas and expressions can change much faster within a paraculture, while the mainstream, where more education is needed to make the world safe for people who are different, will be much slower to catch on. No group can achieve acceptance and inclusion in social institutions (such as transpeople want in the form of employment rights, medical care, and social safety) while its members continue to thumb their noses at the system in which they want to be included. They have to win that system over, and then bring it along by championing values that allow everyone to be themselves and maximize their potential. I think it is wrong to ask for rights and safety for only certain transpeople—only the straight ones, only the gay ones, only the middle-class ones, only the transpeople of color, only the white ones, only the crossdressers, only the transsexual ones, only the ones we want to invite to our parties, only the young, attractive ones, only the older, impoverished ones, the affluent ones, only the FTMs, only the MTFs—or even for only the transpeople. We all must learn to value and advocate for anyone who is different from the stereotypical, over-simplifying sex and gender definitions with which we were indoctrinated. Transpeople must learn to value and cooperate with others who do not share our gender-variant experience.

By the time my neo-adolescence was over, by the end of 1993, I had helped provide a more stable structure to the FTM group, started building alliances with other individuals and groups, and traveled extensively in the U.S. and Europe at my own expense, contacting transsexual people and medical professionals to increase my knowledge base. I knew clearly that one couldn't just get a sex change and go mow his lawn. I saw so many aspects of society where change needed to happen, and so many people suffering and struggling to make a difference for themselves and others, that I knew I had to try to help in a new way, a way that would help bridge the gaps between FTM and MTF, between gay and straight, between men and women, between Anglo and Other, between those who have money and resources to help themselves and disappear, and those who end up on the streets, who are not able to access the medical technology they need, who are multiply-oppressed through belonging to multiple marginalized categories.

Stepping Up to the Plate

Transmen didn't begin to enter the activist picture in significant numbers until the death of Brandon Teena was reported in early 1994. The circumstances surrounding this brutal murder are most clearly presented in Susan Muska and Gréta Ólafsdottir's astounding documentary film, *The Brandon Teena Story* (1997), and in Kim Peirce's powerful fictionalized version, *Boys Don't Cry* (1999). Hilary Swank's portrayal of Brandon in the latter film earned her the Best Actress Oscar in 2000. This murder case was the actualization of many FTMs' deepest fears, and although it was widely interpreted as a lesbian story in both the mainstream and gay press, it mobilized many trans-identified, female-bodied people to begin speaking out against persecution of all transgendered people. It also prompted Dallas Denny, a well-known MTF writer, activist, and founder of the American Educational Gender Information Service (AEGIS), to encourage transmen to organize our own national conference. She offered a challenge grant of $500 to the first FTM group that could raise matching money and would commit to putting on an FTM conference within eighteen months of the award. Also in the spring of 1994, our newsletter designer, Stafford (his full name), suggested we change the name of the group to FTM International in recognition of the ever-wider range of networks we were creating with the *FTM Newsletter*, with over six hundred subscribers, then, and reaching seventeen countries. With an infusion of energy prompted by reaction to Brandon's murder, as well as the success of recent public hearings to investigate discrimination against transgendered people, and all the favorable publicity accorded to Stephan Thorne, Loren Cameron, and David Harrison, the local transmen and our larger subscriber base responded quickly to Ms. Denny's challenge, and we were soon on our way to planning the first large-scale FTM conference ever to take place in the U.S.

The first "All-FTM Conference of the Americas" was held in August 1995. We called it that because I knew national conferences of FTMs had previously taken place in other countries like Australia and the United Kingdom, and possibly Germany, and even though those conferences resulted in attendances not much larger than one of our monthly meetings, I did not want to dismiss those events by claiming ours as the first National FTM Conference, or the first International FTM Conference. I wanted to extend the invitation to all FTM-identified people in North, Central, and South America, and not imply that our situation ended at the U.S. borders. I also wanted the conference to be open to everyone, not just FTMs, but I wanted everyone to understand that the focus of the conference would be FTMs and their partners and families, that MTFs were welcome, but would not be permitted to dominate discussions. In contrast with the hotel-based, MTF-focused conferences that I'd attended, we tried to come up with innovative ways to cut expenses and maximize attendance. Instead of booking a hotel, we secured donations of classroom space at an alternative school in which to hold our workshops; we obtained donations of food so people would not go hungry, and we held the conference in the Mission neighborhood where there were scores of good, inexpensive Mexican and South American restaurants. We kept our registration charge at a maximum of $100 ($50 and $75 early registration periods were an extra incentive) so we could bring in more people, and offered scholarships to anyone who volunteered to help administer or monitor the various aspects of the three-day event that needed attention. Many local people offered housing for visitors. We developed programming to meet the wide variety of needs we'd identified through our local meetings and the correspondence we'd received over the years. And we hoped to inspire as well as inform our attendees. I suggested the theme "A Vision of Community," and the organizing committee agreed.

Jason Cromwell and I thought we'd be lucky to get a hundred people to show up for this first conference, and the local organizing committee planned accordingly, but in the two weeks immediately prior to the conference it became apparent that we would have many more people, and our conference manager, Sky Renfro, had to scramble to find us larger quarters in which to hold the sessions where all the attendees would be in the same room.

We were astounded that nearly four hundred people attended, at least seventy percent of them FTMs. We had 372 official registrants, but judging by the building capacity there were times during the weekend when there were many more bodies in the space. Never before in the history of the world had so many FTM people been in the same place at once. People came who had transitioned over a decade earlier and had never seen another FTM. People came from Germany, Australia, and Japan, and all across North America. People came who had just started their transitions, as did some who were hoping to start soon. People brought their partners, wives, husbands, and children. People looked in each others' eyes and knew that we could never again be isolated and mute.

In the late 1990s a new generation of transpeople began to emerge. Though some transpeople have long identified as "queer" to signify their difference from the mainstream, like Silvia Rivera and other transpeople who—without the label "trans," but only the inclusive label "queer"— fought the New York City police at the Stonewall riots in 1969, young "genderqueers," as some youth self-define more than thirty years later, are still tearing down the old boundaries, smashing old paradigms. Young and old voices are calling for a world without gender, or a world with three genders, four, five genders, anything other than two, while others simply advocate for the right to express whatever gender(s) an individual feels. Transsexual men are still coming forward to introduce themselves to the rest of us as men who only want to live as men and leave the rest of the baggage of transsexualism behind. Not every transperson is "genderqueer" or even progressive, no matter how old or young they are, and they can react against any kind of "inclusive PC rhetoric" as vociferously as any militant conservative. How many times do I need to say there is no one way to be trans? As for community, I still feel we are trying to create it just by naming it, as I said in my keynote address at that first conference in 1995. Though we have made great progress, I still don't believe we have a real community yet; but I believe that we should keep invoking it, keep trying to build it, because we are on our way to achieving it, though it may not ultimately look like what we have previously known community to be. All I ask along the way is that everyone respects each other's gender identity and expression.

There is nothing wrong with wanting to break away from gender stereotypes; I definitely advocate doing away with gender-based oppression. There is also nothing wrong with gender variance or with having a gender identity that is different from one's genitals. I won't call someone else "wrong" for wanting to be gender-ambiguous or refusing to state a gender. Likewise, I won't be called "wrong" for knowing that I am a man and for ensuring that others can see me as a man, for valuing my masculine gender, for loving both women and men in the different ways that I love them, and for appreciating the difference between masculine and feminine. But our collective battles won't be won until there is a language for transgendered children to use to express their feelings, their fears and concerns when they are young, until none of us is afraid to tell the truth about ourselves to our parents, friends, pastors, doctors, employers, or school administrators, until we no longer fear being cast out like miscreants. The condition of being transgendered will probably never be eradicated from humankind. I believe it's a natural condition, part of nature's standard variation. Those of us who are compelled to change our sex as the best way for us to manage our transgenderedness are only a small fraction of the potential community of people who acknowledge the experience of gender variance, but that shouldn't mean we don't count.

For me, community exists when I don't have to be afraid to let others around me know who I am, when I don't have to worry about surviving hostility simply because I am different in some way, whether that way is gender- and sex-related, or because of the color of my skin or my family background or my occupation. I want a community in which I receive the same respect I give to others, and the same level of services and opportunities that others receive, a community that is conscious, caring and respectful of all life and all human expression that is not harmful to others.

I want this kind of community for everyone around the world. Regardless of anyone's personal identity or expression, I want violence and oppression to end.

When we held the first All-FTM Conference of the Americas, and San Francisco's conservative Mayor Frank Jordan issued a proclamation declaring the weekend of August 18–20, 1995, "FTM International Weekend in San Francisco," no one was more amazed than I at how far we had come in just a short time.

4
Body of Knowledge

Surgery is not what transsexualism is ultimately about. Transsexualism is about life. It's about relationships, and not just intimate ones. Being a transsexual is not something we do in the privacy of our own bedrooms; it affects every aspect of our lives, from our driver's licenses to our work histories, from our birth certificates to our school transcripts to our parents' wills, and every relationship represented by those paper trails. Still, for many of us, surgery is a crucial part of managing our gender variance.

Some people have characterized transsexual individuals as highly conservative conformists who "buy into" the binary gender system and gravitate to the extremes of stereotypical, culturally-defined gender behavior, and the fact that some of us want surgery is used as evidence for this theory. I'm sure there are individual transsexual people who are like that—who think of themselves as inadequate if they don't measure up to particular stereotypes of gender roles—just as there are non-transsexual people who feel the same way: for example, the woman I saw on some television magazine show who loves Barbie so much she's had scores of plastic surgery to make herself like Barbie; and then there's Arnold Schwarzenegger and Sylvester Stallone. Body modification is a complex phenomenon. People have done it since the beginning of time, for various reasons and with various results. Changing one's sex is just one way of changing one's body, and a sex change is not necessarily part of a search for perfection or a reification of stereotypes. The reality of gender is that anyone who has not opted for androgyny has usually accepted the binary gender system by age three, and no one makes much of a fuss about it, so why imply that transsexual people have any greater share of responsibility for reinforcing that binary? When it comes to generalizations about bodies, that binary is a given. It's what one does with the social aspects of that binary that count. What most people fail to understand is that, because of their gender variance, most transsexual people are not normatively male or female either before or after transition. Most of us are not seeking perfection when measured against external stereotypes; rather, most of us are seeking an internal sense of comfort when measured against our own sense of ourselves. When we undertake a sex transition (which in some cases may look or feel like a gender transition) the purpose, usually, is to facilitate our being perceived socially by others as the men or women we know ourselves to be, even though we may acquire or retain physical differences from other men or women in the process. Rationality and vanity may play equal parts in the quest for a body that is pleasing, both to oneself and to others.

Before embarking on a transition, transpeople have homework to do. We must know when and how to find a therapist or gender program that can help us sort out the issues and, if we need it, initiate access to medical technology. We should also have an idea about the legal and other social issues involved: what our legal status will be; how we change our records, how we obtain healthcare beyond the transitional time. These topics are covered in other publications (e.g., Bergstedt, 1999; Brown and Rounsley, 1996; Denny, 1994; Ettner, 1996, 1999; and Whittle, 2002), or may be explored in networking groups. I always emphasize that medical transitions are not right for everyone; nonetheless, people always have questions about hormones and surgery, and information specific to the FTM transition is often difficult to find. This chapter will cover some of the basics.

Modern hormonal and surgical sex reassignment technology has been available in the United States and Europe for well over sixty years (Meyerowitz, 2002). But the process is not perfect. No one can tell exactly what will happen to any particular body when *any* hormone is administered. No one can predict, as pre-adolescents, what we will look like when we grow up, and neither can we know precisely what cross-sex hormones will do to our bodies. Doctors know only generally what results may be expected from hormone therapy. Neither are surgical outcomes uniform or consistent. I'm not a physician, so nothing I say here should be construed as medical advice. Consider this a report from one explorer of the territory.

Access to Treatment

The fact is that people do change their sex to confirm their gender without hormones or surgery. It is questionable whether it is legally possible in the U.S. to do this (at the present time), but it is socially possible. Musician, bandleader, agent/promoter, husband, and father Billy Tipton is just one example of a man with a female body that very few people knew about until he died (Middlebrook, 1997). Given the nature of human beings, if there is one who has done it there must certainly be others (Cromwell, 1999). There are transsexual people who elect not to have surgery, and others who are precluded from undergoing hormonal or surgical sex reassignment due to pre-existing medical conditions or deeply held religious beliefs. None of these factors—economics, medical conditions, or religion—invalidates a transsexual person's condition. In other words, it isn't undergoing sex reassignment that makes someone a "real" transsexual, even though the medical establishment uses this criterion—the occasion of someone coming forward requesting medical treatment—to determine whether to apply the label.

For those transpeople who do want to make use of available technology, the first obstacle is access. In the United States, access requires information and/or money. In some western European countries, where transsexualism is a recognized medical condition (Great Britain, France, Germany, The Netherlands, Denmark, and Sweden, for example), access to medical treatment is through the national health systems. In many other countries (Middle Eastern and African countries and Pakistan come to mind), transgendered people are tortured, jailed, and sometimes offered a choice between surgical sex reassignment or execution by the state (Yusefi, 2000). Even in the U.S., gender-variant people can experience similar treatment.

Another point about access, in the U.S. in particular, is that hormones (including insulin, thyroid medications, and estrogen) are some of the most frequently prescribed substances because hormonal imbalances or deficiencies are extremely common. Yet it's only transsexual people whose hormonal imbalances or deficiencies are restricted from treatment under insurance plans. Some surgical procedures are treated similarly; for example, men with "too much" breast tissue, a condition called gynecomastia, can have this tissue removed, and some women may have healthy breast tissue removed as a prophylactic measure if there is a history of breast cancer in their family. But transsexual men cannot have their breast tissue removed because that process is called a sex change, which is nearly always excluded from coverage, even though the procedures are technically almost identical, particularly compared with gynecomastia. Further, sex reassignment is done routinely without the patient's consent in cases of intersexed children, yet transsexual young people and adults are not allowed to have surgeries at their own request. Such policies seem to me to be blatantly discriminatory, and, whether this bias originates in prejudice, ignorance, or sex-phobia, these policies need to be changed to improve access to healthcare for transgendered and transsexual people, and humane treatment for intersexed people, too.

Similar ironies exist in other countries such as the United Kingdom, where all the medical treatments are covered as part of the national health scheme, yet quotas or limits on services force some people to "go private," paying for treatment out of pocket anyway. Also in the U.K., the government has long refused to change the identification documents of transsexual people to match their gender and presentation. As a result, post-operative transsexual people have not been able to marry partners of the opposite sex, often have difficulty with employers, have trouble getting their pensions when they retire, and are often embarrassed and harassed when their required identification documents don't match their appearance or social identity. This kind of official treatment is deeply harmful to people who are simply trying to live within the laws and customs of society. After a thirty-year battle involving successive petitions from transsexual British citizens, the European Court of Human Rights recently (2002) issued an order to the British Government to change its policies and procedures to recognize transsexuals' new sex/gender status (Whittle, 2002). I think in many cases of official disregard, the perpetrators are well aware of their passive-aggressive behavior, and they enjoy thwarting and chipping away at a transperson's self-esteem. Almost every transsexual person has a story about having to reveal their transsexual status to a clerk or administrator or employer who apologizes for not being able to accommodate some minor request, all the while smiling and implying the requestor was naïve to expect anything different, as if transsexual people deserve only rejection. There are distinct analogies here to the civil rights situation of gay and lesbian people. Parallels may also be drawn with the struggle of any oppressed minority, whether the distinctions are racial, religious, or related to disability. When the majority turns a cold shoulder toward a group they don't understand or don't consider valuable enough to receive resources—even basic civil rights—it is our bodies that cause the offense in others, and our bodies that suffer the indignity and pain of ridicule, rejection, or hatred.

The stigma attached to gender variance, and particularly to transsexualism is exacerbated by the establishment of categories of mental disorders that include something called "gender identity disorder." Like many other topics I can only touch on in this book, this one deserves a full treatise of its own. I can summarize my position, however, in four points. First, I'm sure there are people who have psychic disturbances that could be classified as "gender identity disorder," but I suspect only a small percentage of those people are transsexual. Second, not all transsexual people are psychically disturbed, and those who are not should not be forced to carry a psychiatric diagnosis for what is essentially, for them, a medical condition. Third, just because a person wants to change her or his sex, this is not a reason to assume she or he is psychologically disturbed. Fourth, it is problematic that physicians and surgeons who treat transsexual people must rely on psychotherapists to do their patient screening for them, but right now I have no better idea how they can be certain that patients are good candidates for hormonal and surgical sex reassignment, that they have the inner fortitude it takes to end up as healthy human beings following such treatment. Most surgeons are not equipped with the time or training to make this assessment. Perhaps one day when society is more comfortable discussing matters of sex and gender, and more adept at accepting gender variance, people will be qualified and able to request sex reassignment on demand—the way they can now request many other types of reconstructive surgery without permission—because they will understand the consequences (and maybe the surgical techniques will be better, too). But for now, consulting with a knowledgeable therapist seems the best compromise, admittedly one intended to protect all parties to the process. Inappropriate medical treatment can be harmful psychologically as well as physically.

The purpose of seeing a therapist is to help separate the issues so the client may be sure that she or he is clear about their motivation to change sex, and clear about what to expect in the process. The therapist will want to establish that the client is not trying to solve unrelated problems by changing his or her sex (which never works) and that the client has a stable personality and the necessary social support network to ensure a successful outcome. Clients should be able to discuss their fears and concerns in a non-judgmental setting, and get answers to the questions they have about the social ramifications of sex-changing treatments. A knowledgeable therapist will be able to help qualified candidates locate medical professionals to initiate treatment; transpeople can also locate treatment facilities through community resource networks (see Brown & Rounsley, 1996).

Hormone Therapy

Surgery is dramatic, and very necessary for many, but it is not always the most profound aspect of a person's transition from one sex to another. Transsexual people are greatly benefited by hormone replacement therapy (HRT) because our bodies have the internal, cellular receptors to process the hormones so that our minds and bodies connect, extending the brain into the body so that we feel the connection resolving the conflict between body and mind. HRT doesn't make us into someone we are not, but enables transsexual people to be more of who we are, to be more at home in our bodies, the way we imagine non-transsexual people feel in their bodies since their sex and gender are aligned. Surgery can be the final confirmation of what we know to be true about our gender identities. Hormones are the oil in the machine that keeps it all running, and this is a fact for everyone, transsexual or not, undergoing HRT or not—all human bodies run on hormones.

One thing is certain: taking testosterone will not make a social female into a social male. It will change some sex-differentiated characteristics that are interpreted socially as male, but it won't make a man of anyone. Being a man is more than looking like one. It requires knowing what is expected of a man, and choosing how to go about meeting or not meeting those expectations at any given moment. It also requires being comfortable in the body of a man, and that is something testosterone can certainly assist, but only if it is within the individual's comfort zone. Some people start taking cross-sex hormones and realize it does not feel "right" or good for them, while for others, like myself, starting testosterone makes them feel relaxed and balanced.

Incidentally, I also think that being a woman requires exactly the same thing: being comfortable in the body of a woman, knowing what is expected of a woman at any given moment, and choosing how to go about meeting or not meeting those expectations. Strong women, just like strong men, are capable of doing the unexpected—that is, breaking gender boundaries—and still being womanly, or manly, or even gender-free in the process, depending on the situation and on their own particular identification and/or intentions. I have never condoned thoughtless conformance to stereotypical gender roles.

So, why change one's body? Possibly because the body is where we live and through it we communicate to others. The reaction our bodies receive from others affects how we interact. I wanted to change my body because I felt invisible. Inside a female body, I felt as if I couldn't fully exist, as if the masculine part of me was compressed inside me to a degree that was not just uncomfortable, but downright painful. We all have hidden components of our personality or selves that we either want to protect or yearn to have others see. We all also have to find the balance for ourselves, bringing out those hidden attributes or somehow finding that place of comfort in our own skins, in our own lives. We all want to find fulfillment. For some people that means something as simple as changing hairstyles or driving a certain car, for others it means serious exercising and buying a new wardrobe. For still others it means giving up a boring job and attempting to change careers, or going back to school to get that MBA or Ph.D. For some people it means adopting a new religious practice or confirming the one in which we were raised. For others it means adopting an androgynous or overtly confrontational style of dress and grooming. For some of us it means changing our sex visibly, legally, internally, and externally—fundamentally and dramatically changing our bodies.

What is it that testosterone actually does? For me, it balanced my emotions and allowed me to feel at home in my body. I had been so afraid of it, frightened that it would make me into an obnoxious ogre, concerned that it would cause cancer, so worried about the mystery of it that I could not allow myself to approach it for decades. I had my first experience with testosterone in 1982, when the bodybuilder boyfriend of a friend of mine presented me with an unopened vial of pharmaceutical testosterone. I took the little bottle from him and held onto it. I was thirty-three years old. I was unsure of myself. "You'll have to get your own syringes and needles," he said. "Can you do that?" I thought of my friend Michael, who then lived an eight-hour drive away. "Sure," I said. "I think I can do that." Still telling myself I was doing research for my novel, I called Michael that night and arranged for Samantha and me to make a weekend visit so that he could give me a few syringes and teach me to self-inject.

It seemed sleazy; I felt like some kind of junkie sneaking around with my little bottle of masculinity. "Let's get it over with," I said, almost as soon as we arrived. "Yeah, you boys go take care of business," Jane teased us as we retreated to the bathroom.

"It's easy," Michael explained, ripping open the sterile package and pulling the plunger on the syringe to fill it with air. He then pushed the needle through the rubber cap on the vial, injected the air in, and then aspirated the golden oil into the barrel. "Fill it up to here," he said, showing me the line marked 1cc. "Now, drop your pants and rub some of this alcohol all around on your hip there. We're going to put it right in that muscle there," he indicated. I was giddy, nervous, laughing, fearful, anticipating.

"Relax now," he said.

I blurted out, "I can't watch!" The needle slid into the gluteus muscle with a slight stinging sensation.

"Hold still now," he said. "It's thick, so it will take a few seconds to push all the testosterone in. You can't do it too fast. . . . Hold on. . . . Still going in. . . . There!" He pulled the needle out of my hip and slapped a cotton ball on the hole where a drop of blood was beading. "Hold that," he said. "Rub it just a bit and it'll stop."

As Michael cleaned up all the sterile wrappers and disposed of the used needles in his sharps container, I waited, listening to my body, trying to see if I felt anything. "How is it?" he asked.

"Fine, I guess. I don't feel anything."

"Really? I always feel a kind of rush from it."

"I don't feel anything at all. Nothing." I was vaguely disappointed, yet relieved.

"Well, you will eventually. It'll do its work. You're gonna like it, I just know it." We returned to Samantha and Jane, who looked at us expectantly. I shrugged my shoulders. "Nothing yet," I reported.

Samantha and I drove home the next day. I still felt nothing. Michael had given me some syringes and told me to give myself another injection in two weeks. I regarded my body with some trepidation, as if I expected it to go out of control, to surprise me with its Mr. Hyde transformation. Still nothing. About three days later, as I was walking down the hall at work on an interdepartmental errand it suddenly hit me, but in an unexpected way. I found myself thinking: "So this is what normal feels like." I had to stop moving and just sense myself from the inside out. Anyone seeing me there would have thought I had forgotten something, would have imagined that I was recreating my previous steps in my mind to remember where I had left something. It was true that something was gone, but an invisible something new was in its place. I felt centered and balanced and whole for the first time in my life. I had never realized before that I didn't know what this felt like. "Wow," I whispered. "This is what normal feels like."

According to protocols developed by the Harry Benjamin Gender Dysphoria Association (Meyer, et al., 2001; the latest edition of these professional Standards of Care is available at *www.hbigda.org*), the Tom Waddell Health Center (part of the San Francisco Department of Public Health), and FTM community lore, the hormonal preparations most commonly prescribed for female-to-male transition in the U.S. are testosterone cypionate or testosterone enanthate. The cypionate is suspended in cottonseed oil, is usually faster acting, and causes more acne if one is prone to it. The enanthate is suspended in sesame oil, is more gradual in its effects, and may cause less acne. These substances are administered by intramuscular injection, typically prescribed in a concentration of 200 mg/ml at 1 cc every fourteen days at the beginning of treatment. Compounding pharmacies can suspend the cypionate form in sesame oil, if requested, and it is less expensive that way than brand name enanthate. Patch and gel delivery systems are also available at considerably more expense, but these may be worth that expense for those who are fearful or weary of needles. Available oral testosterone medications are not recommended because the high dosages necessary to produce the desired effect would be harmful to the liver. Any of these preparations may increase the patient's risk for coronary artery disease by increasing LDL cholesterol levels, liver conditions (particularly if the liver is already compromised), and the incidence or symptoms of uterine fibroids and ovarian cysts. Polycythemia (overproduction of red blood cells), headaches, and water retention are reportedly common complications (I have experienced none of these). After a baseline test prior to starting hormone treatment, many physicians recommend that patients have blood tests done every six months to monitor cholesterol levels and liver function; it's also recommended that

FTMs have regular gynecological exams as long as they have female internal organs, and watch their weight and intake of fat, sugar, alcohol, and other harmful substances (as should anyone). After a year or two, provided all is well, many physicians think blood tests can be done annually, or even less frequently in some cases.

The desirable side effects are that menstruation stops, the voice drops (this effect is irreversible), the hairline may recede, more body and facial hair may grow, muscle density increases, body odor changes and skin texture may become rougher due to pore enlargement (after the oily, adolescent period ends in a few years)—Steve Dain once told me that the difference between the feel of a man's skin and a woman's skin was like the difference between cotton and silk. One's body temperature may seem to increase, but it is actually a metabolic change that makes one feel warmer. The clitoris becomes enlarged, increasing in size to roughly an inch long on average when flaccid, and over half an inch across at the corona—a relatively dramatic change, actually; in some people the erection is enough to achieve penetration during intercourse. Sex drive increases, which may also be a dramatic change for some individuals. Body fat is usually redistributed to a male pattern (around the stomach rather than the hips), but subcutaneous fat is not eliminated: if a person has cellulite before testosterone, he will have it afterward, too. Facial bone structure can change somewhat over the years. All of this takes time, and everybody has different responses and different rates of change.

I didn't know all this when I began with that first injection in 1982. Because I was not under medical supervision, I was nervous about changing too rapidly, so I waited four weeks, instead of two, to take my second injection. I had to call Michael and have him talk me through the process. I was afraid even to open the syringe package without him. I wanted Samantha to do the injection for me, but she refused. It was awkward putting the phone down to do each little movement, then picking it back up again to ask, "Okay, now what?" But I got through it, and still I felt nothing immediately after the injection.

A few days later I developed the worst case of acne on my face that I had ever seen. Thirty-three years old, and acne like an exploding teenager. No. I couldn't tolerate it. And because I was taking testosterone illegally I couldn't exactly go to my doctor to ask for help to treat the acne. I decided

I couldn't take any more testosterone. I wasn't ready to deal with the consequences of a visible transformation.

As the testosterone was processed through my body and gradually disappeared from my system, the acne cleared up, and my next several menstrual cycles were particularly painful. Weeks later, when the testosterone was definitely depleted, I found myself responding to the most subtle emotional stimuli in completely inappropriate ways. I would cry uncontrollably over nothing. I was inconsolable. Worse, I could observe myself behaving in this irrational way, and I was powerless to stop it. I just had these *feelings* . . . and I had to let them out. Fortunately, this lasted only a week or so, and then it stopped, too. I assumed my system was doing a pendulum swing from the masculine to the feminine, and then it found what passed for the center once again. It didn't occur to me that I might be feeling depressed over the withdrawal of a stabilizing hormone that was vital to my system, or over my failure to carry through with what I really wanted. I went back to my usual patterns, taking care of everything around me, trying not to feel anything too deeply. Later that year, Samantha and I made another weekend trip, and I delivered what was left in the bottle to Michael, returning his unopened sterile syringes. At that point I didn't think I would ever do it again. I would find some way to live in the—in *my*, I had to remind myself—female body. I was still incapable of admitting to Samantha or to myself that I wanted to change my sex. It would be six more years before I could muster the courage to do what I needed to do. I do not advocate illegal steroid use. Bodily changes of this magnitude should only be done with the support and supervision of a licensed physician.

By the summer of 1988 I was so ready to embark on a permanent transition that I could barely stand waiting for the medical approval to come. It took five months from the time I began the application process with the sex reassignment program until I got the go-ahead. By that time, I was determined to do it right. I thought at the time that I wanted sanction, I wanted approval, I wanted legal status, and I wanted to be a real, honest man, not someone who snuck around evasively, worried he was going to be caught at something he wasn't supposed to be doing.

Often when people begin a hormone regimen, it is the culmination of a long period of deliberation, soul-searching, and possibly a long period of searching for a provider as well. By the time people have found the courage to embark on this path, they are usually hoping for quick results because they don't want to prolong their anguish. In their excitement people often expect changes overnight, and when those changes don't happen fast enough they sometimes think over-medicating will help. But with testosterone (and probably any hormone), more is *not* better. A unique property of testosterone is that the human body converts what it can't use into estradiol, which for FTM transsexual people produces effects exactly opposite of those intended. It can complicate reactions in the body, and send emotions on a roller-coaster ride through hell, which is not exactly pleasant for other people nearby.

Some people have achieved some hormonal rebalancing or masculinizing that is perceptible and satisfactory to them using DHEA (dehydroepiandrosterone), androstenedione, and various herbal preparations. I don't know anything concrete about these substances, so I can't really comment on this practice. I suspect, however, that the attainable degree of masculinization would not be sufficient for most transsexual people, though it might be fine for some who simply want to manifest more androgyny and may not want surgery or legal male status. Although it is possible to stop taking testosterone and maintain a male appearance, most transsexual people will need to take the required hormone for the rest of their lives. Anyone's dosage may need adjusting over time, because the body needs the proper amounts of various hormones to maintain physical health, including guarding against osteoporosis. Testosterone does this for men as estrogen does it for women. The important thing for anyone (transsexual or not) is to maintain systemic hormonal balance, which can vary at different ages, or with other metabolic changes such as those brought on by exercise, inactivity, stress, etc.

When I started my medically monitored program of testosterone, the doctor prescribed the enanthate preparation to minimize the acne response. Although the acne was not eliminated, being able to speak to a physician about my condition improved my outlook considerably. By that time, too, I had been getting information from Steve Dain, and I knew the early effects would pass, and that my body was going to adapt and change, just the way it does during adolescence.

The emotional effects of hormones are not completely understood, and western culture does tend toward flagrant sex stereotyping regarding the effects of testosterone and estrogen. Estrogen jokes are far less tolerated since the Women's Movement of the 1970s endeavored to show that women are more than their biology, but testosterone is still targeted by female chauvinists and male apologists as a source of poor socialization and other evils, even as male HRT for "andropause" is thought to promise a multi-billion-dollar annual market for pharmaceutical companies (Groopman, 2002). I cannot claim to understand these so-called sex hormones better than endocrinologists do, but I can confirm that they are powerful substances, capable of dramatic effects. Those effects are not uniform in all people. Testosterone acts on receptors that are present in the body. If those receptors are not present, no effect occurs. The body simply cannot use the substance. If a person does not have the gene for male pattern baldness, testosterone will not cause male pattern baldness to occur. Testosterone will not cause heavy beard growth or a buff physique in someone who does not have the genetic capacity to grow a heavy beard or attain muscle definition. Some FTM people say they experience less emotionality, that they cry less, or that they can be emotionally colder with testosterone in their systems. Others do not have this experience at all, and are instead very much in touch with their emotions or cry easily. Some people feel that testosterone makes them more ready and able to express anger than they were before. This may be true, but at least in some people this may be a psychological outgrowth of the act of self-assertion required to declare oneself as transsexual, or the license given by the knowledge that one is male, rather than purely the effect of testosterone. Human organisms are complex, and the only guarantee is that, unless one has no receptors for testosterone at all, emotional and physical changes *will* occur. Even in the realm of sexual response, sexual fantasy, and sexual behavior in general. Some people who were capable of multiple orgasms prior to testosterone will experience only one orgasm in a lovemaking session, while others may have exactly the opposite experience. And the kind of sexual behavior they enjoy may change, too, along with the object of attraction. That is, people who were once only attracted to females may be surprised to find themselves attracted to males instead or as well. Sex hormones are indeed powerful stuff for human beings to process, and they are no more dangerous for transsexual people than they are for anyone else. They are powerful expressly because they affect so many aspects of our social behavior, and they don't cause precisely the same reaction in every person. But that doesn't mean they are unsafe, even for cross-sex transformation. The largest study done to date to monitor the effects of hormones in transsexual people includes over ten thousand patient years of medical histories and shows that there is no appreciable risk in medically supervised hormonal transition (Gooren, 1999).

Hormonal changes may not be enough; surgical modifications to confirm one's gender may be necessary. Some kind of genital reconstruction to conform to the designated type is usually required for a legally recognized sex change or gender confirmation, though whether this should be ultimately necessary is a matter open to debate. When I came to grips with my need to change my sex, I knew I wanted to take testosterone, and I wanted to have my breasts removed. That was all I wanted at the time. And once I knew that was what I needed to move forward in my life, I could hardly think about anything else. I didn't think I wanted genital reconstruction; I was a little afraid of what the hormones might do, and I was definitely afraid of surgery. Any surgery is a risk.

Approaching Surgery

People have all kinds of fantasies about sex reassignment surgery. They ask, "Where do they get the parts for the transplant?" as if we salvage cadavers or perhaps we find someone of the opposite sex who wants to be a donor or to swap with us. It doesn't work that way. There is no such thing as a single, discreet "sex change operation" for FTMs. There's "top" surgery: a bilateral mastectomy or other breast tissue removal procedure and contouring of the chest. Then there's "bottom" surgery: removal of the internal female reproductive organs and/or genital reconstruction. It takes years to go through this transition, to master the changes each step of the way. And that's without taking money into consideration—each step costs a significant amount of money, tens of thousands of dollars. Even in countries where the procedures are covered by national health plans, there are long waiting lists and people often "go private," that is, find a surgeon outside the system and pay for it themselves if they can afford it.

Once you undergo one of these surgical procedures you have *altered* your body. Your skin, nerves, and possibly muscles will have experienced a wound. At that site, your body will never be the same as it was before. Before approaching surgery, it helps to understand our existing bodies. We must be realistic about what our body is before we enter the surgical suite, we must know what we want it to be when the surgeon's finished, and we must know what questions to ask the surgeon and how to ask them. Our body may never live up to our self-image, no matter who the patient and surgeon are, or how much money the patient has. The surgeon works with flesh, and we have to acknowledge that our flesh may not present the ideal working conditions for the surgeon. Second, we must understand the surgeon's techniques well enough to discuss the desired outcome, and have some idea of what to expect to see and feel when we awaken from the anesthesia. We should find out directly from each surgeon how she or he approaches the various difficulties that may be encountered in each procedure. And last, but not least, we need to get into the best possible physical shape before surgery to assist the surgeon in shaping the body and to aid in our own healing. Except for some revisions or "touch-ups," all the surgeries associated with gender confirmation or sex change are invasive procedures performed under general anesthesia. It is always advisable to ask any surgeon about the risks associated with surgery in general, as well as with specific procedures, but this is often difficult when we are nervous. As transsexual people discuss issues with physicians, we must always be on guard for signs of disrespect or of dismissive, abusive treatment. All too often, transpeople are willing to "take it" in the interest of getting through the surgery.

"Top" Surgery

There are four primary techniques used in removal of the female breast: keyhole, drawstring, pie wedge, and double incision. Surgeons experienced in working with FTMs may employ one or more of these techniques. Some surgeons have new techniques or variations that they find effective, such as the "inverted anchor" technique of one New York surgeon I've met. There are surgeons who have never had an FTM patient who are fully capable of performing these procedures. They may have used them on men with gynecomastia or on women at risk for, or who have, breast cancer, or with breasts that are so large they might cause damage or stress to the supportive structures of the back. A surgeon experienced with FTM procedures will evaluate the patient's body and recommend the best surgical technique for removal of the breast tissue and contouring of the chest wall to ensure a masculine appearance, preserving or revising the nipples.

If the patient has very small breasts, that is, *very small* (A cup or *smaller*), the surgeon *may* recommend the keyhole or drawstring techniques. These methods leave little or no noticeable scarring, but will rarely yield optimal results if breasts are larger than A size or if the breast tissue extends close to the armpit. However, some larger breasted people have undergone this procedure and been pleased with the results, so I think the most rational advice is to arm oneself with education. If one is compelled somehow to select a complex or potentially inappropriate procedure for his body, then he must be prepared either to live with the results or undergo revision surgery.

When performing a keyhole procedure, the surgeon makes an incision around all or part of the areolar ring, inserts a liposuction device and essentially vacuums the fatty tissue out of the breast. Alternatively, some surgeons may make an incision in the armpit through which to insert the cannula. With this technique, mammary glands are usually left intact. Drawbacks are that small deposits of fatty tissue may remain in the chest (which may possibly be reduced by a technique called feathering), or the finished areola may be disproportionately large in comparison with the nipple on a typical male chest (which is fine for some people, but unacceptable for others). Furthermore, since the breast tissue is not removed, breast cancer screening may be appropriate for individuals with a family history of breast cancer. Advantages are little or no apparent scarring and retention of nipple sensation. In the drawstring technique the areolar ring is lifted away without disconnecting the nerves, the breast and fatty tissue are scooped or suctioned out, the excess skin is trimmed and then pulled taut toward the center of the opening like a drawstring bag. The nipple is then reattached, covering the opening. Disadvantages are the same as for the aforementioned keyhole procedure, plus the nipple placement may be low on the chest. With either of these two procedures, if the breasts are too large the result may be unsatisfactory due to puckering, poor nipple placement, or overly large nipple size, though these results may be perfectly acceptable for certain patients.

The pie wedge technique creates a scar from the outer edge of each nipple toward the underarm, or sometimes straight down from the nipple. Usually this procedure is done with small to medium breasts. Many transmen are dissatisfied with the appearance of the scars because they are so symmetrical and obviously breast-related.

The most common technique for FTM breast removal is the double incision. In this procedure, each breast is opened horizontally across the chest below the nipple. The top panel of skin is peeled back to expose the chest muscle wall, and the breast and fatty tissue is cut and scraped away. The top skin panel is then brought down smoothly and the skin is trimmed and sutured to the lower panel at the incision. One nipple is reserved for later use, and the other is discarded (sent to pathology for analysis first) along with the extraneous skin; or, both nipples may be retained. The nipple in reserve is reshaped to form both new nipples (or the two original nipples are trimmed), and then grafted into place. Surgeons have varying techniques for shaping and placing nipples; candidates are advised to look at photos of former patients (or see them in person, if possible) and discuss his or her technique with the surgeon *before* surgery. This procedure leaves a long horizontal scar, or, depending on the shape of the original breasts and the surgeon's technique, the scar may form a UU shape that displeases some transmen. Muscle development after healing *may* hide the scars beneath the pectoral fold. Disadvantages are scarring and loss of nipple sensation, though some nipple sensation may return over a period of months or years. Some men are not disturbed by the scars which *may* be covered by hair or may appear to have been caused by an accident or other medical condition such as a collapsed lung. Surgery to revise scars may also be practical, and the scars will generally fade over time. Dissatisfaction with nipple size, shape, appearance, or placement is always a possibility. However, this method offers the most thorough removal of breast and fatty tissue because the chest wall is well exposed and contouring is emphasized.

For FTM patients, bilateral mastectomy is usually performed as an outpatient procedure. This practice reduces costs, and also acknowledges the fact that we are usually quite happy to have this surgery, and our optimistic attitude aids in our rapid healing. The costs for "top" surgery range from $3,500 to $8,500, depending on the surgeon's fees and operating room expenses associated with the technique he or she will use. The procedure usually requires two to three weeks rest, and limited pectoral and shoulder activity for a period of up to three months. Time off work varies from two to six weeks. Incidentally, 18,548 non-trans men had breast reduction surgery in 2001 in the U.S. at an average cost (surgeon's fee only) of $2,747 (Marini, 2003).

The bottom line when it comes to "top" surgery is that no surgeon can give a transman precisely the chest he "should have been born with." Everyone's skin and tissue type and composition are different. Even using the same surgeon, no two men will have identical results. Regardless of which technique is used, the patient may require follow-up or touch-up procedures to clean up any residual fatty tissue, puckering, or excessive scarring. And while he may have a great-looking chest when he's dressed, he may always have a sensation in his skin that there was a wound, especially if the incision was a large one. If a surgeon says a specific procedure won't work for a particular patient, it is not usually a conspiracy or an arbitrary attempt to turn the patient toward a technique the surgeon prefers. If the surgeon can demonstrate successful results using a variety of techniques through photos of his or her work, the surgeon probably knows what he or she is talking about. For more information on "top" surgery, see the article "Creation of a Male Chest in Female Transsexuals" by W.R. Lindsay, *Annals of Plastic Surgery*, July 1979, vol. 3, issue 1, 39–46. This is an old article, but it is one of the clearest on the subject by a surgeon. Another good pictorial resource with details of the surgical process is *The Phallus Palace* (Kotula, 2002). All too often people will be so desperate to get through this transition, or to force it into a certain timeframe ("I have to have my surgery next month because that's the only time I can get vacation," or, "I'll be between jobs, then, and no one will have to know," etc.) that they will settle for the first available surgeon without checking others out at all.

"Bottom" Surgery

Doctors have performed the first reported penis transplant at the Nil Ratan Sircar Medical College Hospital in Calcutta in late February 2003 (Rahman, 2003). The patient was a seven-month-old child born without a penis, and the donor was a one-year-old child born with two of them. The surgeon was Dr. Ashok Ray, a noted pediatric surgeon, so surely this will eventually receive more attention, but as of this writing, there have been no follow-up stories on the success of the procedure, and it remains to be seen how each of these children will fare as they grow. This is not the same as a transplant in an adult. Transsexual people are just as prone to fantasy about the procedures and the results as are non-transsexual people. Realistic expectations and realistic decisions can only be based on real information about what is possible.

The bottom line with "bottom" surgery is that no surgeon can give a transman the penis that he should have had at birth. So what's the reason for having genital reconstruction at all? Some FTMs think there's no acceptable reason to have "bottom" surgery. Some of us want desperately to have our bodies altered so we can indulge in sex in a "male way," or so we can get our new birth certificate and have legal male status. Some are afraid of being caught with female genitalia, with nothing in our crotch, or of being caught sitting in a toilet stall, unable to stand and void at a urinal. Some are afraid of being perceived as female, or of being discovered to be "a woman after all"; they believe their penises will prove they are men, even though they know that unless they spend a lot of time in locker rooms and public showers no one will see it besides them, their lover(s), and their doctor(s). Most transmen I know are terrified of landing in jail or of using a changing room at work or at a gym, for fear of having to expose themselves or reveal genitals that will mark them as targets for abuse. There are a lot of reasons to have lower surgery, not the least of which is the desire to have one's entire body match one's gender identity—to feel whole, as some describe it. And there are many reasons *not* to have it. Genital reconstruction is a lot more expensive and risky than a bilateral mastectomy. Few surgeons do genital reconstruction, fewer are truly good at it, and fewer still provide their services to FTMs. Loren Cameron's electronic book *Man Tool* (*www.lorencameron.com*) offers clear, technically excellent images of postoperative genital transformation. Other websites, like FTM Surgery Info and Transster provide snapshots of surgical results and allow FTMs to share their experience and opinions concerning surgery. *Caveat emptor* is a valid concept in matters of this magnitude. Given the present technology, there are trade-offs in deciding which type of surgery to undergo.

There are two general types of genital reconstruction, or genitoplasty, available to transmen: phalloplasty and metoidioplasty.

Phalloplasty
Phalloplasty techniques were pioneered in the first half of the twentieth century to treat men whose penises were lost by traumatic amputation. The first type of modern phalloplasty was the pedicle flap. In this technique, a flap of skin from the abdomen, groin, or thigh, is raised but never fully removed from the body in order to maintain the blood supply. The surgeon manipulates the flap to shape it and "walk" it from its source to

the genital area in successive procedures, always keeping the flap attached to the body at some point (the pedicle). The technique was first applied to female-bodied people in Germany in the 1930s. In 1945 a British surgeon, Sir Harold Gillies, applied his "abdominal tube" technique, in which a flap of abdominal skin is rolled into a tube and left hanging like a flaccid organ, to an FTM patient in England named Michael Dillon (Gillies and Harrison, 1948).

Gillies adopted and popularized surgeon Maxwell Maltz's "tube-within-a-tube" phalloplasty that provided for a urinary canal. Maltz also developed the "suitcase handle" technique, in which the rolled tube of skin is left attached top and bottom on the abdomen for six weeks to ensure adequate blood supply to the neophallus. The upper attachment is then severed and the "handle" swung down and reattached over the clitoral base. This resulted in better retention of the neophallus, which otherwise was prone to wither and fall off (Hage, Bloem, and Suliman, 1993)! Frequent complications of fistulae (leaks) or strictures (blockages) in the urinary passage caused surgeons to continue seeking other solutions.

These early pedicle flap phalloplasties (which some surgeons still perform) required the use of a stent (silicone rod or bone stiffener) inserted in the shaft to achieve erection. This neophallus has no feeling, so care must be taken during intercourse that the stent does not punch through the end of the penis. These penises often do not have a very natural appearance. Urethral extension is rarely done with this technique in the U.S., but some surgeons may be able to provide urinary ability through a subsequent procedure rerouting the urethra. Some surgeons leave the female genitalia completely intact below the neophallus, while some will create a scrotum (scrotoplasty) using a pouch of abdominal tissue bunched up between the neophallus and the pubic mound. Some surgeons will use labial tissue to form the scrotum, but this only creates a realistic appearance if the neophallus is positioned close enough to the scrotal sac, which is not always accomplished. This procedure can cost from $13,000 to $25,000.

The more contemporary phalloplasty technique is called the free tissue flap transfer (FTFT), pioneered in China by Dr. T.S. Chang and Dr. W.Y. Hwang. This technique has been made possible by the advent of microsurgery in the 1970s, and the development of the fine art of connecting dissimilar nerves and blood vessels (anastomosis). A flap of skin and muscle tissue (usually from the forearm or thigh) is transferred, with its existing nerves and blood vessels, to the genital area, and the nerves and blood vessels are connected microsurgically to the nerves and blood vessels of the pubic area. For example, the brachial nerve of the forearm is connected to the pudendal nerve (the nerve providing erotic sensation). The glans of the clitoris is removed to provide access to the pudendal nerve. This results in a penis of an appropriate adult size that may have feeling, but is not capable of achieving an erection. Although implants are available to create erection, they may occasionally be problematic due to infections, rejection by the body, or breaking through the skin either outside or inside the body (extrusion and intrusion). Without an implant, a stent is required to erect the shaft of the neophallus. This penis still may not have a natural appearance; in fact, with all phalloplasties the sculpting of the glans often leaves something to be desired, and it is usually this feature that exposes the organ as one that has been constructed. Several surgeons have overcome many of these problems, notably those who work in countries like the Netherlands and Belgium where transsexual surgery is an accepted procedure. They get more practice with the techniques, plus the aftercare for the patients is better and more consistent, with more physician observation, and the healing process is not so rushed. Reportedly there are excellent procedures being done in China and Taiwan, based on the excellent and thorough anastomosis techniques developed and practiced there.

The advantages of FTFT are that microsurgical techniques can provide a phallus with erotic sensation, and one that is closer in size to that of the average penis, as well as providing for urinary extension (Hage, 1992). The risks, though, are many: damage to the remaining nerves of the donor site (the arm or thigh from which the muscle and tissue is taken), damage to the pudendal nerve that results in a numb organ, death of the graft, loss of function in the donor site (loss of dexterity or mobility in the affected hand, arm or leg), disfigurement at the donor site (though some techniques mitigate this), and the development of fistulae or strictures in the urinary passage. Other factors are the inability to achieve or sustain an erection without a stent or an implant; the possibility of excessive donor site scarring; the fact that these procedures usually require *multiple* encounters with general anesthesia; the results *may* be aesthetically poor; and there can be severe pain and long-term discomfort associated with the donor site as well as the genital area. The risk of infection is greater when there are large areas of the body opened up, and when recovery time (in the U.S.) is often spent in non-sterile hotel rooms with no nursing care. Also, for most transmen, FTFT is cost prohibitive, ranging from $25,000 to $40,000 in the U.S., plus months or even years spent in recovery and/or undergoing revisions, sometimes totaling $100,000 or more in cumulative costs should complications arise.

Metoidioplasty

A transman's natural advantage over a penis-less man is the clitoris. Dr. F.G. Bouman in the Netherlands and Dr. Donald R. Laub, Sr. in the U.S. independently realized in the 1970s that since the clitoris and the penis were homologous organs, they could make use of this erectile body rather than ignoring it, as surgeons had in the past. The two surgeons virtually simultaneously developed the metoidioplasty technique, which is the only type of genital reconstruction that actually transforms the female genitalia into male-appearing organs, as opposed to burying the clitoris (as in FTFT phalloplasty) or attaching the penis above it and otherwise ignoring the presence of the vulva (as was usually done in abdominal tube phalloplasty at that time). Dr. Laub coined the term "metaoidioplasty" by combining Greek expressions that mean "changing form." Dr. Laub told me that, in its application to an exclusively FTM procedure, he intended the term to be construed as "a surgical change toward the male form." In the early 1990s, Dr. Laub began contracting the spelling to metoidioplasty.

The original clitoris is tucked under the pubic bone. Enlarged by testosterone, its length may be enhanced by performing a clitoral release—or "free-up"—severing the suspensory ligaments that hold the erectile bodies down, and advancing the crura (or internal "legs" of the clitoris—now the penis) outward. These "legs" can be repositioned forward with respect to the pubic bone, and a flap of abdominal skin used to cover the newly exposed tissue on the clitpenoid shaft. This technique preserves the natural glans, corona, and shaft, producing a sensate organ with erectile capability. The clitoral release effectively gives the transman a micropenis, a term I despise because it conjures an inaccurate image of an organ visible only through a microscope. Rather, it is a significantly smaller-than-average sized penis, that otherwise functions normally. This condition occurs in 0.6 percent of male-bodied individuals (Silver, 2000), for whom cutting the suspensory ligaments is also being done more frequently.

For transmen, the scrotum is formed by joining the labia majora and using silicone testicular implants, sometimes preceded by tissue expanders. The primary risk with metoidioplasty is that when the surgeon advances the crura out, it is possible that the pudendal nerve may be damaged and the organ rendered numb, though such an occurrence is *extremely* rare. The advantages are that the penis, though small, is otherwise typical in appearance (an intact foreskin, where possible, can contribute to girth), and the scrotum can provide weight and mass in the crotch through the use of testicular implants that are proportionally sized to fit the body rather than the penis. Another advantage is that sexual function is not lost; the man can have natural (i.e., not mechanically assisted) erections and orgasm. Although surgeons have been quoted as saying this penis is too small to be used for intercourse, it is possible to achieve penetration, and simultaneous orgasm, although this ability cannot be expected in every patient or with every partner.

Following a clitoral release, it's possible for the neo-phallus to retract. A surgeon can manually stretch the neo-phallus and tack its base to the pubis. This technique is also used in males with "hidden," "concealed," or "inconspicuous" penises (Alter and Ehrlich, 1999). Surgeons who specialize in dealing with the FTM population are developing enhancements to the original techniques that may result in larger organs; one such procedure is called the "Centurion."

Metoidioplasty can be performed on an outpatient basis and also costs less than phalloplasty, usually running $10,000 to $25,000. If tissue expanders are used for the scrotum, expect a second procedure, costing approximately $2,000 to $3,000, to remove them and replace them with the actual implants. Each procedure requires about ten days of absolute rest, and the initial reconstruction requires a further healing period of one to three weeks when limited activity may be necessary. Many variations are also possible, with common configurations consisting of clitoral free-up only, free-up with testicular implants, free-up with urinary hook-up only (no scrotum), free-up with vaginectomy (removal of the vagina) only, and other combinations. Actual prices and recovery times should be obtained from surgeons on an individual basis.

Urethral extension in metoidioplasty poses the same problems it always has with phalloplasties: some surgeons are more willing to attempt it than others, and one hundred percent success is not uniformly achieved.

Several surgeons have been working on new techniques to eliminate strictures and fistulae, one of the most promising being developed in Sweden by Dr. Gunnar Kratz, who is working on cell regeneration for urethral tissue, similar to that used in regenerating skin for burn patients. This technology may one day allow transmen to grow their own penises larger, too. Tissue engineering experiments at Harvard Medical School focused on penis generation are reportedly promising for people born with ambiguous genitalia, but scientists are still far from experimenting with human tissue, and they say these techniques will not work for female-to-male sex change procedures because "women don't have the right cells" (Westphal, 2002). Language like this indicates complete ignorance of the experience of transmen, and indicates a bias against working with them as subjects. Cells alone do not determine whether one is a woman or a man. Female bodies that do not have the clitoris enhanced with testosterone may very well not have the pre-existing condition necessary to increase penis size, but the body of a transman may be perfectly capable of benefiting from this treatment. Tissue-engineered penises for transmen are probably at least ten years away.

When transmen are searching the medical literature for ideas about how to technically improve phalloplasty, they should not be misled by descriptions of penis reconstruction techniques used for loss of erectile function caused by other diseases. These methods presume the presence of an organ that is not easily mimicked by tissue from other parts of the body. Instead, they should look for Kallmann's Syndrome (one of many conditions that results in micropenis) or hypospadias repair; these conditions are far more analogous to transmen's physical situation. Also, any man should watch out for promises made of fat transfers: packing one's penis with one's own fat can make it difficult to erect and less sensate. The fat can also migrate, clump in unattractive places, or even die.

Additional Procedures

There is one further type of "lower" or "bottom" surgery of which transmen will often avail themselves. This category includes hysterectomy, salpingectomy/oophorectomy, and sometimes vaginectomy. These procedures may be performed through an abdominal incision, through a vaginal entry, or using laparoscopy. Some jurisdictions may require that oophorectomy be performed to render the transman sterile before granting legal recognition as a male. Some transmen feel they need to be rid of these "female" organs for psychological reasons, and some need to have them removed because the testosterone therapy may aggravate existing pre-cancerous conditions in that tissue. Some transmen believe these are unnecessary surgeries and will avoid them.

When deciding whether or not to have the uterus and ovaries removed, there are a few things to consider. First, because the FTM population is not well studied, we don't know the long-term impact of testosterone therapy on female internal organs. If one is in a high-risk group for cancers of female organs, prone to ovarian cysts, or has a history of problems in these organs, these are good indications for removal. Also, people who live in small towns may run into problems obtaining medical treatment for "female" problems while presenting a male appearance, so having the organs out when one can do it simply (while still presenting or classified as female) precludes ever having to deal with them again. Sometimes big cities aren't any easier than rural areas on the physically incongruent, either.

Considering the three different surgical approaches, there are many factors to weigh. The abdominal approach is the least desirable because it induces more trauma, sometimes leaves a noticeable scar, and may interfere with a later phalloplasty via abdominal tube; however, in cases where the organs are difficult to remove or there are large fibroids or other growths, this method may be necessary. The laparoscopic approach can only remove the ovaries and fallopian tubes; it is more expensive than the abdominal method, and not all gynecologists are skilled in the technique; it leaves some scarring. The vaginal approach leaves no external scar, causes less trauma, allows for more rapid healing, and is convenient if the surgeon is also performing a vaginectomy and/or anterior vaginal flap urethroplasty (the most effective technique to date for urethral extensions); one prerequisite is that the vaginal opening must be large enough to accommodate the surgical instruments.

Some doctors recommend removing the vagina (like the other "unnecessary" female organs) to avoid infections and cancer. But transmen not undergoing urethroplasty might consider retaining the vagina in the event an anterior vaginal flap urethroplasty is elected in the future. Some people who are accustomed to vaginal response during orgasm may want to retain the tissue to avoid loss of that particular sensation. Another factor to consider is that the vagina is well-vascularized, making blood transfusions necessary in some cases of vaginectomy. Some surgeons will ask patients to have some of their own blood drawn by prescription, well in advance of the surgery date, so that the patient's own blood is available should a transfusion be required. Because it can be a difficult procedure, and because it can compromise future reconstructive options, I believe a vaginectomy should not be mandated for social reasons. In 1997, a Canadian transsexual man sought my help in his struggle to attain legal male status when officials suddenly adopted the requirement of vaginectomy. I helped him frame the issues and referred him to legal scholar Stephen Whittle in England, who submitted an affidavit on his behalf. The man's petition was successful, and the affidavit appears in *Respect and Equality* (Whittle, 2002).

Decisions, Decisions

Understanding the surgery one is seeking requires accepting the fact that one is altering his body and that he will never have the body with which he should have been born. This means accepting the limitations that his body has before he gets on the operating table, and accepting that he will not come out of this scarless, without wounds, or without compromises. That is not to say that transmen can't keep working and hoping for improvements—we can and we do. But we have to live in our bodies one way or another. We need to know how much imperfection we can handle. Identifying as transsexual means we have signed up to consider these questions. Not to do so is to invite disaster, which may occur *anyway* under the knife.

I've undergone a bilateral mastectomy via double incision, a hysterectomy and oophorectomy via abdominal incision, and a metoidioplasty without urethral extension. None of these procedures was a walk in the park; I was apprehensive going into each of them, though in different ways. Each time I had no reservations about it, but I knew I might not wake up. I had no idea how the results would actually look. I remember that after my genital reconstruction, Dr. Laub came to inspect the results the following day. He removed the dressing and exclaimed, "It's beautiful. No bruising. Excellent!" He and his assistant surgeon, Dr. Gail Lebovic, stared into my crotch, smiling. I felt oddly disembodied. Then Dr. Laub asked, "Do you want to see?" "Sure," I replied. He held up a large mirror so I could inspect myself. I looked and I wasn't sure what I was seeing. Everything was flat, compressed, shriveled. "Doesn't it look great?" Dr. Laub prompted. "Yeah. Yeah, it looks great," I said. I think I was a bit in shock. I didn't see a penis, but I didn't see a vulva, either. At least it wasn't bloody or covered with huge stitches, but I wasn't sure what I was seeing. The happy surgeons departed, and within hours my penis and scrotum had swollen to the size of a hacky-sack perched atop a softball. I worried that I would never walk again, let alone ride a horse or bicycle. The swelling was normal, and subsided after a week or so, but I had had no idea to expect it and it frightened me. There are many things surgeons forget to tell us, but I don't think they deliberately omit information. They've never gone through the experience from our point of view, so how can they know exactly what we will feel? In 2000, I asked two Belgian men who had undergone phalloplasty procedures if there was anything about the surgery or recovery that surprised them, or that was not explained to them beforehand, and they both mentioned the paralysis of the hand on the donor arm. Both were surprised by the swelling and loss of motion, which lasted for up to a month. One of them experienced a serious panic condition when he realized he was paralyzed; no one had told him to expect it. Fortunately it was temporary.

Some people who say they desperately want surgery are still waiting for the surgical techniques to improve, and I think there likely will be some significant improvements in surgery over the next decade or two, but the results may not be what some people imagine, at least not for quite some time. Right now, our choices are essentially constant size (phallo) or natural spontaneous erection and orgasmic potential (an organ that is small but increases in size with erection—metoidio). I was willing to make a choice back in 1990. I thought that I wouldn't want to wait until I was fifty or sixty to have this surgery. I knew I didn't want to continue living in a self-imposed underground because my body didn't fit either male or female criteria. I had grown too weary of living in that limbo state, though I know many people are just fine in that space, and I respect their choice to stay in it. I opted for metoidioplasty because I wanted to get it over with, to stop having to worry about not having genitals that matched the rest of my body and soul, because I wanted to experience my genitals outside my body, because I wanted to have erections and orgasms, because I wanted to have genitals that a woman who was interested in being with a man would be able to relate to (even though I figured whoever she was, she would still require a period of adjustment), because I wanted a procedure that was not terribly invasive, because I wanted the rest of my body to be unscarred (except, of course, for the scar I already had on my chest), and because I could afford it. For me, it was the best option, and I'm very pleased with the result and glad I did it. I'm not saying that anyone should rush out and have the same type of surgery I did, or do things for the same reasons I did. Others will know when the time is right for them, and they'll know what procedure is right for them, too. I'm just reporting what I did and why. Everyone has to make his or her own decisions about his or her own body, and if we can express our opinions without implying a value judgment on others, so much the better. There is no reason to invalidate anyone's choices about how they live their life, yet transsexual people often do this to each other, consciously or unconsciously, when they speak about their choices with respect to surgical procedures.

People do ask how much it all costs. I've cited cost ranges above for specific procedures, but surgery isn't the only aspect of transition that costs money. For the record, in 1991, I tallied up the money I'd spent over my surgical transition. Costs quoted to me by providers and consumers alike in 1988–1989 hovered at less than $4,500 for "top" surgery (outpatient bilateral mastectomy, or chest reconstruction), and roughly $6,000 for the metoidioplasty. In my newly found conviction to follow through on my self-realization as a man, I figured I could easily afford to pay $10,000 to $12,000 over a period of two or three years. Hell, at the time it was just like buying a new car, right? Wrong!

I didn't realize it as it was happening, but the true dollar cost of the sex reassignment process can be much more than each specific surgery along the way. At the outset, I didn't anticipate the hysterectomy, which later proved necessary because of fibroids and pre-cancerous cell generation in the uterine wall. Not everyone will require a hysterectomy. In comparing these costs with other published estimates or records, keep in mind that phalloplasty costs much more than the genital reconstruction I had. The range I was quoted most often in 1990 was $10,000 to $50,000 for phalloplasty. Currently, prices run in the $13,000 to $100,000 range, averaging $40,000 to $60,000. Advance payment is almost always required for any procedure not covered by insurance. Also, every procedure is not always successful; revisions are often required. If these can be handled in a clinic environment the costs are frequently less than $3,000, depending on the problem at hand. And men who do physically demanding work may want to take more time off to ensure good healing with minimal scarring. The amount one will want or need to spend on therapy or clothing may be more or less than what I've listed here. As one's body changes, one's self-image changes; anyone may need or want to experiment with different styles, or they may make fashion errors. Clothing is very important to one's presentation, and it can be very expensive, even if it's purchased at discount or second-hand stores, but it's a cost of transition that FTMs often don't anticipate.

Summary of Costs (1988–1991 prices)

[1988–1989]

$400	initial evaluation by Gender Dysphoria Program, Inc.
$34	breast binder (to assist in pre-surgical cross-living)
$312	annual cost of Delatestryl (brand name for testosterone enanthate; brand name depo-testosterone [Cypionate] or generics of either type usually cost less)
$200	rough annual cost for physician visits and blood cholesterol tests
$100	prosthetic penis to wear under clothing (not for sex) [I only wore it once and felt ridiculous so I sold it to someone else.]
$4,242	"top" surgery: operating room, surgeon, and anesthesiologist
$4,250	rough annual cost for psychotherapy (fifty sessions)
$500	estimated cost to augment wardrobe (size changes: neck and shoulders bigger, hips smaller)

$10,038   **total expenses during the first year.** I also spent three weeks on disability following surgery.

[1989–1990]

$ 200	rough annual cost for physician visits and blood cholesterol tests
$312	annual cost of Delatestryl
$4,700	surgeon's fee for metoidioplasty
$1,385	anesthesiologist's fee for 5.5 hours of surgery (metoidioplasty and total abdominal hysterectomy)

$3,000   OB/GYN surgeon's fee for hysterectomy

$500   surgeon's fee for mastectomy scar revision (done simultaneously with surgeries listed above)

$11,000   operating room and hospitalization (four-day stay due to hysterectomy; not required for metoidioplasty alone)

$300   pre-operative lab work and post-op pathology

$4,250   rough annual cost for psychotherapy

$500   cost of a decent business suit and serious shoes

$26, 147   total expenses during second year. I also spent eight weeks on disability following surgery.

[1990–1991]

$ n/c   series of office visits to surgeon over three to four months to fill expanders in scrotum and stretch skin for testicular implants to come later

$1,150   surgeon's fee to remove expanders and place actual testicular implants

$725   operating room fee

$200   rough annual cost for physician visits and blood cholesterol tests

$312   annual cost of Delatestryl

$136   filing fee for Superior Court for Change of Name and Sex, and Issuance of New Birth Certificate

$80   required publication of Order to Show Cause (part of court proceedings)

$25   fees for official copies of judge's decree and new birth certificate

$4,250   rough annual cost for psychotherapy

$6,878   total expenses during third year. I also spent another two weeks on disability.

$43,063   total cost of transformation from spring of 1988 to spring of 1991

[Ongoing]

$2,700   projected annual maintenance costs, post-transition: physician visits and blood work/ongoing testosterone therapy/periodic psychotherapy if required. I actually have spent much less, closer to $500 annually

Expense Summary and Comparison to 2003 Costs

	2003*	Total	1988–89	1989–90	1990–91
Physician visits[1]	1,000	1,000	600	200	200
Surgeries[2]	35,750	27,002	—	—	—
Top surgery	8,500	—	4,242		
Metoidioplasty and Hysterect./ Oophorect.	25,000	—	—	20,885	—
Implant Insertion	2,250	—	—		1,875
Testosterone[3]	1,488	936	312	312	312
Accessories[4]	1,800	1,134	634	500	
Legal filing costs for sex change[5]	300	241			241
Psychotherapy (fifty visits/year)[6]	18,750	12,750	4,250	4,250	4,250
Total Costs	59,088	43,063	10,038	26,147	6,878
Ongoing maintenance[7]	4,383	2,700			

* The 2003 column contains estimates of the same costs adjusted for inflation. In cases where the costs are known, that data is used rather than an estimate.

1. Costs estimated include initial evaluation, physician visits, and lab (blood) tests.

2. Costs estimated for services provided in west coast region, including pathology costs.

3. Cost shown is for brand-name testosterone enanthate at $93 per five-dose vial (sixteen vials over three years). Brand name cypionate costs $1,040 (eight vials over three years); compounding pharmacy cypionate in sesame oil costs $360 (eight vials over three years).

4. Items included are clothing, binding, and prosthetic devices.

5. Estimated court filing and notice publication fees, plus notary fees, etc., post-judgment. Will vary by region or jurisdiction according to local requirements.

6. Cost estimated at $125 per visit, fifty visits each year, for three years.

7. Annual cost estimate includes brand-name testosterone enanthate, psychotherapy at twice a month, regular physical check-ups, occasional new clothing. Costs could be much lower, e.g., $500 or less.

Genital Geometry

We know anecdotally that many transmen don't have genital reconstruction. That puts a lot of people in an interesting position with respect to the definitions of sex and gender, and gets lots of other people very confused. I don't advocate surgery only to alleviate the confusion of others. I also don't believe that genital configuration (or genital geometry, to borrow a phrase I like from Stanford biology professor Joan Roughgarden) is what defines either one's sex or one's gender (Roughgarden, 2004).

There's no denying, however, that genital geometry is an important marker in our understanding of sex (when applied to others) and in our relationship to our own body/sex/gender composition. Some transmen feel a tremendous amount of pressure to have genital reconstruction because they feel incomplete without a visible penis. Whether that penis can be two inches or six inches, sensate or functional, is another matter, which depends on finances, one's physical characteristics, the expertise of the selected surgeon, and sometimes plain old luck. Other FTM-identified guys wouldn't let a scalpel near their genitals, while still others are in a holding pattern until science advances enough to give them a throbbing Jeff Stryker look-alike that they imagine would appear completely natural even on a five-foot, one-inch 110-pound body. In any case, people with female sex organs who appear in every other way as men sometimes live in a state of fear lest they be discovered, sometimes live in a state of complete comfort with their bodies, and sometimes gravitate between these poles in varying states of self-acceptance.

This seems to be the crux of the matter: self-acceptance. In combination with what each of us believes about the definition of maleness and femaleness or masculinity and femininity and our relationship to these features, self-acceptance is the key to our decision-making process when it comes to any body-altering procedure. Consciously or not, we evaluate what we understand about the procedure in question, and, basing our judgment on what we expect to be the possible outcomes, we decide what we can live with or without as part of ourselves. Self-acceptance and self-esteem are crucial factors in our ability to achieve our goals in life. For those of us who struggle with gender issues, putting together the pieces of our individual puzzles can be a complex challenge.

Whether we are men, women, or in between, we are always engaged in a social process of being accepted by others as well as ourselves. We form cultural agreements about what is recognizable and acceptable as masculine, feminine, and androgynous, we decide where our comfort zone is for ourselves, and then we form friendships with people who accept us for who we are and with whom we enjoy spending our time.

We do not form our friendships based on genital geometry. Sure, people who are sexually attracted to men are usually interested in the erotically stimulating qualities of the penis, but they (usually!) do not form social relationships with men by examining their penises first (though I know it can happen that way). Plenty of penis-less transmen manage to engage in sex with penis-equipped gay men or penis-focused straight women, and these non-trans partners are often surprised to realize that a penis is not what defines a man, that the lack of a penis does not mean a lack of masculinity, manliness, or male sexuality. A big penis is not always better than a small penis; likewise, the desire to have a larger penis (or unhappiness with a small one) is no reason to ridicule someone else. Neither is someone's ability to be satisfied with having a small penis. It's the balance we find in ourselves that matters.

Are hormones enough? Is it the clothing, the beard, the body hair, the muscular density, the odor of male sweat, the attitude of "man" that connects with others and makes for social acceptance or sexual attraction? All those secondary sex markers have a very real function in communicating with others about our sexuality and the nature of our psyches or our psychological sex and gender identities. We all make extensive use of these complex communication systems, though for the most part unconsciously. More to the point, though: is gender identity enough? Does a butch lesbian who prefers men's clothing and gets called "sir" have to feel so responsible for other people's confusion that she must conclude she would do better as a man? No, she does not. If she knows and accepts herself, she can claim her space as a woman who looks like a man, and that may very well be what makes her happy and attractive to others. What is her (or his) gender identity, and who gets to define it: her or himself, or someone observing her or him? Gender identity belongs to the person who lives it, but we cannot deny that observers will make assumptions about us based on their understanding or comprehension of gender signals. We need to encourage people to be less concerned about "fixing" others, either by labeling, classifying, or punishing them. For transsexual people this means legitimizing the transformed body; for all people it means legitimizing the self. The debate is over territory, ownership, and the power to define. For physically disabled people, the question once was whether to regard the person as their body (and its obvious or invisible limitations), or as their mind and their human capacity to dream, to relate, to achieve, regardless of what they look like or what accommodation must be made to put them on a relatively equal footing with people who are physically advantaged. For babies with ambiguous genitalia, our medical establishment wonders how can we possibly relate to them, or how will they ever manage to get along socially if doctors don't make those babies look like other people? Instead, the question we ought to ask is how we can make sure these unique individuals get the love they deserve from the people who brought them into the world until these babies become people who can consider the consequences of treatment with which they are willing to live and be an informed party to decisions about what happens to their bodies. Who decides whether our experience of ourselves matters? Who decides what constitutes "quality of life" for me and for people like—or unlike—me? I am the one who has to live inside my body. This is my body of knowledge.

5
Transparent Feelings

I forbid it," my mother sputtered, slamming her tiny fist against the arm of her easy chair. It was a warm Saturday in the spring of 1988, and I had just told her I intended to apply to a medically supervised program for surgical sex reassignment. I'd only seen her this angry a few times before: when I told her in 1978 that Samantha was my family and that therefore we were lesbians, and in 1984 that Samantha and I planned to have a baby. This time I wasn't frightened of her rage. I no longer had anything to hide, and I was ready to face the consequences of becoming myself.

"I know it feels like I'm doing this *to* you, Mom, but I'm doing it *for* me. You haven't wanted to see it, but I've suffered with a dichotomy between my body and my gender all my life. Now I know what I need to do for myself. I know it's possible to change my sex from female to male, and I owe it to myself to at least check it out. It's not an overnight event; it's a long, slow process, and if at any time it doesn't feel right, I can stop."

She stared at me, both her fists white-knuckled, and said, "Don't tell your brother; he won't be able to take it."

I smiled. "Yeah, Mom; like he's not going to notice."

Soon after, I did tell my brother, who I've always called "Mr. Normal." He's much bigger, and nearly four years younger than I am. His immediate reaction was to say, "Well, if that's what you need to do to be happy, you've always been my big brother anyway."

Denial

My mother commanded me not to tell the neighbors, not to tell any of our other relatives, and not to tell any family friends. I agreed, anticipating that this would be a temporary arrangement. If this were anything like my previous revelations, she would get over it once she saw that I was the same person, and that the world did not come to an end.

I could not help but think back to when I'd told both my parents that Samantha and I were lovers. My father was sitting in the leather easy chair that time, with his long legs stretched out on the matching ottoman, while my mother curled her short legs under her on the loveseat across the room from him. It was December, and the occasion for my coming out at that particular moment was the upcoming Christmas holiday. Because I had lived out of state since starting college, it had never seemed critical to tell my parents anything about my intimate life, but since Samantha and I had moved back to the Bay Area there was no hiding the fact that we were building our life together. Her parents knew the nature of our relationship since Samantha had come out to them when she was still in high school, but mine did not. I had resisted telling them primarily because I'd been hearing some anti-gay remarks, especially from my father, and particularly since there had been more frequent and vociferous confrontations occurring between Anita Bryant and the gay community in the local and national news. California also had the Briggs Initiative on the 1978 ballot, a proposed law that would prevent gays and lesbians from serving as teachers in the public schools. My father would say, "No queer is going to teach my grandson," referring to my newborn nephew, and in practically the same breath he would encourage me to become a teacher. I wasn't sure how to confront him, so I just avoided it. The Briggs Initiative lost, and Anita Bryant's forces retreated to Florida, so some pressure was removed, but by Christmas the situation was unavoidable; my mother wondered why Samantha couldn't just go be with her family and why I couldn't just spend Christmas with my own family. Why, she asked, did I need to spend part of the holiday time with Samantha's family, and why should she be coming to our family events?

"Because we are each other's family," I explained, standing in front of the fireplace so I could see both my parents clearly.

"What?!" my mother exclaimed, stiffening.

"We are partners," I said. "We are lovers; we are each other's family and we want to spend the holidays together with each of our families."

Mom swung her feet down to the floor and leaned forward. "It's a phase! You'll get over it! She's using you! You can't go on like this!"

I'm ashamed to say that I was frightened. I had so much fear in me about my parents' response that I let it come forward in tears and a defensive outburst: "Well, at least I'm not telling you I'm changing my sex!"

"You'd better not," she ordered. Then she turned to my father: "What do you think about this?"

Dad sat silently for a few seconds and then he looked at me with sadness. Slowly and deliberately, he said, "I'm sorry that my attitudes made it so difficult for you . . . to tell me something so important about who you are."

I think my liberal Democrat mother was disappointed that my conservative Republican father was not more indignantly opposed to the substance of my confession. But my father stood firm, as he always did when he had made up his mind, and declared, "Of course you are both welcome here, and of course you will be here for Christmas, and with her family, too, when you need to be."

My father never said another anti-gay word in his life; he always showed affection to Samantha and Morgan, who was two years old when her Grandpa Green died of a heart attack in 1987. Later I realized I'd been subconsciously debating whether to apply to the sex reassignment program when he died, and I wish he'd been alive when I found the courage to go forward. I'm sure his presence would have made it easier on my mother.

Partners, parents, and children are our closest relationships, the relationships people are most fearful of losing when they contemplate changing their sex, unless they've already been lost in the process of asserting evolving identities. In spite of my father's accepting stance in 1978, in 1987 I was still concerned about his reaction to my transsexualism. My own mother resisted every step of the way. Long after I was clearly male and every androgynous trait had vanished from my appearance, when I was comfortable in my body at last, she still insisted on using feminine pronouns in reference to me. She also insisted on calling me by the feminine name they had given me as an infant, which I had privately replaced with Jamison at age fifteen. She had respectfully called me Jamie or Jamison since I announced my new name when I entered college at seventeen. Now she was trying to reclaim me as the daughter she wanted, and in public she tried to humiliate me into giving myself up to her vision of me. But it only made her look addled as people wondered why she couldn't see as plainly as they could that I was a man.

It took my mother over five years to refer to me consistently as her son, and my transition caused her to withdraw from me, forever changing the tenor of any conversation between us, limiting our topics to the weather, other family members, and purely logistical matters. We stopped discussing books and ideas, and she never wanted to hear about any accomplishment of mine that particularly recognized either my masculinity or my transsexual experience. I know she couldn't help feeling the loss of the idea of me that she had developed over forty years, and she was trying to manage it as best she could. It was hard on me to upset her and watch her struggle with it, too, but I stayed present for her because she needed both my brother and me after our father died, and because I hoped one day she would see me as I am. I have seen far worse reactions from some families. I've also seen better ones.

Fear

Since the early 1990s I've met, spoken, and corresponded with literally thousands of transgendered and transsexual people—far more than most clinicians or researchers ever meet. I've listened to their stories, and I've also listened to the stories of parents, partners, and children of transpeople, many of whom also contact me looking for information, referrals, and reassurance. The most common theme in these inquiries is fear. Transpeople are fearful of losing contact with people they love, and their loved ones are afraid of that, too, and more. Among the fears that have been voiced to me are that partners of transpeople worry that people will think they (the partners) are homosexual or, if gay or lesbian, heterosexual, or crazy for loving such a person; that courts will force them to divorce or restrict them from marrying; that their transsexual partners will not be able to support them (or hold up their ends of any economic partnership) because they (transpeople) are sure to lose their jobs. Parents of transpeople fear that their children will never find anyone who will employ them or love them, that their children will be harmed by the hormones or surgery, or by a vicious, insensitive public. Children of transpeople fear losing their parent, fear for their own security. Both partners and children fear that their transsexual family member will stop loving them, because transness can sometimes take precedence in a person's life for a while, and people worry that the period of self-absorption will never end, or that the transperson will become someone so different from the person they once knew that all connection will be lost.

Some people are afraid that the transgendered individual is mentally ill and that supporting their desire to change sex makes the insanity worse. There are some cases in which a person's desire to change her or his sex actually is a manifestation of mental disturbance that is not gender variance, and in those cases people may be causing irreparable damage to themselves by attempting to transition, but that is hardly true of all transsexual people. Family is often nature's way of teaching us to get along with people we would not otherwise choose as friends. In many cases, simple acknowledgment and acceptance of a transperson's experience can ease tension in the family and allow healing to occur, though that may be easier said than done.

For some people, the consequences of a transperson's assertion of his or her identity are simply too frightening because it threatens their own position within a particular community of ideology or faith. Others are able to stretch the boundaries of their experience to admit transpeople, and while in the long run they may find it liberating or deepening, they may also find the experience challenging or frightening as well. The transperson has had years to experience and come to terms with their transness and, at least to some degree, know what acknowledging it will mean in the world beyond themselves (even though some transpeople can seem remarkably naïve about the consequences of particular actions, regardless of their age). The partners, families, and friends of transpeople generally have not had the same opportunity to prepare. Some transpeople will unnecessarily cut themselves off from their families because they are fearful of confronting them or guiding them through the transition. Family members may be the most difficult to approach because losing them would be the greatest loss, so we impose that loss on ourselves rather than have it visited upon us.

Yet some parents, partners, and family members are not surprised by their loved one's revelation. My own brother was, I think, more comfortable with me as a brother than as a sister. Certainly he was more comfortable introducing me to his co-workers and associates once I had transitioned.

When I had a female body it was much more difficult for others (like my brother) to make sense of my gender presentation, so when I appeared to be a masculine woman it was easy for them to assume I was a lesbian. In a male body, my attraction to women looked "normal." My brother was not exactly disapproving of my sexual orientation, nor was he resentful of my ability to pitch in with his friends on construction projects or to manage home electrical problems, but he was much more comfortable when he didn't have to explain me anymore. This is not a reason to transition, as far as I'm concerned, but it is a fact that an appearance of conformity with normative gender behavior does cause less social friction, a fact that every child has had drummed into her or him from earliest consciousness.

Parents and Trans Children

The first time a parent, the mother of a transman, came to a San Francisco FTM meeting to meet her new son's friends and learn a bit more about what he was going through, she was welcomed with rousing applause, a few tears, and a chorus of thank-yous for her willingness to accept her child for who he was. This was in 1993, when we members of the local FTM group were still grappling with our collective fear of being rejected by everyone, when people would talk about wanting to disappear, transition, and then reappear as a different person so no one who didn't share it with them would ever have to know about their past. Several people in the group, most of whom were in their twenties and thirties, had not had contact with their families for years. They either knew or had decided that their families would not approve of their transition. In spite of my own mother's reaction, I felt strongly that we should not be made to hide who we were, and I encouraged people to endure the often painful process of educating their families, when they felt safe enough to do so, so they might have the continuity that contributes to a stable life. Even when a break with the past is necessary for survival, as it certainly has been for many people, I believe it's important to be realistic about what has happened and to psychologically incorporate it in a way that preserves the individual's integrity rather than allowing fractures to persist and destabilize either identity or social function. Now, a decade later, I've met quite a few supportive parents from around the country, and heard reports from numerous transmen, especially younger ones, about their supportive families.

One of the best experiences I had with parents of a transman was with John and Mary Boenke. They had long accepted their daughter's lesbianism and had become active in PFLAG (Parents, Families and Friends of Lesbians and Gays), a national organization with chapters in many cities. Joining with other parents of gay children to help support families was Mary's way of using her post-retirement time and energy. She wanted to help make the world safer for her child. When her daughter came to her to say that he had realized he was a transsexual man and he would be transitioning, she was startled and worried. She and her husband were visiting the Berkeley area in 1995 and invited me to lunch. I brought along another FTM friend, Jeff, and his partner, and we had a very serious conversation about the processes, possibilities, risks, and benefits of transitioning from female to male. Later Mary told me that seeing us, seeing that it was possible to live a healthy, happy life and find partners as transmen, brought her so much relief that she began advocating within PFLAG for the organization to include support and education for families of transgendered and transsexual people. In 1996 the Transgender Special Outreach Network, now called Transgender Network (T-Net), became an active component of PFLAG national programs. In 1998 transgender became an official part of PFLAG's mission statement, and in 2002 PFLAG resolved to support only protective legislation that encompasses all GLBT people, becoming the first national organization not started by transpeople to take both steps. PFLAG offers e-mail, phone, and in-person support for family members of transpeople, and T-Net's booklet *Our Trans Children* is a useful resource for families. Another resource for parents is the book *Always My Child: A Parent's Guide to Understanding your Gay, Lesbian, Bisexual, Transgendered or Questioning Son or Daughter*, by Kevin Jennings, executive director of the Gay Lesbian and Straight Education Network (GLSEN). Other resources with more transgender-specific content will surely be developed, but for now the best way to learn is still to meet other gender-variant and transsexual people.

Since the phenomenon of transsexualism has become more openly discussed in the U.S., I've heard from parents or relatives of at least a dozen FTM-identified children who are younger than ten years old. Some of these situations are terribly sad, like one in a southern state where the parents are frightened by their child's depression and they cannot find any doctors who will listen and confirm the child's self-knowledge. But others are having better success, like Susan and Howard, whose child, Ryan, has confidently asserted his male gender identity since the age of three. I met these parents at a regional transgender conference in their midwestern state, where they had come seeking information when Ryan was seven. They were frightened about what the future would be like for their female-bodied child who was so clearly and confidently male, but they were also inspired by seeing several healthy and successful FTM adults. I was able to offer them some referrals to resources and some encouragement. A year later, Ryan's mother wrote to me: "A lot has happened since we last emailed. Ryan has truly transitioned in every way possible for an eight-year-old. He came out to his peers at school last year (1st grade), and when the kids from school forgot about the pronouns over the summer the school principal and I went to every classroom to educate/remind all the kids (1st–8th grade). The support has been unbelievable. The kids have been so compassionate and have no problems 'getting it.' One middle school class wrote a beautiful letter to Ryan about his courage and their admiration for him. His own class, which consists of eighteen 2nd and 3rd graders, were so incensed about the advice Dr. Phil (a television therapist) gave a mother of a child with GID that they became little activists and wrote him a letter. Other than educating the school, my husband and I have spent a good deal of time speaking out on the subject and just trying to provide some kind of normal (in an abnormal situation) childhood for both our kids" (Private correspondence, 2003).

Another mother, Evelyn, whom I met at a transgender law conference in Houston in 1994, documented the successful MTF transition of her own child (Evelyn, 1998). Evelyn has also participated in efforts to create local school policies and state legislation that would protect the interests of transgendered children.

The fact that parents are able to hear their children and recognize their identities as valid is overwhelmingly rewarding. After experiencing my own parents' denial and attempts at training me to "act like a girl," after hearing horror stories about children whose "non-conformance" (as if their gender expression was simply rebellious behavior, and therefore change-able with practice and discipline) was met with hospitalization, psychiatric institutionalization, or plain old-fashioned brutal disciplinary beatings at the hands of both well-meaning and vicious parents, teachers, religious leaders, or even "friends," it is a relief to know that at least some parents are learning to spare their children years of grief and torment. Of course, many of these parents are frightened for their children's welfare, since they know that school administrators, teachers, doctors, and other parents and children don't understand and may want to exert authority over their child. These parents want their children to be safe at school and in the world, and they're negotiating a difficult path between the risks of an ignorant society and the risks of forcing their own child not to be who he or she is out of fear of others' inability or refusal to understand difference. When spared an adolescence that doesn't correspond with their psyche, transgendered or transsexual children can thrive psychologically from an earlier age by integrating appropriately with their affiliate gender. Without support from parents, the medical establishment, and school administrations, it is difficult for children to manage early transitions. Yet some individuals do manage them successfully, while others who are thwarted are either crushed by "the system" or they manage to wait until they are out of high school and strike out on their own.

Almost any transsexual man who had a clear conviction of his masculinity as a child might have benefited from an early transition, though certainly we would be different people as adults because of the different circumstances we would have dealt with over the years had we transitioned at a younger age. Stories about contemporary men who had the conviction to live as men as soon as they could get away from home are documented in Cromwell, 1999; Self, 2000; and Kotula, 2002. Had my own home situation been more adverse than it was, I might have done the same thing, which is not to say that I believe female-bodied people seek sex reassignment as a result of childhood abuse. There are plenty of female-bodied children who are abused who are not transsexual. I don't believe that transsexualism is created in people by their circumstances, but circumstances may influence the intensity with which a transsexual person feels the necessity to seek treatment.

Most children know their gender identity from an early age, whether or not they are transsexual or transgendered. Most people are not transsexual, but for those who are, accommodation should be available. Professionals must use caution in evaluating transsexualism as voiced by children, but it is inhumane to deny social and early hormonal transition (or estrogen blockers to delay puberty until testosterone can be started at age sixteen, if medically indicated—unfortunately, an expensive process) in cases where family stability is demonstrated and clear, consistent signals about the child's gender identity indicate that the stress of living in the wrong gender could be alleviated with treatment. When parents are clearly aware and accepting of their child's gender identity, and agree with the child's wish to have her or his sex align with her or his gender, this should be honored.

Parents and psychologists should also be aware that it is possible to safely allow children (and adults) to "try on" the gender they are asserting to see if it "fits." It's not uncommon for children to express the desire to be the opposite sex, and sometimes when something is forbidden it becomes more attractive. If society were less concerned about the consequences of gender-variant expression it could be much easier for children to navigate their own gender identity and to experiment safely. For example, just allowing little Betty to be called Bob and to participate in some "boys' " activities, if that's what she wants, could easily allow Betty to see that she'd rather be Betty after all, if that were the truth for her. The "danger," of course, is that Betty might just really like being Bob. But is that really a danger? Why? Are we really so unsure of our gender identities that we think everyone would want to change their sex if they could? If that's the case, we'd better take a closer look at our assumptions about gender, sex, and identity. However, I don't think that's really the issue; I think fear is a knee-jerk reaction. Transitions are not accomplished overnight (sometimes a gradual process is better in the long run, and some surgical techniques are potentially more effective when the body is mature), but the goal of any treatment should always be to improve or maintain quality of life according to the subject's own assessment, not some "expert" opinion of what that quality should look like.

When I was in the fourth grade, just nine years old, I was instructed to leave my regular classroom for an hour two days a week for a special reading session—at least that was how it was presented to me. Twice a week I entered a room with a female speech therapist and several other children who had real speech impediments. My problem was that someone had determined that my voice was too low, and that my speech patterns were not appropriate to my assigned gender. In this special class I was asked to read some doggerel aloud, and urged to raise the pitch of my voice, to force a singsong cadence, to end my phrasing with an upward tonal flourish. I remember wondering why I, one of the best readers in my class, had to engage in this embarrassing practice with other children who stuttered and lisped. I liked the sound of my voice—in fact, other boys in my class admired it so much that some even offered to trade their higher pitched voices for mine. I was confident in my reading, and I enjoyed the power of words to create images and ideas. I tried to read the way the speech therapist wanted me to, but it felt horrible. Worse, the boys got to read verses about baseball, while I and the few girls in the room had to speak the language of fragrant bouquets tied with lacy ribbons.

After several weeks of increasing tension between the speech therapist and me, school officials recommended I be taken to a throat specialist. Dutifully, my mother made an appointment and took me to see a man whose office was like a dentist's, but instead of a drill next to the chair, there was a small gas flame. The doctor would use the flame to heat his little mirror, which was like the one the dentist used. Then he would grab my tongue with a coarse paper towel and pull it, hard, and stick the hot mirror in my throat. The heat kept it from fogging up, so he could examine my vocal cords. Mom and I made at least three visits to this man's torture chamber, after which he told my mother he could do surgery on my vocal cords that would give me a fifty percent chance of having a soprano voice. He implied that this would result in more people reflecting femininity back to me when I spoke. Only then did I realize all this was about making me into a girl. I was relieved when my mother said, "No, thank you." This is nothing compared to what happens to many other gender-variant children (Burke, 1996; Scholinski, 1997).

Transpeople as Parents

Many transsexual people who grow up in environments of denial or of abusive punishment for gender variance will make every effort to conform to what is expected of them—to the point of pursuing careers, entering marriages, and having children according to their prescribed gender role—trying to behave "appropriately" thinking their psyches will adapt, that they will eventually accept the "correct" role and behavior for who they are "supposed" to be. Some people make compromises and find that they are able to adapt as long as they're permitted some measure of transgression, such as crossdressing either full- or part-time, or establishing gay, lesbian, or bisexual relationships. Some people are never even given the chance to compromise, or are incapable of it; the most unfortunate in these kind of situations may be ostracized, brutalized, battered, or tormented, so they may never be visible in polite society. They may kill themselves in despair, or be killed in disgust. The incidence of such atrocities is hidden by institutional refusal to recognize transgendered lives.

Isolated from others like themselves, transpeople often assume they're the only person on earth who feels as they do, so it must be wrong. They may work hard to "do everything right" hoping that the feelings of difference or transness will go away; or they may take themselves away—emotionally, mentally, or physically. Getting married and having children is one way that all kinds of people (not only transsexual people) try to normalize themselves. Transpeople also fall in love and desire children regardless of the state of their gender/body dissonance; not every marriage of a transsexual person springs from denial or overcompensation, but may very well arise from genuine love for another person.

Although I was born with a female body, I never wanted to bear children—but I did expect to be a parent. When I was an adolescent, I assumed I would adopt, partly because the idea of giving birth was incomprehensible since I didn't experience myself as female, and partly because I had been adopted myself and had enjoyed a moderately privileged, happy childhood. Later, in the early 1970s (my mid twenties), when I thought I might be a lesbian, I resigned myself to the common belief of the time that homosexual people did not raise children, unless they had gotten them through prior heterosexual relationships.

Samantha, however, was intent upon giving birth to her own children without the participation of a man. When she told me that she wanted to raise children, I apologized to her for not being able to give them to her; secretly I felt relieved, because I thought my life was my own and I would never have to accommodate the constraints of parenting. But her desires did not wane, and mine actually changed as we built a life together that was economically and emotionally capable of sustaining a child. By 1983 Samantha and I were at the forefront of what was to become the "lesbian baby boom." At the same time, I was gradually becoming more deeply engaged in an internal struggle between my lifelong sense of myself as a man and my desire to demonstrate the feminist principles that having a female body did not mean one could not hold a responsible job, love a woman, and raise healthy children.

At that time, I thought I would not have to change, that I could be satisfied living as a masculine woman, or a female-bodied man. I wanted to be able to do that; I wanted very much to avoid the ravages of hormones and surgery and the stigma of transsexualism. I wanted to avoid the struggles and readjustments that I knew transition would bring. Samantha says I never voiced any of this to her. My memory is that we discussed it frequently. I didn't realize at the time—and couldn't have discussed the fact—that it was easier to focus all my emotional energy on Samantha and our efforts to start a family. It was safer for me to believe that everything I did was about managing the responsibility of bringing a child into the world, and about not selfishly focusing on my own feelings or needs.

We went to the Sperm Bank of Northern California in Oakland and selected a donor who resembled me as closely as possible. I purchased the semen in little liquid-nitrogen–immersed vials with the donor's identification number on them. We took the vials home at the appropriate time, and performed the insemination as a ritual, accompanied by candlelight and champagne.

It took eleven months for Samantha to become pregnant, by which time we had long given up on the champagne. On the occasion at which conception actually occurred, I changed another element of the ritual. Typically, while Samantha waited, meditating in the candlelit bedroom, I would run tap water over the vial until it was thawed, then aspirate its contents into an insulin syringe without a needle. This time I decided to forego the running water and to just place the vial in my pocket, holding the cold little seed against my thigh for about twenty minutes, bringing it to life with my own body heat. On some level I wanted to infuse the sperm with the virility of my spirit, the fecundity of my dreams. I was so proud when the conception was confirmed a few weeks later, feeling that our success happened expressly because I had put something of myself into that semen.

And then I panicked. Like classical fathers in television sitcoms, I was beset by worries about my ability to provide for a family, to protect it, to give my dependents everything I knew they needed. Always more comfortable taking action than examining my feelings, I decided the best thing to do while waiting for the baby to arrive was to buy a house. That certainly kept Samantha and me busy. Then there were repairs and remodeling to be completed well before the baby arrived, so there would be no chemical residue, noise, or fumes, nothing to disturb our newly nested family.

When she finally arrived, an unanticipated daughter, we were ecstatic. At the time, we had been told that most donor-inseminated births are male because of the insemination timing: the Y-bearing sperm are faster swimmers, so when you impregnate at the optimal fertile moment for the egg, the sperm most likely to score would be one most likely to produce a male child; yet here was this baby girl. I had never known such a complete feeling of unconditional love as I felt for this child. Our beautiful, miraculous Morgan was the most important person in the world to us. I knew the moment I held her and she looked straight into my eyes that I was willing to die for her. And I knew it was time for me to really take responsibility, for my own life as well as for hers.

Over the next three years I grappled with my place in this now all-female family: Mother, Daughter, and Other. I was listed on Morgan's birth certificate as her father, but I had no legal relationship to her. We thought about second-parent adoption, which was still a risky proposition in the mid-1980s in Alameda County, now one of the jurisdictions where this is easily accomplished. But back then co-parent adoption had only been granted to one other lesbian couple, and we weren't sure we wanted to risk the rejection or notoriety. My own concerns regarding my gender identity were being brought slowly, though sharply, into focus. Whenever someone would refer to me as Morgan's "other mother," I would feel agitated, angry, and invisible. I never owned the label of "mother." I would always correct anyone who bestowed it on me by saying, "She has a mother, and it isn't me." I wanted to say I was her father, but I felt I couldn't say anything that would cause Morgan herself to be confused.

After what felt like a herculean effort to maintain a female identification to reinforce our lesbian family, I was astounded when Morgan first called me "Daddy." It was wonderful to hear her strong little voice calling me who I was, and yet I could not reinforce a behavior that I knew could cause her embarrassment and grief.

It would be an oversimplification to say that this was my pivotal moment, the moment that moved me off the androgynous fence and into the male camp. It was only another candle in that very dark cave I'd been groping around in since I was two years old and refusing to wear dresses. Because my feelings of parental responsibility ran so deeply, it weighed heavily on me that my daughter perceived me as male (as most children did), and I had to tell her this perception was incorrect. I didn't like invalidating her feelings: would she come to doubt herself, or would she come to doubt me? On top of that, I was experiencing increasing distance from my own body during this period. Often I couldn't recognize my own reflection for a moment as I watched myself walk by shop windows. Every time a stranger called me "sir" or "Mr. Green" in person or over the telephone—something that had been happening for decades already—I felt as if I was less and less able to laugh about it. It seemed I was becoming a man in spite of myself; yet because my body didn't match my own or most others' perceptions of my gendered self, the constant feeling of having to explain or justify myself as either female or not male created an emotional conflict in me. I didn't want to face that conflict, but it continued to present itself, to rise up and fall away like a boat bobbing in the waves—and it was making me seasick.

I think what really knocked me off the fence was our effort to have a second child. We were able to get the same donor so our children would be full siblings, and we thought the odds were that this second child would be male. But I was disappearing. My female body was swallowing me up. I worried constantly about raising a son and placing on him the burden of reconciling our shared masculinity with my female body. I didn't want either of my children to witness people taunting or challenging me—I didn't want them to feel they had to defend me or to be ashamed of my difference. I didn't want to hear one more person refer to me as the "other mother" with the insipid smiles of condescension that came from some straight people (as if they were saying, "you only think you're a parent, but we'll humor you") or the smiles of inferred conspiratorial complicity coming from gay and lesbian people starting to warm to the idea of gay and lesbian families, as if they were finally realizing having a child is not just a heterosexual privilege.

I had been tentatively researching transsexualism for many years, long before children were a part of my landscape. Samantha and I had discussed my male spirit frequently in the dozen years we'd been together. She even wrote a song in 1980 about her lover changing sex which declared, "I'll stand by my baby no matter who don't understand," even though I'd been thoroughly resistant to the idea of physical transition from female to male. I assumed this song was evidence of her understanding, though she later said it was about Michael and Jane, not about us. Long afterward, Samantha said my decision to change my legal sex was a complete surprise to her because of my pride in being what I then called cross-gendered. But she did try to be supportive of me, wondering whether she could make the adjustment to my transition. As for Morgan, she was three years old when I told her I wanted to change my body so I could really be her dad.

"Remember when you called me daddy and we told you I couldn't be your daddy?" I asked her. She nodded. "Well, I really do feel like your daddy, and I'd like to be your daddy. So I found out that I could go to a doctor and have an operation to become a man, and then I could be your daddy. How would you feel about that?"

Perhaps she was thinking of her Grandpa Green dying in the hospital the previous summer, and how sad I was then: she cried and said she didn't want me to have an operation because she didn't want me to die. I hugged her and consoled her and told her not to worry, I wasn't going to do it right away; I was just thinking about it, but even if I did do it I wouldn't die.

I let a month or so go by, and then I asked her if she remembered the conversation we had had about me maybe having an operation and becoming her dad. She scowled at me. "Yes . . ." she said, with some trepidation.

"I'm still not doing it, but I wondered if you thought about it any more and if you had any other ideas about it."

"I don't want you to do it," she said firmly, "because you'll grow very tall and I won't recognize you." No tears this time.

"Well, no, if I do it I won't grow very tall. And although there is an operation, the changing takes a long time. You would always recognize me. After all, you know that you are such a little girl right now, and you are probably going to grow up to be tall like your mother. You are going to change as you grow up, even more than I would if I had this operation, and I will always recognize you. We will always recognize each other."

"I still don't want you to do it," she said.

"I'm not doing it now," I told her. "I might do it, but I haven't finally decided, so I just wanted to talk with you about it."

I had already submitted the application to the sex reassignment program, but I didn't know whether I would be accepted as a candidate, so there was still a possibility that I would be remaining in my female body. I waited another month or so and then I asked Morgan one more time if she remembered the conversations we had previously had. This time she rolled her eyes.

"Have you thought any more about it?" I asked.

"Do Mama and I have to become men also?" She looked at me apprehensively.

"Absolutely not!" I replied. "You and Mama are definitely girls, definitely women, and that's wonderful. But being a woman doesn't work so well for me. This doesn't happen to very many people, so just because it happens to me doesn't mean it's going to happen to you. But because of the way I feel inside, I think I would be happier if I became a man. You and Mama are happy being just the way you are, and I love you both just the way you are."

"Okay, then, I don't care; do what you want." And she went back to her own interests, playing with some coloring paper and crayons on the floor.

She was afraid of losing me. Change itself was the fearful thing, the unknown, and beyond that: how will this affect *me?* That was the question most people seemed to ask, even if not out loud. What will the neighbors think? How will your actions reflect on me? When Samantha and I went to inform her parents, Samantha's father said, "But that would be like my wife waking up one morning and telling me she was going to become a man. I don't know if I could take that."

"Not exactly, Dad," Samantha explained. "I've known all along that Jamie is essentially a man. This isn't a surprise to me. Mom's a woman; her suddenly saying she's a man *would* be a shock. But not Jamie."

"But you're a lesbian," he said to his daughter.

"Yes," Samantha said. "I am."

"Well, that might be difficult," her mother said. "What's going to happen to your relationship?"

"We don't know what's going to happen," Samantha acknowledged. I had to concur.

"I hope we can stay together," I said. "I want to stay together."

"We can try," Samantha said.

But it didn't work out. Signals that the relationship was ending began to come in, but I did not interpret them correctly. On the night before I was to start taking hormones, I asked Samantha, "Are you sure this is okay with you?" Her response was: "If you don't go through with this now, because of me, you'll always resent me." I interpreted her statement as one of support. I didn't want to hear the underlying message. Samantha was already pregnant with our second child. Complications arose with the pregnancy, though: the embryo was too close to the cervix. She was told to stay off her feet and avoid sexual activity for several weeks, until the doctor could be sure the placenta was attached appropriately to the uterine lining, or else she might lose the baby.

I had been taking testosterone for nearly two months when the doctor told us everything was all right with Samantha's pregnancy, and that it would now be okay for us to be sexual. One fairly immediate effect of testosterone is an increased libido, so I was definitely ready. I remember that night as one of the best we ever had together. It was very close to our thirteenth anniversary. But unlike all the years we'd been together, I was ready for more the very next night. Prior to taking testosterone, I had rarely been interested in sex. Now I was ready every night and day. Samantha rebuffed me on the third night, and I probably made stupid jokes like, "Ahh, come on, it'll make you feel good." I probably acted like a teenage boy, and probably thought I was cute doing it, before I relented and went to sleep. When I woke up the next morning Samantha was already awake, lying stiffly on her back, staring at the ceiling.

"What's the matter?" I asked.

Without moving she replied, "Don't ask to have sex with me, and if you want to save this relationship you'll get us a counselor."

I felt an adrenaline rush of impending doom, like freefalling for miles. I telephoned our family doctor that day for referrals to psychotherapists who might be familiar with transsexual issues and couples work, and I set up a series of appointments for us to interview the ones who seemed receptive. I didn't realize that Samantha's interpretation of my libidinous interest was not the same as mine. I was reveling in my sense of myself and felt like I was able to really give myself to her now that I was connecting with my body. She felt like I could have been jumping anyone, since all I seemed interested in was sex. Years later she told me she felt deeply discouraged and insulted, but however we discussed it at the time we were not able to make ourselves understood. We had apparently reached an impasse.

When we found a counselor she wanted to work with, the first thing Samantha said was, "I lost sexual interest in you three years ago. I think I should end the relationship, but I'm afraid to make a decision before my baby is born." As soon as she said "my baby" I knew she had already made up her mind; she behaved as if she had decided, but verbally she denied it. Therapy did nothing to restore our relationship.

For the next several months, Samantha distanced herself emotionally from me, while I tried to be more present for her—calling from work several times a day to see how she was doing, coming home early—hoping that she would see how much I cared for her and change her mind. We both tried to conceal our angst from Morgan, who was sensitive enough to know something was wrong no matter what we said. We didn't fight with each other, but we definitely weren't connecting the way we had before. A sense of peacefulness was absent from our home. Mitchell was born in April 1989, and Samantha barely spoke to me after that. I thought she was just tired, so I took care of Morgan and gave Samantha the space she seemed to need. Friends would come by to see the new baby, and they'd ask me, "What's wrong with Samantha?" "I don't know," I'd reply. "Postpartum depression, maybe? I don't know. She doesn't want to talk to me, though."

We'd had Mitchell at home a week, when I couldn't bear the icy silence anymore, and I asked Samantha what was going on. "What's going on?" she repeated. "I'll tell you what's going on: this relationship is over."

Though friends warned me against relying on her, Samantha had promised to stay with me through my chest reconstruction, which was scheduled for June. I kept hoping that staying together would allow her to realize that I loved her, and that I was still the person she had wanted to have children with, but the surgery only further distanced her from me. While I recovered from the procedure, which was moderately painful and required keeping my arms close to my sides for two weeks, I took care of Morgan while Samantha and Mitchell spent much of the time away from home. On July 1, 1990 we put our house up for sale, and Samantha moved out. I became a weekend dad for Morgan, and visited both kids one evening each week, first at Samantha's parents' home, and later at the apartment Samantha shared with her new lover, a woman who had once been my friend, and who had accompanied me to my first FTM meeting. I also found out Samantha had been clandestinely involved with her for several months before Mitchell was born, and now it was my turn to feel betrayed. With both of us feeling wounded, my communication with Samantha was confined to logistical arrangements concerning the children. I became depressed over the loss of my relationship and the separation from my children, and I managed the depression by keeping myself busy at work, busy looking out for other transpeople, and busy trying to build a life that would provide a solid foundation for my children to rely on: trying to be a good father, even when absent. It was a difficult time.

I know other transsexual men who've lost contact with children they were co-parenting before they transitioned. I know transsexual men who've lost the right to see the children they gave birth to from their former female bodies. I also know transsexual men who have custody of their children and are doing very well. Even families with a transsexual parent have typical family problems that have nothing to do with transsexualism. Some transsexual men's children don't know their fathers once had female bodies, or may even now have female genitalia. All these fathers, like male-to-female transpeople who have fathered children before their transitions, share the knowledge that—even if we were not present when our children were conceived, if we fathered, however briefly, even someone else's child through adoption or just our physical presence—we have contributed to the developing consciousness and quality of life of another human being. Some aspects of parenthood are still largely an abstraction to me, and perhaps to other non-biological fathers, adoptive fathers, or stepfathers. I wonder what it must feel like to look at your child and know that part of your body is inside every cell of theirs.

Certain fathers know the physical experience of childbirth: fathers who are transsexual men who also gave birth to their children. There was a time when the fact that a person had given birth to a child would have prevented medical professionals from diagnosing the individual as trans-sexual and providing treatment. The assumption was that "true" FTM people had such abhorrence of their female bodies that they never would have permitted themselves to be impregnated, let alone endure nine months of pregnancy and the birth process: it was just too much reinforcement of the female archetype. Clinicians' framing of FTM experience as a rejection of femininity would not allow for it in what they called "true" or "primary" transsexuals. But there are plenty of transsexual men who did just that, sometimes in the vain effort to avoid transsexualism (as occurs with MTF people and is clinically accepted behavior), sometimes fully knowing they would transition in the future, but wanting to have children of their own who they believed could not be taken away. Sometimes their conscious awareness of their transsexualism came later in life. In any case, many of these fathers are comfortable with the continuity between their selves as mothers and their male selves—and some are not. I know of transsexual men who transitioned when their children were teenagers, when their children were pre-adolescents, or when their children were infants. It's certainly easier when the children are younger because they're so much more accepting—but even older children can understand and manage a parent's transition if the quality of their relationship is strong, supportive, honest, and loving. My own eleven-year-old nephew had no problem with my change from his aunt to his uncle. His father—my brother—was nervous about telling him: "Well, your aunt Jamie is going to become your uncle Jamie." But the boy took it in stride: "Uncle Jamie . . ." he pondered this for a moment. "Okay," he said, shrugging his shoulders. His understanding of me was clear and he did not see my change as a threat to his own identity or social functioning.

Some people apparently think it's more important to reinforce gender norms than to consider the individuals involved when it comes to raising children. As I told people at work about my impending transition (1988), one male co-worker reacted by bursting out laughing when I told him I was a candidate for surgical sex reassignment. This wasn't the typical reaction that I'd experienced up to that point: usually people were stunned or curious, but no one before (or after) this man had laughed derisively. I noticed a photo of a smiling woman with an infant on the credenza behind him, and I decided in that moment to respond to his laughter by calmly saying, "I have a wife, too, and a three-year-old daughter and another child on the way." He sobered and stared at me for a few seconds. Then he said, "Well, you're doing the right thing, then." Though we continued to have a cordial working relationship, I didn't pursue a friendship with him. In the moment I had appealed to his anti-gay feelings, it's true, and I didn't want to have to persist in facing them. Making a project of reforming his disdain for homosexuals was something I couldn't take on at the time; I was embattled enough just then.

In 1999 Matt Rice, an FTM who had been rather public, announced to the community via email that he had stopped taking testosterone in order to conceive a child and that he had given birth to a son, whom he and his partner Patrick Califia, another FTM, planned to raise together. Instead of congratulations and good wishes, he was vilified on numerous internet lists for bringing embarrassment upon those of us who regard ourselves as men because "men do not have babies." A flood of vitriolic messages berated Matt and Patrick, and some even wished the child dead.

From the correspondence and opinion postings I read, I understood the primary objection to be a fear that others (particularly the medical establishment) would use Matt's childbearing to invalidate the masculine and male identities of all FTMs. Matt's behavior was seen as reifying the female bodies that most male-identified people sought to escape. Matt was told he could no longer call himself an FTM, he could not call himself a man, and he could not expect understanding or acceptance in the community of men. As a result of asserting his own identity as a man and saying that some men could have babies, Matt was ostracized by many who accused him of trying to speak for all male-identified people who had once had female bodies. No one speaks for all of us; that is impossible. We can each speak only for ourselves; but we can talk about our observations and our experience, and Matt is as entitled to his identity and experience as any one of us. If we have to worry about following *any* prescribed path in order to be ourselves—no matter who prescribes it: the trans community, the medical establishment, or the non-trans assumptions of stereotypical (and therefore socially validated) gender behavior—we are only setting ourselves up to be judged by an arbitrary standard that can be changed at any time by those to whom we've delegated authority over our own authenticity.

When it comes to parenting children, it shouldn't matter whose body a child came from. People who want to be parents, whether they are trans or not, or whether they are straight, gay, lesbian, or bisexual, should be as entitled to be parents as all those people who are parents but who didn't want to be. For children who have a parent who's transgendered or transitioning, *Out of the Ordinary: Essays on Growing Up with Gay, Lesbian and Transgender Parents*, edited by Noelle Howey and Ellen Samuels, is a useful resource. Once a child is on this earth, the most important things any adult can give her or him are love, security, and education, and those things are possible to give regardless of sexual orientation or gender identity. They are possible to give even when one is a non-custodial parent.

So I persist in my parenting. I have shown up on Samantha's doorstep at the appointed hour, mailed my child support check so it arrived on time, left work early one day each week to pick up Morgan after school, run errands, have dinner, talk about what is going on, and maintain a real continuity between us. She is starting her studies at a university now; her life is her own, and the time we spend together is more relaxed. Watching her grow up is one of the most rewarding experiences of my life. And her brother, though I watch from a greater distance, is another joy to me. Since Samantha is single again, I've had more, though still infrequent opportunities to spend time with Mitchell. He and I are still just getting to know each other, but I'm glad for every chance I have to see and speak with him, and I hope he'll come to regard me as at least a trusted friend. Not too long ago he told me, "I think it's cool that you're famous."

"I'm not famous, Mitch," I said.

"Sure you are," he insisted. "If you go into any bookstore and look in the transsexual section, you're in every book!"

I just laughed. Not that many bookstores have transsexual sections. The important messages in his statement were that he was curious about me and that he was proud of me.

It never occurred to me, as doctors often caution transpeople to consider, that I would regret the sterility caused by my transition to male—that I would regret that I could never bear children. That desire never did come to me. Ironically, though, I did experience something else, which may be a sign of awareness of mortality more than anything: I realized, well after turning fifty, that my genetic line would end with me, that my genes would never merge with anyone else's (female or male) to create new life. Of course I had always known this, intellectually. How could I not be aware of it when I knew all my life that I had no blood connection with any of my loved ones—not with my adoptive parents, and not with my children? Yet it struck me in a deeper way not too long ago, not as a wish so much as an ache, a physical feeling that something inside me was reaching out for biological continuity. I never experienced this until my body had been male for well over a decade, but now I know: I would like to have given my seed to my wife, to have had her bring a child of ours into the world. It sounds clichéd perhaps—and it was a genuine surprise to me because I thought I was intellectually beyond such notions—but I sensed that my body would have liked to have been extended for another generation. The feeling passed, or perhaps my logic overpowered it. It is too late: I am sterile, so even if there were some way to make my gametes fertilize my partner's egg, I have no gametes left. And I am too old for childrearing all over again: it takes so much energy, and I would not want my children to feel superseded by a new baby. I am married to Heidi, a woman who is younger than I, and who has chosen not to have children. I am fortunate to have my children—and a wife who is loving toward them—and though they do not share my genetic structure, they share my life, my hopes and dreams, as I share theirs. I am as proud of them as any parent could possibly be. Grandchildren will be enough, if Heidi and I are blessed with them. Even though they will not be extensions of our flesh, they can be extensions of our life and love.

My parents adopted me when I was one month old. When they held me for the first time, there was no blood connection between us, but their love was unconditional and our bond secure. When I held each of my newborn infants, when I kissed their exhausted mother in gratitude and admiration, the widening of that circle of unconditional love was as firm a bond to me as any other.

6

Consummate Presence

When I was growing up, there was virtually no discussion within my family about sexuality. My brother and I were taught respect for the autonomous physical space of others, and that our bodies were private and not to be violated. We were left to infer what violation meant. I learned about sexuality from the other children in my neighborhood and from my own body. I learned from gradual experience the difference between exciting, satisfying, gratifying, private, dirty, offensive, wrong, harmful, and hurtful. I learned the difference between lust and love.

When I was fourteen, a new family moved into the house next door to mine. I have no recollection of the adults, nor of the family name, but I remember the girl Linda and what her presence did to me and to the other boys in the neighborhood.

Linda was sixteen. She went to a private school, so we only saw her coming and going, and we never had much chance to get to know her. No other girl in the neighborhood was like her. She had thick, wavy dark hair that just brushed the top of her shoulders. She had breasts that looked heavy, firm, and round. "Look at those handfuls," we'd say as she walked from her father's car to her front door. She ignored us as we moved off the road when her parents drove through our ballgames. We stood aside and stared at her, holding our best rebel poses. "I'll bet she's got hair on her pussy," Craig said once. We were stunned, silent at first. But he had done it: Craig had given us all permission to expose our lust.

When we couldn't gather enough boys to compose opposing teams, we would sprawl beneath the redwood tree in my front yard and talk about what we'd like to do with Linda: "I'll bet she does it." "Think she'd do it with you?" "Sure!" "No way!" "She'd do it with *me!*" "No way." "What do you think she looks like when she does it?" "I'll bet she jiggles great." "I'd stick mine in her just to see that." "Yeah." I suspect we all felt the delicious erotic pulse and vibrancy through our young bodies; but it was all talk, no action. We wanted to see her undressed, and we dared each other to hide in the bushes outside her window, climb up in the branches of the bushy cypress that shielded her bedroom from the sun.

I was the one who finally did it. Tommy went with me, but he never climbed up high enough to see in. I saw her in her white slip, white bra, and pale yellow panties. I was terrified that she might see me, so I scrambled down before she turned.

"I saw her," I whispered to Tommy as we ran out of her yard.

"Well, does she?" Craig asked later. "Does she have hair on her pussy?"

"Yeah," I said, grinning like a dog. "She does." I didn't even know what "pussy" meant.

"Damn," he said. "I wish I'd seen that. How come you get to be the one who sees her?"

"'Cause I'm the one with guts," I sneered. *That* I knew well enough.

In that time of awakening lust, my boyhood was secure, but awareness was descending on me: as the realities of female adolescence imposed their fate on my developing body, I felt that my dream of attaining manhood would never be realized. My status among the boys in the neighborhood as a leader, as an equal (even occasionally superior) team member, and as a strong arm and strong will, was firmly established. The difficulty for me—and for Craig and Tommy and the other boys—was that as we were growing older our worlds were being populated with many other kids who didn't understand who I was, didn't realize that I was the power hitter, that I was the best wide receiver, that I was the superior strategist in battle. These boys from the surrounding neighborhoods made the boys from my neighborhood feel stupid for permitting what they thought was a girl to participate in their sacred rituals and games. My friends weren't strong enough to stand up to them. In our neighborhood it was business as usual; but in more public space they would disavow me, at worst joining the other boys in teasing me, at best pretending that they didn't see it happening.

It wasn't until roughly two years later, when I was nearly sixteen, that

I was finally barred from the neighborhood equivalent of the boy's locker room in a pile-up at the scrimmage line when Tommy gave my breast an aggressive, painful squeeze and shouted, "Hey, she's got 'em! She's gonna be a girl after all!" Mortified, I extracted myself from the pile of boy bodies, dragged Tommy up to standing, punched him hard in the stomach and stomped home. That was the last conversation Tommy and I ever had. I would soon have my driver's license, so screw them. I had bigger plans, dreams more vast than could be sustained by trivial neighborhood games—though it did hurt to feel betrayed by my body and cast out by my friends. Alone in my room at night I often wondered how I would ever find people who would accept me for everything that I was. My thoughts would drift from mourning a childhood slipping away to creating a future full of adventure and independence. In those days I wrote stories about mountaineering, mystery tales full of natural disasters, westerns in which I was the boy-hero who always won the affection of the pretty girl by saving her life. But like the Lone Ranger, I always rode away without her.

At school there were girls I had my eye on: Suzie, Diane, Vicky. I observed the adolescent mating dances they all engaged in with various boys, I listened to their critiques of the male sex, as I was able to do for much of my adult life, ensconced within a female body, my presence often, though not always, overlooked when conversations among women turned erotic: I could be a spy in the house of love. I watched how those boys gravitated toward the objects of their desire. "Oh, he's so stupid," they would laugh—boys were like meteorites caught in the magnetic pull of powerful planets—"all he thinks about is himself"—and once they entered the girls' attractional fields there was no escape. I observed it all from a safe distance. Being different from both the girls and the boys, I was reluctant to engage in interspecies contacts.

I spent a lot of time driving around, listening to the radio, imagining a woman next to me who loved me, who would want to kiss me and stroke my body. I didn't think too much about genitals. I knew mine weren't right for me, and I didn't think it would ever be possible to make them right. I was eighteen before a woman ever kissed me and let me touch her breasts, but I was hooked long before that on the idea of taking a woman in my arms and ravishing her while simultaneously protecting her. When that first kiss finally came, though, I knew I had a penis very much alive inside me.

The first two women with whom I had long intimate relationships (three years each) considered themselves heterosexual. They were attracted to and had been dating men, and didn't understand why they found themselves drawn to me. While they of course knew I had a female body, they each said that it was the male in me with whom they had fallen in love. The first woman suggested that I have a sex change—the one who I had told, "Only crazy people do that," insisting that she never raise the issue again. The second woman I was with frightened me when she told me she wanted to have my babies. Oh, I was flattered, too, all right. I knew she was saying that she trusted and valued me, that she wanted to merge with me in that deep, life and death way. I believed I could never give her children (sperm banks were a thing of the future then), and I would therefore always be a disappointment to her; looking back I can now see how I held myself in check. Although I loved her deeply, I was afraid to commit because I didn't yet know how to be myself. I'm still ashamed of the way I extricated myself from that relationship, which was, in short, to pretend to myself that we had discussed it, and then to simply leave. I thought I was sparing her the pain of a breakup and the shame of a childless future, but all I did was hurt her and deceive myself. She continued to date men. I decided to give lesbians a try.

I don't presume to know what women feel when they are horny. I only know what I have felt. The one thing that has always been consistent for me when I think of physical pleasure is a desire to place myself inside a woman, to feel the difference in her skin—her smoothness, her resilience, as opposed to my muscled rigidity—the wetness of her mouth, of her vagina, sucking me in where I can expand and swell and work the magic of connection, give her all the impact of my body and soul.

All the driving around I did as a teenager was the perfect metaphor: I was a heat-seeking missile looking for that chink in a woman's armor. My desire would have been so much more obvious if I could have reached inside myself and pulled out my hidden penis. As it was, I learned self-restraint. I could only rarely allow my lovers to touch the female-looking genitals I hid beneath my jeans—certainly there could be no penetration, not of me. That was too female; it would not have maintained my difference from them. To emphasize the similarities between our female bodies would have made for a completely un-sexy experience for me. What worked for me erotically was when a woman admired my strength, my hardness, when she would find the roughness of my hands exciting. Usually attractions would start out this way—but most of the lesbian women I was with would quickly try to soften me, try to give me what they themselves wanted from a partner. Their attempts to emphasize what they saw as a strong *womanliness* always felt to me as if they were trying to make me into someone else, as if I wasn't good enough as I was. I became, again, invisible; and, again, I didn't know how to address it. Eventually my escapades with lesbians would fizzle out like so much lesbian bed-death, initial passion resolving into deep friendship with waning sexuality on my part, and frustrated desire to be with a woman on the part of my lovers. I tried for over twenty years because I loved these women, but I lost sight of desire. I lost touch with the raw male lust that had fed my teenage years. As I relaxed into the comfort zone of each new relationship, I privately resumed my own internal concentration on hiding my discomfort with my female body, and therefore my failings as a lesbian, rather than enjoying the bodies of my partners. Though I didn't know it at the time, I couldn't give to them a self I didn't have.

What I hadn't anticipated about the transition from female to male was that it would take me back to that point in my adolescence where I had shut down and give me a second chance at life. It would revive my desire to express myself intimately with the kind of strength and energy I had known as a youth.

Testosterone fuels the sex drive for both men and women. Men have—on average—about ten times as much testosterone in their systems as do women. This doesn't mean that women don't want sex—far from it! There are many factors that contribute to the *gestalt* of desire, and these factors vary tremendously between individuals. Regardless of the measurable amount of testosterone in individual systems, there are men who are not terribly interested in sex, and women whose desire is insatiable. Yet hormones do change us; we just don't know precisely how that change will manifest itself. Prior to my transition, I was more interested in intimacy than in sex, per se. I would feel profoundly sexual when I found myself attracted to someone, and during the courtship phase—but once the relationship became emotionally committed, my interest in sex would subside dramatically. Without something to accomplish, which was usually "winning the girl," I didn't feel much motivation to engage in sex.

That changed once I started taking testosterone.

The initial effect of testosterone on my body was that it allowed me to feel "normal" for the first time in my life. And once I got comfortable with that feeling, once I started to relax and accept that my natural self was finally being affirmed, along came libido. It came pushing out the front of my body like an engorged cock, and it made me feel sensibly connected to my body as I never had before. My penis started to grow—that is, my clitoris became enlarged, eventually to the size of a small penis—and after about a year I had a cock I could really grab onto. The genital reconstruction surgery I was contemplating then would later reposition this new penis more appropriately for intercourse, but even without all that, for the first time I could imagine enjoying a woman giving me head. I could relate to my body as a locus of sexual pleasure, emanating from my genitals and spreading through me and beyond, out into the universe of female flesh and orifices. Before having this body, I never realized what people meant when they said they were horny, and I never understood the value of sexual expression in an ongoing relationship.

Penises do lie. Sure, it's obvious when a penis is erect, but there's no reliable way to know what that erection means. An erect phallus is the most consistent visible symbol of desire that humanity has managed to agree upon cross-culturally. Yet it is possible for a man to feel romantic or erotic, sexual or lusty without inciting an erection, and erections sometimes do occur when they are least expected. I relish my erections and crave release from them the same as any other man. But it is not a penis that makes me (or anyone else who has one) a man. A man's penis is a specialized, appreciated, and sometimes maligned part of his anatomy, nothing more. Without it, a man would still be a man. With it, if he's lucky, he's a man who can urinate in a standing position, deposit sperm close to a cervix, and enjoy orgasm—important activities, no doubt, but there are other ways to do all of those important things. These are not the requirements for being a man.

In the beginning I marveled at my penis and my newly rediscovered desire; like an adolescent boy, I was delighted with my performance. I was able to make love with Samantha twice before she told me she was no longer interested in me; I didn't have partnered sex again for two years, when I had been through all the stages of surgical sex reassignment, and was clearly ensconced in the full second psychological adolescence that transsexual people are privileged to endure. Meanwhile, I masturbated, as most young men do, while emotionally vacillating between despair at the loss of my partner and elation with the growing congruity my body and soul were achieving, reveling in the powerful release of my own energy, and then remembering I was alone and sinking into depression.

It was lust that saved me. It was lust that kept me centered in my body, informing me that I was alive and could go on. Gradually I began to notice again that women existed in the real world, outside the pages of the pornographic magazines that I kept beside my bed and in my car. Gradually I began to see that real women were starting to notice me, expressing interest in me. I was shy, still trying to break free of that second adolescence, but I had to recognize that women were seeing me as a man at last—not as a boy, not as a lesbian, not as an androgyne, but as a bearded, hirsute, solid physical man with something to offer them. And I began to realize that men were noticing me, too. Gay men were attracted to me. Would I? No, I didn't think so. I liked and desired women. But I wasn't threatened or offended by the interest of men; I thought of it as a confirmation of my maleness that men who liked men would find me attractive. Women and men would compliment my appearance, would flirt with me—and I didn't know what to do. I had never experienced anything like it. For the most part, I would just smile and blush, or say "thank you" if I was aware enough. I was still too shy and unsure of myself to know how to respond any other way. I was forty-two years old with so much to learn! I didn't even know how to date because I'd never really done it before; at least I'd never done anything like what one sees on television or in the movies. I didn't know how to meet someone and experiment with intimacy without assuming that each incident was "it," the one with whom I ought to try to stay.

Desire versus Identity

I was fortunate to meet Marcy Sheiner at a moment in my life when I needed someone like her. For seven years, Marcy and I had a relationship that was crucial to my development and maturity as a man. She had a realistic, practical, and even spiritual connection with her own sexuality that she was willing to share with me. She encouraged a level of openness in me that was only possible for me since my body had become more masculine. She acknowledged my transness and the special awareness and abilities I had because of my trans experience. I was ready for a relationship then because I was finally in touch with and happy with my own body, and, like many an adolescent, I was interested in experimenting with it.

Marcy identified as bisexual, with her predominant attraction toward men—though, like many women, she often found men irritating and exasperating. When we met, late in 1990, she was a writer for a variety of publications, many of which featured sexual or erotic content. She went on to become a well-known editor of anthologies of erotic writing, as well as an advocate for disability rights, and the author of her own non-fiction books. Primarily through Marcy, but also through my increasing activism on behalf of FTM people at the time, I met many of the leading figures in San Francisco's sex-positive community: Joani Blank, Susie Bright, Pat Califia, Loraine Hutchins, Lani Ka'ahumanu, Carol Queen, Gayle Rubin, Maggie Rubenstein, Annie Sprinkle, David Steinberg, and Kat Sunlove were just a few of the writers, thinkers, artists, and educators about sexuality who have influenced our culture's methods of analyzing, discussing, and relating to this complex topic.

When I first met her, though, Marcy had conjectured that FTM people were probably misogynistic, homophobic, miserable bull dykes. We met early enough in my transition that there were liminal moments when she thought she could still see the "woman" in me, and this in-between-ness, the quality of "morphing" that she experienced as she searched my face for something feminine—while simultaneously feeling my masculine energy—was new to her. But within the first two years we were together, that androgynous person disappeared as the maturing man within me materialized. Marcy would tell interviewers like Amy Bloom, "I'm convinced—I know otherwise, but I'm convinced—that he was never really a woman" (Bloom, 1994). She had thought that in a relationship I would be different from other men, but that proved not to be the case. Nonetheless, she was willing to discuss with me all of the permutations of sexuality that I experienced within myself or came across among FTM-identified people. Through her I learned that my previous assumptions about relationships were simplistic and naïve—probably because my own parents created such an ideal, "normal" environment, never fought, never even disagreed in front of the children, and disapproved of divorce. It was true, as Marcy accused me of several times, that I wanted a relationship that resembled that of my parents. I don't know that this is such a bad thing, really; after all, they did love each other deeply. It was also true that there was no way

I would ever have my parents' kind of solid, calm, self-assured relationship with Marcy. Our personalities were just too conflictive, and ultimately neither of us could tolerate the stress of our divergent worldviews. Marcy saw sex as perhaps the only pleasure in a horrid, brutal world (until years later when her grandchildren brought her a fresh perspective). I saw the world as a ground of endless possibilities and hopeful futures, in spite of the sometimes painful and even frightening experiences I was sharing through listening to more and more transpeople.

The first transpeople I had met were all fairly private folks who were interested in living ordinary lives, unmarked by transsexualism. Their transitions were something they went through and left behind. If they discussed sexuality with acquaintances, it was usually because they were in a position to help others demystify the sexual interest and capacity of transsexual people, such as would be demanded by the need to respond to questions about genital reconstruction and sometimes about hormonal changes. Nearly everyone I met in the late 1980s, other than Lou Sullivan, claimed a heterosexual orientation. People were very circumspect about their personal lives, and concerned that they be perceived as normal representatives of the gender to which they felt they belonged. The late 1980s and early 1990s brought a new wave of challenges to gender norms in many social quarters: hair dyed bright blue and other unusual colors; piercing in places other than earlobes; the increased popularity of musical artists who cultivated androgyny or deliberate, often confrontational, cross-gender expression; and the increasing presence and power of women in business and politics. It was almost as if the level of challenge to the patriarchal status quo had finally risen enough to overflow the dam that had been erected in the 1950s in order to reinstate white males in the place of superiority they had collectively lost in the trauma and decimation of World War II. With Clinton's election in 1992, it seemed the dominance of the immediately–post-war worldview was beginning to die out, and baby-boomers hoped that old paradigm would now be replaced by less constricting attitudes. I think the rise of the transgender movement in the 1990s is directly connected to all the other movements in politics, art, and society that reflect people's individual and collective desires to be seen for, and expressive of, who they are.

By the mid-1990s I felt transsexual men had still not found a safe "place" to talk among ourselves about every aspect of rebuilding our lives.

While our collective community-building was a movement based on identity, I felt that the dominant feature of a community had to be values rather than any particular sub-identity, or else we'd become hopelessly mired in identity politics, which does very little—if anything—to alleviate the actual pressures, stresses, and problems people face in their daily lives. Speaking about our lives meant, for me, being able to speak frankly about sexuality, because sexuality is a significant aspect of being human. It was important to me to cultivate the ability to listen to and be empathetic with people whose experiences I didn't necessarily share, whether that experience had to do with sexuality, spirituality, race, or class, or education, or occupational interest. I didn't need to have *everything* in common with another person in order to respect him or her, or possibly to be of assistance. Our lives as transsexual men have been pathologized, which already renders us subject to judgment and evaluation. I resented that scrutiny, and I refused to perpetuate or advocate that kind of colonialism among my peers. From my perspective, trans inclusion in gay/lesbian/bisexual space was crucial. I began to focus on it, though I recognized that straight transpeople would need to learn to be less homophobic (and gay transpeople less defensively superior and cliquish) and that there would be problems for transsexual men being subsumed into the category of transgender, which is sometimes too broad a category for specific purposes. This would represent a threat to identity for transsexuals, but I always have held that those of us who are transsexual need to take responsibility for speaking up for ourselves. Many of us are most vulnerable when we are young, androgynous, transgendered, and undecided about our futures; I wanted to be sure that people in that questioning stage (add Q to LGBTI), no matter how old they were, would feel safe in asking the questions they needed to ask. Thus, I tried to make space for diversity and to promote the value of respect for differences. As the trans community in San Francisco became more vocally political in 1993 and 1994, the place where we found political allies was in the queer community (the source of yet another Q tacked onto LGBTIQ), where people began to realize that anti-gay attitudes were our common enemy. And today, that fusion of consciousness that recognized gender variance as being a part of queer political responsibility seems to be taking hold more and more, even though queer politics do not even begin to encompass transgender identities or issues. Trans activists' political work with straight people mostly takes place in more private spaces, at professional associations, or in conference rooms at our city halls or state capitols, because straight people don't organize politically around their sexuality unless they're intent on separating and protecting themselves from anyone who's different from themselves. Because they live in their own heterocentric world, most straight people, I've found, don't have that much of an issue with other people's sexuality—as long as they don't have to see it. Straight people may be concerned about issues that are a consequence of sexual behavior, such as abortion rights, rape, or issues affecting children and families, but rarely do they openly discuss sexuality as a component factor. As a result of this omission, unspoken assumptions about sexuality are given free reign.

When it comes to discussing, or even just acknowledging, sexuality, people are forced to confront their fears and assumptions—and this can be very uncomfortable for most people. When people make their sexuality obvious, some people react in a range of negative ways, from squeamish discomfort and giggling to violent anger and assault. There are two key problems here. One is that people aren't sufficiently educated about sexuality to realize that it's not necessarily something to fear. The second is that sometimes people interpret things as sexual that are not necessarily sexual. Both of these problems affect transpeople as much as they affect anyone else—either as those being misinterpreted or those doing the misinterpreting. Transpeople don't know more about sexuality just because they are trans. In some cases we may know even less because our own confusion and fears have allowed us less sexual experience. We have just as much misinformation about ourselves, misapprehension about others, and misunderstanding in our relationships as anyone else. But we *are* more often the targets of other people's fears, and we share with gay and lesbian people the scourge of vile disgust that some non-trans heterosexual people feel toward us.

One of the primary strategies that the gay and lesbian community has employed for combating anti-homosexual policies and beliefs is the concept, "We're just like you; it's just that we do something different in the bedroom, and what each of us does in our bedrooms is no one else's business." This is a reasonable statement, but it doesn't apply to all gay or lesbian people, and it led to the creation of the "gay stream"—mainstream gays and lesbians—inviting people who could pass for straight to come out of the closet to show how normal and ubiquitous they were. This newly emancipated segment of the gay and lesbian world gradually came to dominate the visible gay culture and set the agenda for the gay civil rights movement in the 1980s. As their political goals were realized incrementally, this dominant group didn't want any public association with the "sexual fringe": leather daddies, drag queens and kings, people who "flaunted" their sexuality. I suspect they didn't even think of transpeople as part of their community because they understood transpeople to be "men who wanted to be women," and that wasn't gay to them. Gay people, in the common understanding of the category, wouldn't change their sex. Identity politics requires a stable identity—so another primary strategy for combating homophobia is the theory, "Sexuality is an immutable characteristic; one is born with it, and it cannot be changed." Because their sexuality is sometimes more fluid, transpeople undermine this paradigm, so they had to be silenced. The AIDS crisis shifted this a bit in the late 1980s, but silencing of sexual overtones continued.

Transpeople began to find our voice again in the 1990s, and we brought forth a number of messages, including our experience that sexuality can change, but it cannot be changed from the outside. It changes from within, and every person, gay, bi, or straight, is subject to the possibility of change in her or his sexual desire, response, or interest. We've just been too sheltered to know this as a society, or too fearful and judgmental to discuss it. The idea is frightening because, contrary to the beliefs of some religious people, we don't have the power to determine, by force of will, the changes that happen to us. Changes occur without warning, and they are beyond our control. Some gay people may be fearful of transpeople's validation that sexuality can change, thinking that it undermines their anti-homophobic strategy. But transpeople's experience actually validates civil rights for all LGBTIQQ people because it emphasizes the fact that we have no control over the nature of our sexuality, no control over to whom we are attracted or with whom we fall in love, no control over what it is that "turns us on." We do have control over our expression of sexuality, and society's challenge is where to draw the line. Do we draw it with procreation, as some would have us do, limiting sexual intercourse only to that activity intended to conceive offspring (which not all straight people practice, by the way)? Do we draw a line against any sexual activity that harms another person—and then how do we decide what constitutes harm when some people find bondage or various practices that look violent to others to be mutually satisfying? Do we decide that we must circumscribe our circle of eligible partners to include only people of the opposite sex—and if so, how do we determine the "opposite" sex? If we did that, we might just as logically require all people to choose their partners from only people of the same sex or the same race, for all the sense certain restrictions make when we look at the reality of human sexuality—and the power of love.

In the 1970s, the feminist movement's response to rape was an excellent example of the way society draws and redraws its lines. Defending their actions, male rapists claimed that women "asked for it," either by the way they looked or behaved. While it is true that some women have accused men of rape after consensual sex, more often than not the "she wanted it" defense was designed to evoke notions of "woman as temptress," and for centuries many have believed this myth. The Women's Movement, however, illuminated the ways in which sexism limited women, perpetuating a patriarchal power dynamic that subjugated women, and exposed how the male rapist was trying to invoke that very power dynamic as a defense by blaming the victim. Very convenient; it must have been effective when we were all uneducated, when women and children were thought to be without souls and were considered chattel, to imply that rape was about sex when it was really about power. But as society gradually accepted the idea that women could be equal human beings to men, could be intelligent, capable, competent, and deserving of respect, the effectiveness of that "blame the victim" defense was increasingly diminished. Much of our society has redrawn the line and acknowledged that women do not, under any circumstances, deserve to be raped.

Likewise, the homosexual panic defense that people use to justify bashing and even murdering gay, lesbian, bisexual, and transgendered people—the defense people use for trying to "cure" young children from their cross-gender expression, and maybe even the rationalization of "normalizing" by surgery and coercion the sex/gender experience of intersexed people—is slowly being disempowered in the face of new awareness about gender, about sexuality, and about the nature of healthy development of the human psyche even in the face of difference from what we think of as a norm. Relativism—the application of varying criteria for evaluation based upon differences between subjects—does exist, and our society is gradually learning to live with it. Torturing or killing people because one doesn't like the way they look, because one thinks they should express themselves differently, because one thinks they are expressing something about sexuality that one doesn't like, because one couldn't tell what sex they were, because their sex/gender congruity was not what one expected, because one thinks genitals must appear a certain way, because one was surprised by something one didn't expect, is simply not acceptable—yet it still happens. Reacting with violence because one found out someone was attracted to him is just as wrong as reacting with violence because one found out someone was not attracted to him, no matter who the parties involved are, or what kind or shape their genitals may be. Society has not yet adopted this line, though. Consensus was more easily reached concerning the violence of rape against women; we have yet to deal openly with sexual crimes against men. We have still not faced the realities of violence that society justifies by fear of difference or fear of sexuality, whether that sexuality is gay or not, real or imagined, or rooted or not in our own desire.

The "Threat" of Sexual Uncertainty

Sexuality is rife with power dynamics, which usually relies on the concurring awareness of partners about the rules of the game. Males usually have greater muscle strength than females. Someone is usually (though not always) penetrated (somewhere, or at some point) in sexual activity. That can be good or bad, depending on how one expresses or experiences it, and on how power is used by the people involved. Much has been written on sexual power dynamics (see P. Califia, 1994; Roxxie, et al., 1994; G. Rubin, 1992 and 1993; and most feminist literature critical of male dominance). Certainly FTM transpeople run the gamut in their relationships to power as an aspect of sexual expression. There are heterosexual-identified FTMs who are misogynistic and gay-identified FTMs who are misogynistic, just as there are heterosexually-identified FTMs who are egalitarian, or who subordinate themselves to the women in their lives, and gay-identified FTMs who have feminist values yet subordinate themselves to the men in their lives, and both gay and straight FTMs who are dominant with their partners, too, or dominant in the bedroom but egalitarian or deferential in public. In other words, none of the characteristics of any particular type of sexual expression are solely the province of any particular type of person. Furthermore, not all people behave consistently from one relationship to the next; any new mix of partners may bring out hidden or repressed desires, or awaken new possibilities for sexual fulfillment and other types of intimacy. While I suspect that most people believe they are consistent in their relationship style, I also think that, for most people, transsexual people personify the threat of uncertainty, of change, and of unstable power dynamics.

Lesbians can sometimes have a particularly problematic relationship with the concept of FTM people, though the experience of individuals may differ widely. Lesbians who participate in butch-femme roles express a specific kind of angst that is exacerbated by FTMs: femmes worry that FTMs are stealing all the butches, and butches worry that FTMs are stealing all the femmes. In other words, femme-identified lesbians sometimes feel threatened that their very masculine partners will see FTMs and want to join them in becoming men, and butch-identified lesbians sometimes feel threatened that their feminine partners will see FTMs and be more attracted to their testosterone-enhanced masculinity, which may seem to be more of a threat than non-transsexual men (Munt, 1998). It's a similar kind of angst to that which many people feel about bisexuality—ultimately a kind of insecurity. The threat is what's perceived as the direct competition, and when someone is honest about being attracted to the sex other than that of his or her partner's (or when one has a history of being, as is the case for many gay and lesbian people, attracted to the opposite sex before realizing they are attracted to members of the same sex), then their partner's insecurity may be projected into the notion that the other partner is somehow untrustworthy. Lesbians may also fear association with FTMs because of what they fear the existence of FTMs says about them: they can be afraid FTMs reinforce the common misperception that lesbians want to be men. While it is not true that lesbians want to be men, it is true that some apparent lesbians do feel like men. What if they would be more comfortable being men? What if there were (as there are) apparently straight women who feel like men and would be more comfortable being men? Should they have been lesbians instead? How could they be lesbians if they are attracted to men? The assumption that one thing *always* leads to another, that gay sexual expression leads to gender incongruity, or gender incongruity leads to shifts in sexual orientation, or that any of these things is inherently wrong if it were to occur, is illogical. Learning about sexuality as a dimension of human experience and to understand ourselves does more to alleviate misunderstandings and eradicate fear of difference than does hiding from sexuality or pretending it is not a factor in our lives.

Gay men have also had varied reactions to the existence of FTMs. Some, like anyone else who does not understand transsexual people, dismiss us as less than men, or not real men. Others find themselves attracted to individuals who happen to be FTMs and are stunned when they realize the object of their desire was not born with a male body. Their initial shock may elicit various reactions: some remain interested in the person to whom they were attracted, while some are deeply offended and may become as violent as some straight men do when they realize they've been attracted to transwomen. They respond as if they've been betrayed when what they are feeling is their own embarrassment over not being able to recognize a man "pretending to be a woman," which brings out their homophobia. Some gay men feel the same way: that their attraction to an FTM implies that somehow they are straight, and they may feel betrayed by the FTM whom they interpret as a woman trying to infiltrate their masculine domain, bringing out their heterophobia, or perhaps misogyny. Others find FTMs intriguing and deliberately incorporate them into their schemata of desire, as some gay, straight, and bisexual women have done, too.

Sex and Validation

Some FTMs seek gay sex as a way to learn about men, or at least about penises, even if they don't identify as gay. It is not unusual in many large cities in the U.S. to find young transmen who are willing to turn tricks with gay or bisexual men, particularly to give blow jobs because they don't have to get undressed and reveal that they do not have a penis themselves. If they are willing to give a blow job without a condom they can make more money, too. This means transmen may be at risk for HIV infection—yet there is virtually no institutionalized effort to reach transmen in HIV prevention education except in cities like New York, Boston, San Francisco, and Oakland, where transpeople are employed as public health workers. Some nonprofit organizations like the Ingersoll Gender Center in Seattle or the Los Angeles Gay Center encourage health education programs that are inclusive of and sensitive toward transgendered and transsexual experience.

Several gay transmen I've known have written about their feelings and sexual experience—most notably Michael Hernandez and Shadow Morton (Hernandez, 1994, 1996 and 1997; Morton, 1997). I always loved Shadow's story he would tell in presentations about revealing to a man with whom he was about to have sex that he was an FTM, a transsexual man. If the other man said he couldn't have sex with him because he was a woman, Shadow would say something like, "Tell you what: we'll fuck, and then you tell me if you feel like you were with a woman. I guarantee you'll know you were with a man." He was talking about the sense of innate maleness or femaleness that each of us has, that is not reliant on the shape of the genitals for its expression; he was talking about the sense of maleness a man can have and project even if he doesn't have a penis.

One gay man told me about a friend of his who picked up a handsome young man at a bar and took him home only to discover the young man was an FTM who had not had genital reconstruction, but he was so attracted to the fellow he took him to bed anyway. The young man liked to have his vagina penetrated, and the gay man was not accustomed to vaginal sex, but looking down at the very attractive, very masculine-looking young man looking back at him, looking down at the young man's hairy chest and belly, and then seeing his own penis entering the young man's body was one of the most exciting sexual experiences this man had ever known. He'd never liked sex with women, but he clearly felt he was having sex with a man, and the man's vagina fit his penis perfectly. His mind reeled with the deliciousness of it. Like others who have had erotic experiences with transmen, this man realized that genitals are not necessarily the defining element when it comes to gender, sex, or sexual orientation.

When I broke up with Marcy, I determined that I wanted some time to myself for a while, but about six months later I suddenly fell in love with a young woman from Sweden. She and I were together for about eight months, and when she left me I was crushed. It took me several months to recover and to want to engage emotionally with other people again. During that time I also declined to run for re-election as president of FTM International, and on August 1, 1999, I resigned from the Board of Directors after eight and a half years of service. I decided, now that I was over fifty, that it was time for me to learn how to date. I had always gone from one relationship to the next; I had never consciously spent emotional energy getting to know more than one person intimately in a given timeframe. I also began to consider having a relationship with a man. I thought that because my communication with men had always been good, perhaps a relationship with another man might be more stable and rational, more emotionally supportive than the relationships I had recently had with women: perhaps a companionable and sexual relationship with a man wouldn't be as complicated and difficult as my relationships with women had been lately. I was beginning to acknowledge a bisexual potential that I had not thought I had before. I knew it wasn't fear of homosexuality that kept me from being sexual with other men, any more than homophobia in a female body kept me from being sexual with other women, and I wondered what was at the root of my resistance to male attention. I concluded that the underlying issue for me was always visibility—the fear that I was or would be invisible. I couldn't be with a man while I had a female body because I assumed any man would always perceive me as a woman. Some women could perceive my masculinity then, as I knew some men could, too, but I felt safer with women because the *gender* differences between us were greater, so my chance of being seen as myself were greater. When with a man (while I had a female body) the *sexual* differences between us would be greater and I believed men would always see my female body as definitive of who I was. Once I had a male body—more accurately, once I had *matured* in a male body and established my self-confidence and autonomy—I had no fear that my identity as a man would be overwhelmed by that of a male partner. I ultimately realized that men's interest in me was as a man, and that I could respond without fear of disappearing, just as I would no longer disappear when I was with a woman. So I incorporated dating men along with dating women in my new training. I was absolutely open to finding the right person to engage in a committed relationship, whether that person was male or female. Bottom line, though: I promised myself I wouldn't focus on the first person who came along, as wonderful as she or he might be, just because doing so would relieve me of the anxiety of dating. By not evaluating people's suitability over time before trying to enter a committed relationship, I had been preventing myself from learning valuable social skills that others had learned as young adults.

I dated several people over the next few years, most of them living in cities far from my own, which made it easier to resist the urge toward exclusivity. I dated—and had sex with—gay men and bisexual and straight women: all terrific people; and I'm very appreciative of the time and intimacy we shared. With each and every one of them I had to explain about the differences in my body from other men's bodies, and I know that just that requirement alone prevents many transmen from dating or entering intimate relationships. It can be daunting to anticipate the rejection and potential humiliation, but (maybe I was just lucky) none of that happened to me. Every person I connected with was respectful and gracious about my unique body. I finally learned that I really do know and accept who I am, and I don't have to rely on my partner's appearance, sex, or gender to validate or reinforce my own identity. It was just as Marcy said once: "We make love to each other, after all, not to organs" (Bloom, 1994, 2002). Ultimately these varied experiences prepared me to recognize the qualities I wanted in the person I would ask to spend the rest of my life with me—who turned out to be a woman.

Having sex with a man—as a man—is different from having sex with a woman as a man, or with a woman as a man within a female body. For me, the erotic charge of difference between body types is a powerful motivator. So is the image of a penis, whether it is my own or another man's. I experience the difference between having sex with a man as compared to having sex with a woman as a different quality of connection. With men, I found sex more like sport, less invested with need by either party. With women, I found sex charged by an underlying vulnerability that my female partners have always expressed, even when they were strong, sexually powerful women. My experience is particular to me and the people I've partnered with, and should not be construed as generalizations about all men and women. The important lesson in all this for me has been that when self-respect and concern for others are conscious choices it is possible to unhook sexual behavior from self-definition and identity and find a healthy balance between sexuality and the other aspects of one's life.

Sometimes people assume that I have experienced sexual gratification in ways that are stereotypical for both women and men, and they ask the question that Tiresias was asked: who enjoys sex more—men or women? I don't think being either a man or a woman predisposes one to enjoy sex more. I think one enjoys sex when one is completely connected to her or his body, and for me that has occurred in my male body. I'm sure, though, that women who are connected to their bodies are every bit as capable of enjoying sex as is any man. To me, it's the joy of being alive and connected to one's body that renders one able and willing to share that body with another person. The idea of debating whether men or women are better at sex or enjoy it more seems pointless to me.

Knowing What's Desired

Of the thousands of transsexual people I've spoken with, the vast majority, while usually enjoying their sexuality, were not motivated to transition because of it. Many older transsexual people say they are even willing to give up sex entirely in order to live in a way that expresses their gender identity. Doctors at Johns Hopkins Medical Institutions have stated, "[F]emale-to-male transsexuals appear to be individuals who are fundamentally homophilic but cannot consciously accept their sexual orientation" (Fagan, Schmidt, and Wise, 1994). I can see it now: in a clinical setting, a transman desperate to be allowed to transition tries to express his "normal" sexuality by asserting his attraction to women and denying that he is a lesbian. Yes, he's telling the truth from the perspective of his gender identity. But what the doctors hear is filtered through their own belief that the body tells us who we are, and this transman in front of them wants to change his body so he can change the abhorrent nature of his lesbian sexuality. These clinicians don't understand that it isn't necessarily his sexuality that is abhorrent to him. Even if this patient fell in love with a man, it wouldn't *necessarily* change his relationship to his own body: in his own self-perception he might then be homosexual after all, even if his body were still female and the body of his partner were male. That wouldn't *necessarily* change his need to transition.

The language that individuals use to express the complex feelings they have about what others might label "gender identity," versus what they feel about what others might label "sexual expression" is highly subjective and may be easily misinterpreted. There probably are people around the world who would undergo (or have undergone) sex reassignment because they believe they need to in order to have what would be perceived by anti-trans observers as same-sex relationships. Researchers can likely find people who would say that was their reason, too, even if it wasn't precisely true, and it is not unusual for researchers to find only what they expect to find.

Complicating matters is the reality that there is no way we can know how we will feel or evolve once we begin a transition. Trans or non-trans, individuals' relationships to sexuality develop and change over time, as our lives or transitions progress, in ways that are often unexpected. Some people's dreams come true, others' don't. Fixed notions of what the future will bring are often as fallacious for transsexual people as they are for anyone else.

The larger FTM gatherings in the United States, since their inception in 1995, have always incorporated frank and open discussion of sexuality. Maybe it's the testosterone. Maybe it's the influence of transmen who have come from the queer and leather communities, where sexual expression has been a primary motivation for the development of community. Maybe it's the deliberate effort most transmen's groups make to ensure the presence of alternative values and viewpoints. Whatever the reason, transmen usually want to affirm the importance of sexuality as a positive factor in our lives.

I know now that I can desire and enjoy a man as well as a woman; I can relieve my lust in a variety of ways; and I prefer monogamy and commitment in relationship. I know I feel most engaged and present when I'm both intimate and sexual with the one person I love who loves me, and I'm fortunate to have a woman who feels the same way about me, who's willing to commit to build a life together with me. When we're together it stirs more lust in me to see and feel her pleasure, the pleasure that she takes from me. We feed each other. That gift of our most vulnerable selves, the movement of my engorged penis inside her and her response to it while we can see each other's faces, is pure communication, an opening to the past and the future, a way of expressing everything. Bodies are different, and some bodies fit together better than others. And every sexual act is different; enjoying the feel of another body in every possible way is an amazing gift: so simple, so easy, so ultimately human. So profound it makes us laugh; so sacred that it invites cheapening by those who are afraid of it or those who have been so damaged by abuse that they no longer see any beauty in life, or that the beauty they might remember has been obliterated by pain.

I don't care what people think about my reconstructed genitals, or about the fact that I was long ago treated as a girl. I don't care whether people think I am reinforcing gender stereotypes because I am in a heterosexual relationship, or if they think I am bravely accosting the gender apartheid system because I've broken the barriers, lived on both sides of the gender fence, and overcome my preconceptions about sexuality. I care about living honestly and passionately, without fear or shame, and that means being unafraid to relate what happened back in 1962, when Linda and her family moved out of our neighborhood.

I sailed past on my bicycle, watching the movers load up the giant van. Linda was standing on the corner, away from the thick, perspiring men who labored under her mother's irritated command and her father's aloof wariness. I couldn't help glancing at her, and she stared straight back at me, telegraphing a message. I knew she wanted to talk. I turned around and pedaled back, stopping at the curb.

"Where are you moving to?" I asked.

"Chicago," she said flatly.

"You don't want to go?"

"No. I never want to go. We move almost every year and I hate it."

I nodded. Chicago was so far away from San Francisco that I could hardly imagine it.

"I saw you," she said. I was confused and gave her a quizzical look.

"Why did you do it?" she asked. Instantly I knew what she meant. I felt like running; I must have flushed deep red.

"You saw?"

"In the mirror."

I smiled stupidly, embarrassed both by what I had done and by how she had caught me.

"Why did you do that? Why did you want to look into my room?"

"I don't know," I said in a panic. "I guess I was just curious about you."

"Well, it was nasty and rude."

"I'm sorry. . . ."

"My mother thought you were a girl, but I think you're a boy. If you ever grow up, maybe you'll understand what a hurtful thing you've done."

"I didn't mean to hurt you."

"It wasn't that you looked that hurt so much," she said. "It was that you stole that look and ran away. I always watched for you to come back, but you never did."

I was speechless. I wasn't sure I understood.

"Linda! Come in here, please," her mother called from the doorway.

"I'm sorry," I said again.

"Just don't ever do anything like that again," she said, turning away toward the house.

That was the last time I saw her, and it was my first realization of how important it is to be present when a moment of intimacy is occurring, and how easy it is to mistake self-centeredness for self-awareness. I think it took me about forty more years to achieve real presence, the kind that is beyond the self; but the only proof of it is in the strength of one's connectedness with others, the kind of connectedness that I could not truly feel until I became a visible man.

7
Visibility

When Billy Tipton died in Spokane, Washington on January 21, 1989, the phenomenon of a female-bodied man did not generate much discussion of transsexualism outside of the transsexual community. Because he had not had any hormones or surgery, it was easy for his story to be adopted by lesbians as an example of women's institutionalized oppression and the lengths to which women were forced to go to be artists or to make a living at all. Everyone saw in Billy Tipton only what they themselves could fathom as motivation, saw specifically what they identified with: lesbians saw another lesbian; transsexual people saw another transsexual. The people who regarded the appearances of Tipton's family members on *Oprah* and other talk programs as entertainment saw only what they were capable of seeing, too: Tipton's strange, incomprehensible behavior that tricked these poor, innocent people who were left behind and forced to explain it. They got to say, "Wow, imagine if that happened to you! How could they possibly not know that he was a woman? I don't believe it, not for a minute!" Acknowledged yet still resisted by Tipton's biographer Diane Middlebrook, FTM-related interpretations of his life were forced to the periphery. Dr. Laub told me, though, that his office received an upsurge of inquiries from other female-bodied men over sixty asking if it was too late for them to have surgery. He said they reported they didn't want their loved ones to suffer the kind of embarrassment that Tipton's family had. They didn't want to make waves; they just wanted to die as men, to be remembered as men.

"So, what do you tell them?" I asked him.

"I tell them it's not too late," he said.

But is surgery the answer to the larger problem? It may alleviate a transman's stress and facilitate self-acceptance, even acceptance in one's immediate surroundings. But I don't believe it will eliminate the possibility of what happened to Billy Tipton. When he collapsed at home, his son called paramedics, who removed some of his clothing and said, "Son, did your father have a sex change?" Ten days later, the story was a media event (Middlebrook, 1997). If Tipton had actually had a medical sex change, there's no guarantee that he and his family would have been spared exposure. It only takes one insensitive or disrespectful attendant or observer, one disgruntled family member or friend to diminish a life by exposing a secret. Surgery does not create a flawless body. Hiding ourselves may serve self-preservation, but it does not address the larger problem of social acceptance, acknowledgment that what we experience is valid. To be believed, we must be seen.

Visibility on Screen

By the time of Tipton's death, a growing number of FTM-identified people in the United States, Europe, and Asia were able and willing to network with each other and discuss issues that affected us. We were starting to acknowledge the frustration that our concerns—our lives—were being erased, but collectively we weren't sure what, if anything, we wanted to do about it. There was a certain comfort in not standing out, not being targets, in just being accepted and living our lives as men, that appealed to most of us. But in 1990 an event occurred that brought visibility to FTM-identified men that was, for some, shocking and unwanted—certainly controversial. Lou Sullivan published a little notice about it in the December 1989 issue of his newsletter. The headline read "*Hustler* uncovers an FTM," referring to the upcoming February 1990 article by Annie Sprinkle entitled "I Love a Woman With a Cock." Sullivan noted Sprinkle's "annoying" insistence on referring to her partner Les as "she" and as a "woman with a cock," but promised that the article would be worth perusing for the photos of Les's phalloplasty surgery alone, such photos being impossible to find outside medical journals.

The *Hustler* article itself brought outrage and an outpouring of defensiveness from within the FTM community. The general public hardly blinked. Les was not the kind of representative that most FTMs wanted the public to see; even the most *avant garde* among us acknowledged that Les was "highly eccentric, *extremely* exhibitionistic and *totally* irrepressible" (*FTM Newsletter,* letter to the editor, Issue #12, June 1990). Of even greater concern for some men was that the photos of Les's surgery did nothing to combat notions of genital reconstruction as mutilation. Far better examples might have been shown, but their owners would not have exposed themselves, even in the name of education. Any educational content in Sprinkle's enthusiastically sex-positive text was probably lost on the typical "reader" of *Hustler.* The article was succeeded by a videotape version of the "Linda, Les and Annie" love story, which Sprinkle dubbed "docu-porn," that the members of Sullivan's FTM group viewed on September 16, 1990. Several people, embarrassed, disgusted—or both—got up and left before it was over.

Transsexual people who held anti-porn beliefs were pitted against transsexual people who celebrated the bravery that Les and Annie displayed in their attempt to recognize the sexual desirability of transsexual bodies. These debates played themselves out in the letters section of the *FTM Newsletter* for over a year, finally dying down when the community's attention turned to Sullivan's death in 1991. The attacks that people had anticipated would result from the spotlight on Sprinkle's work never materialized.

In 1990 I was invited to participate in the filming of a documentary about transsexualism by Xiao-Yen Wang, a feature filmmaker from China. Released in 1991, *The Blank Point—What is Transsexualism?* won numerous awards in film and video festivals around the world, and was exhibited for many years. It still occasionally shows up on educational television channels. It was Wang's first documentary film. She and her husband, writer/producer Andy Martin, were relaxed and respectful on the set. They were serious about letting their subjects, two transsexual women and me, tell the truth about our experience in a way that would communicate emotionally with the viewer. I was concerned about confidentiality so I used the pseudonym "Richard." The end product was a quiet, reflective piece grounded in Wang's own curiosity and vision of what it must feel like to change sex. Her being a newcomer to the United States and mystified by what she perceived as American openness about sexuality were undercurrents throughout the film that helped her connect with viewers who might not have cared otherwise about the subject. The film conveys the sense that transsexual people can look just like anyone else (or anyone can look like a transsexual person!), and Wang's feeling, once she had learned about it, that changing sex was not so strange after all.

Why did I do it? Because I thought it might help someone. Steve Dain's 1984 appearance in *What Sex Am I?* had made such an impact on me, and I hoped to communicate the male perspective in the same spirit as Steve had done to help override the stereotypes and stigma attached to transsexualism. I had no intention of doing more than that one film; I was still interested in putting it all behind me.

In 1992, Kate Bornstein asked me to be in the film about her, *Adventures in the Gender Trade*. I made a brief, talking-head appearance, using the name "Jack Ireland." The film was released in 1993. I was still worried about the potential consequences of exposure: public ridicule or violence against my daughter or me. But by 1994, when Candace Schermerhorn of Northern Light Productions in Boston first contacted me, I had changed my mind about the risks. I no longer feared public backlash because I realized that the public cares almost nothing about transsexual people. The public holds us at a distance and criticizes us or laughs at us when it suits them, and otherwise we are on our own.

Schermerhorn had been inspired by the story of Billy Tipton when she heard a radio interview with his biographer, Diane Middlebrook. She wondered what it would feel like to have a female body and live completely as a man, and she set about trying to find people fitting that description to interview for a documentary film. The only people she could find to talk to at that time were transsexual men, and she was so moved by their stories that she changed the focus of her project to center on the transitions of FTMs. She and co-producer/director Bestor Cram were calling their film "Courageous Hearts." They were using my friends Michael and Ted from Boston, and they needed more people, so Michael had told her to contact me. I suggested to her several men in the community who I knew were willing to be visible, and she selected Loren Cameron, Stephan Thorne, and Max Valerio. In 1995 we began shooting what would ultimately become the award-winning film *You Don't Know Dick: Courageous Hearts of Transsexual Men*, the first mainstream educational video exclusively about transsexual men. It was the first documentary that explored FTM experience in a context outside that of male-to-female stereotypes and allowed some of us to tell our stories without making any reference or comparison to the clichés about MTF people. Released in the spring of 1997, *You Don't Know Dick* is still playing at film festivals and can still be seen on television in the U.S. and abroad. The Gay and Lesbian Alliance Against Defamation (GLAAD) nominated it for a GLAAD Media Award in 2001.

Transsexual and transgendered people were always good for ratings on the exploitative talk shows and *Saturday Night Live* skits in the late 1980s and through the 1990s. These programs were rife with gender ambiguity jokes and sex change stories. Sometimes the transpeople who appeared on talk shows were articulate and informative, and sometimes they were embarrassing. Through referrals from IFGE and other MTF transsexual people who were on various media lists, I received frequent requests from talk show producers to appear on *Geraldo!, Rolanda, Montel Williams, Maury Povich, Ricki Lake*, and local shows, too. I turned them all down, partly because I couldn't stand the format they used (and one never knew with whom one would be appearing on stage) and partly because I was unwilling to drop everything in my life for a "free trip to New York" or just to be on television. I always referred other well-spoken people to the shows, who could decide for themselves if they wanted to appear. I finally did appear on the *Charles Perez* show in early 1995, and was deeply disappointed with the experience (see Gamson, 1998). The only reason I went was because I happened to be available on the requested dates, and because they told me David Harrison would also be there. The producer misled me about the show's topic and about the format, and I was angry when I left the studio. When the show finally aired several weeks later, the only feedback I received was a positive acknowledgement from a cook in a local café, a rugged man who had been stunned to find out that I had once had a female body. The next time he saw me, he shook my hand for a long time and stared into my face. "More power to you, man," he said. "You blew me away. I tell you, the world is full of amazing things."

Another artistic impression of transsexual life appeared in 1996. Filmmaker, painter, and gay activist Rosa Von Praunheim of Berlin released his documentary video *Transexual Menace* [sic], which describes crossdressers and transsexual people from many different cultural, racial, economic, and gender-identity backgrounds in the context of the rise of the transgender political movement in the United States. No other overview documentary to date is as culturally diverse or as political as this one, shot in 1995 in New York, Atlanta, and Washington, D.C. (A&E's "Investigative Reports—Transgender Revolution," first broadcast in 1998, comes close, but it is specifically focused on an American perspective). I was in both the Atlanta and D.C. segments of Von Praunheim's film, and introduced the director to a number of other transmen (and non-trans friends, too) in San Francisco. I enjoyed his hospitality in Berlin the following year, where he introduced me to Charlotte Von Mahlsdorf, the subject of the very moving autobiography *I Am My Own Woman* (Von Mahlsdorf, 1995 tr.), and of Von Praunheim's film of the same title. She is represented as a transvestite in both, because, like Billy Tipton, she had not had hormones or surgery, but I felt I was meeting a woman. She extended her hand and I was struck by its softness, by the gentle weariness in her eyes and her understated, quietly confident, feminine bearing. She was as real a woman as any other I've ever met. After a lifetime punctuated by misunderstanding and accolade, honor and abuse, she died in Sweden on April 30, 2002, at the age of seventy-four (Koskovich, 2002).

New creative voices and are always clamboring to be heard. In 1997 Christopher Lee released his film *Trappings of Transhood*, a vibrant, rough twenty-seven-minute video that captures the burgeoning energy of transmen of color and transmen who identify as gay, bisexual, and/or queer. Society must look clearly at the full range of transgender and transsexual experience if we ever hope to understand it, and help others who will negotiate it. Since the mid-1990s, many other transmen, their friends and partners, and professional documentary filmmakers have made scores more films examining FTM transition, the effects of testosterone, and the peculiarities of FTM experience. Some are destined for widespread viewing on television, like BBC and Discovery Channel documentaries (e.g., *Body Chemistry: Hormone Heaven* by Britain's Channel 4 in 1999, and *Changing Sexes—Female-to-Male* by Film Garden Entertainment for Discovery Channel in 2003), *The Opposite Sex: Rene's Story* by Hensel-Krasnow Productions in 2003 for Showtime television to be broadcast in 2004) and some are presently viewable only in film festivals and arranged screenings (e.g., *A Boy Named Sue*, by Julie Wyman, released in 2000, *Girls Will Be Boys* by Texas Tomboy, released in 1993, and *The Ride* by Bill Basquin, released in 2000).

I've now appeared in eight documentary films, in dozens of news and interview stories on radio and television stations on every continent, and in program segments on venues as diverse as Court TV and PBS's *In the Life*. This exposure has not threatened the peace of my private life, as I once feared would happen. I know from the feedback I receive that these appearances have made a difference for those who have been informed or inspired by them. The extent to which we convey the truth of our experience is the extent to which any audience will receive us, yet so long as other people control the forum, or so long as the analyzing or commenting voices are not informed by direct experience of us, we are still vulnerable to being treated with nothing more enlightened than prejudice. As with any other little-known, easily misrepresented group, it is crucial that transsexual people have some measure of control over at least some of the images of us that are presented to the public.

Visibility in Print

Print is one medium where the voice of the author can be very strong, as opposed to appearing in a film or video that someone else will script, narrate, and edit. Loren Cameron and I had posed for a photo shoot to illustrate a magazine article in 1991, and both of us felt objectified by the photographer, even though I don't think that was her intention. I was working to articulate my experience, hoping to turn it into effective communication, policy, and training, while Loren vowed to teach himself photography so he could depict transsexual men with dignity. His *Body Alchemy: Transsexual Portraits* was published in the fall of 1996. It is a landmark publication for transsexual men: the first high-quality photography book about FTM transsexual people by a transsexual man brave enough to reveal his own body and soul, and to attempt to reveal the bodies and souls of other transmen with pride and respect, not as lurid curiosities or stark confrontations with the ordinary, but as a part of the beauty of humanity. Not only does it present transsexual bodies as dignified and powerful—as works of art—but it also presents concise, moving profiles representative of the wide variety of people who comprise the FTM transsexual community. It is unsurpassed as a work of power, beauty, and flowing composition.

In 1997, Indiana University Press released Holly Devor's *FTM: Female-to-Male Transsexuals in Society*. This text is the first extensive sociological analysis of a diverse group of transsexual men done outside of a clinical setting. Devor's body of work has been extremely important in academically in raising visibility of transgendered female-bodied people and transsexual men, and was the first sociologically meaningful work that allowed FTMs to speak in their own voices and encouraged other researchers to take us seriously. Devor raised complex issues without shrinking from controversy, and was attacked by some transmen who were growing increasingly irritated with having "outsiders" write about us. The only previous studies (Lothstein, 1983; Stoller, 1968, 1972, 1975 and 1982) had drawn fairly unattractive pathological pictures of their subjects, and they issued opinions about all FTM people based upon examinations of a tiny handful of damaged people isolated in clinical settings. Devor worked with FTMs to look at the things that happened to them and the ways they felt comfortable or uncomfortable in their bodies and in their social relationships. It is ironic that transmen would attack someone for exposing them when at the same time they were crying out to be seen and acknowledged for who they are. Even more ironic is the danger of separatist behavior in the trans community—you never know whom you are excluding, because you never know what changes people might be going through. We should be the last to forget this mantra: you don't know to whom you're talking. Holly Devor became Aaron Devor, one of us, in 2002, and I expect he will continue to produce research and analysis about our collective experience that is thoughtful, challenging, reasoned and realistic.

Jason Cromwell's *Transmen and FTMs* is another proud affirmation of lived masculine experience, that also takes an anthropological approach to the concepts underlying the struggle for visibility that many transsexual men confront. Reflecting on the presumption that all transsexual men share a common vision of the masculine and a common horror of feminine that renders us all neat and predictable, he quotes Judith Butler: "Discourse becomes oppressive when it requires that the speaking subject, in order to speak, participate in the very terms of that oppression" (Butler, 1990, in Cromwell, 1999, 108). He examines the literature of transsexualism to show how, if we hadn't conformed to those neat, predictable ideas in the late 1980s, we would not have been acknowledged or treated. We were conditioned to be compliant. Cromwell is also one of the early voices that challenged the status quo after analyzing his own experience. His book is another foundational document underpinning the contemporary movement.

Most transsexual men still express an understandable reluctance to reveal their transsexual status, but in the early 1990s this reluctance was more like a terror. Men often asked me how could I do it, how could I deal with the idea of people knowing about me, how could I risk the exposure, but I felt the potential benefit to gender-variant people outweighed the risk to me. Even after hundreds of classroom lectures, television news interviews, and public appearances at art events and political meetings, strangers rarely recognize me on the street, and when they do their comments are universally positive. After a three-page spread in a Sunday edition of the *San Francisco Chronicle* in September 1997, with nearly a full page of photos, almost no one mentioned it to me. I did receive one unusual phone call that morning—when I said hello, a male voice I didn't recognize asked if I was the James Green who was profiled in the paper. "Yes . . . ?" I replied, wondering what would come next. He said, "You probably don't remember me. My name is . . . and I went to high school with you, and I just want to tell you that there are a lot of people out here pulling for you, and if I ever did or said anything back in high school to hurt you, I want you to know I'm sorry." I told him, "I do remember you, and I know you never did anything that hurt me." We talked for a few minutes and I thanked him for calling; I was touched by his effort to reach out to me. As Marcy and I walked through the San Francisco airport terminal that same afternoon, my face looked back at us from dozens of opened newspapers people were reading while awaiting their flights. People had it on the flight to Honolulu that Marcy and I were on, but no one noticed me. Marcy was anxious, in fact angry with me, at the thought that our privacy might be invaded during our vacation or upon our return, but—as I expected— nothing happened.

At the time I was on hiatus from my work as a part-time contractor doing technical writing for several high technology companies, with one primary client that was a fairly conservative, high-profile organization. I did wonder if I would ever hear from them again after the *Chronicle* spread, but, sure enough, my primary client called me back after the first of the year. A week or so into the new assignment, a fellow writer who was on the corporate staff told me the article had been the talk of the organization for several weeks after it had come out. Still, no one made an issue out of it to me. It can be a strange feeling to wonder who knows and who doesn't, but I figured so long as people were treating me respectfully and using the proper pronouns everything was okay. Ultimately none of us has complete control over what others think about us, so I have come to accept myself as a man with an unusual history. If I am to be visible, let me acquit myself well.

The Visibility Dilemma

With the latest transsexual autobiographies (several MTF books in the U.S. in the latter half of the 1990s, and four FTM books in the U.K. in 1996 alone!), the publication of photographic work by Mariette Pathy Allen (2003), Loren Cameron (1996, 2001), Dean Kotula (2002), and Del Volcano (1999), the increasing popularity of gender studies and numerous academic anthologies with serious content devoted to the topics of transgender and transsexual experience, one might think that the scales of acceptance—if not understanding—were now tipping in our direction. Indeed, progress has been made, but visibility remains a conflicted aspect of transsexual lives. How do we manage visibility? If we are visible we risk being mistreated; if we are invisible, no one will understand what our social or medical needs are. If we are visible, we risk being judged inferior or unreal, inauthentic; if we are invisible, we risk being discovered and cast out, again because no one is educated.

Every time a transsexual man goes into a public (or perhaps even private) toilet he is aware of his history; every time he makes love with a partner; every time he applies for a job or seeks medical care; whenever he is at the mercy of a governmental body or social service agency, he is aware of his history, or aware of any anomalies in his body, and—so long as he must fear the ignorance and hostility of others—he must be on guard against discovery.

Social conventions and institutions support individual prejudice against the rights of transsexual people, adding to the burden of secrecy. These conventions persist because no one has tried, until very recently, to correct them. There are doctors who will not admit they provide services to us. Insurance companies deny medical coverage for conditions relating to "sex reassignment," "surgical sex change," or "transsexual treatments or procedures," which can be—and are often—extrapolated to mean *any* medical condition once a person is known to be transsexual. I've received calls from dozens of men who were denied treatment for conditions like bronchitis, bleeding lacerations below the knee, and bursitis of the shoulder simply because their records stated (or the men themselves revealed) their transsexual status and were told, "We can't treat people like you," or, "This hospital doesn't provide services for transsexuals." One man told me about seeing his medical records within an HMO setting: someone had written "TRANSSEXUAL" in bold red ink across the top of his chart. That meant every clerk, technician, or nurse's aide who came into contact with that chart was instantly invited to inspect him, conjecture about his genitals, invoke their own preconceived notions about what the word "transsexual" means, perhaps even assume that he was a "man who wanted to be a woman," and then treat him according to their own ideas about how he deserved to be treated. This means that when we are unconscious, or when the anomalies of our body may be discovered against our will, we are vulnerable to mistreatment or attack even by those entrusted with our care.

Some institutions or governmental agencies will not allow us to change our identity records to ease our passage through life, thus exposing us to ridicule or attack every time we want to cash a check, travel on an airline, or buy a beer. The justification for this is that to change the records would somehow be a falsification. But there is no similar restriction, in most cases, for adoptions or voluntary name changes or removal of erroneous information. There is no reason to presume that any one aspect of individual history is more permanent than any other, and history is, in fact, the record of change. The pain inflicted by the refusal to acknowledge the lived experience of a person is vicious and debilitating. Some transsexual people have had police making routine traffic stops for minor violations confiscate their identification believing it to be fraudulent. Employers are free to dismiss us because they feel our presence is just "too disruptive"; they apparently don't believe that it's possible for us to function efficiently, or for people around us to leave us alone, whether our transition is in the past, present, or future. As a medical condition, transsexualism is our own business, and our treatment status should be a matter between us and our physicians.

Having stepped out of the transsexual closet myself, I occasionally wonder when certain friends—both trans and non-trans—will feel the pressure of their own awareness that my photograph is on the cover of a book or in the newspaper and decline to be seen with me because they don't want others to presume they are transsexual. I wonder who knows about my transsexual past and who doesn't: have my friends told their friends about me; is that why people seem so eager to be introduced to me? What do they mean when they say, "I've heard so much about you!"? Are they being kind, or are they merely curious? Is it to me that people seem attracted, or is it the exotic trans phenomenon?

Walking down the street in San Francisco or in New York City, Tokyo, Sydney, Paris, or Rome, no one takes any special interest in me. I am just another man, invisible, no one special. I remember what it was first like to feel that anonymity as testosterone gradually obliterated the androgyny that for most of my life made others uncomfortable in my presence. It was a great relief to be able to shake off layers of defensive behaviors developed to communicate my humanity from inside my uncategorizability. It was a joy to be assumed human for a change, instead of gawked at, scrutinized for signs of *any* gender. Now, whenever I stand up in front of a college class or a corporate training session, or make any public statement in support of transgendered or transsexual people, I am scrutinized for signs of my previous sex, even though my gender is perfectly obvious, reinforced by my male appearance. Occasionally my appearance in a public setting has had nothing whatsoever to do with transsexualism, and I have a lurking suspicion that I would not receive the attention I sometimes do for non–transsexual-related accomplishments if I still retained the androgynous appearance I had for the first forty years of my life. In fact, I know that androgynous people, such as I was, have often been passed over as subjects and spokespersons on such topics as women in non-traditional jobs because we didn't appear acceptably gendered, and this applies equally to pre-transition female-to-male people and post-transition male-to-female people.

Now, however, people are quite comfortable with my male presentation. My psyche seems to fit nicely into male packaging: I feel better; people around me are less confused, and so am I. So, why tell anyone about my past? Why not just live the life of a normal man? Perhaps I could if I were a normal man, but I am not. I am a man, and I am a man who lived forty years in a female body. But I was not a woman. I am not a woman who became a man. I am not a woman who lives as a man. I am not, nor was I ever a woman, though I lived in a female body, and certainly tried, whenever I felt up to it, to be a woman. But it was never in me to be a woman. Likewise, I am not a man in the same sense as my younger brother is a man, having been treated as such all his life. I was treated as other than a man most of the time, as a man part of the time, and as a woman only rarely. Certainly I was treated as a little girl when I was young, but even then people occasionally assumed I was a little boy. I always felt like something "other." Can I be just a man now, or must I always be "other?" These are the kinds of questions transmen ask themselves, and sometimes ask each other. Before transition we tend to think that once we become men everything will be fine; we are often surprised to find that some problems may remain, transforming with us.

Transitioning men feel a tremendous sense of relief that marks what is probably one of the most satisfying periods of their lives. While immense challenges arise during transition, and while there may be a sense of urgency to complete the process that can obliterate all other external concerns, the sense of growing into one's self—of really becoming who one is at last—can be so rewarding that it may erase the long-standing pain of having one's gender misunderstood. The transition itself opens so many windows on the gender system that we may be compelled to comment on our observations, which could not be made from any vantage point other than a transsexual (or sometimes transgender) position, and to comment requires revealing that position, present or past.

Transgendered people who choose transsexual treatment may be pathologized and stigmatized because we depend on a system of approval that grants or restricts our access to treatment. That approval may be seen as relieving us of our responsibility—or guilt—for being outside the norm. We then become either the justification for the treatment by embodying the successful application of "normal" standards or we become victims of the treatment, depending on our circumstances. Things can go smoothly: some of us find our inner and outer balance, gain acceptance from self and others, and can lead ordinary, or even exemplary, lives. But if things don't turn out so well for some reason, if something goes wrong with our hormones or the surgery is botched, or we just don't have the innate physical characteristics or body language abilities that translate well through our transition (FTM or MTF), we are forced to realize that we are still very different in form and substance from non-transsexual people, and therefore we still suffer from the oppression we wished to escape when we looked to doctors to make us "normal." By claiming our identity as men or women who are also transpeople, by asserting that our different bodies are just as normal for us as anyone else's is for them, by insisting that our right to express our own gender, to modify our bodies and shape our identities, is as inalienable as our right to know our true religion, we claim our humanity and our right to be treated equally under law and within the purviews of morality and culture. To do that, we must educate—if we have the ability and emotional energy to do so. That is what visibility is about.

Academic Debates

Gender and genitals are strongholds of control binding all people to a social order that has so far had serious difficulty acknowledging diversity. Somebody's got us by the balls and they don't want to let go. Who is that somebody? Who is so afraid of losing control? Of what are they going to lose control if people are allowed to freely express their gender(s)? What is preserved by denying the legitimacy of transsexual and transgendered people? What is destroyed if we are acknowledged? Is it the right of succession? Is it the right to own property? Is it the institution of heterosexual marriage? Is it the ability to know whether to treat another as an equal, an inferior, or a superior human being? The standards implied by these conventions are not necessary to civil society, but are merely used to control or privilege certain groups of people.

In her introduction to the 1994 edition of *The Transsexual Empire*, Janice Raymond postulates a reason that "there are not as many female-to-constructed male transsexuals." She writes that for women "the construction of gender dissatisfaction has been medicalized through promotion of breast implants, hormone replacement therapy, infertility hormones and reproductive procedures, and plastic surgery." She also points out, "Maleness is not so easy to come by, especially because the majority of vendors (professionals) are males themselves and more discomfited in giving it away." These are very female-centered positions that don't allow space for divergent opinions. Raymond states that the medicalization of transsexualism (which I assume to mean the granting of medical treatment) prevents the destruction of stereotypical gender roles and reinforces sexism, presumably by acknowledging that people want to be gender-congruent. In other words, forcing us to live visibly outside the gender boxes (as we were apparently born to do) would somehow eradicate sexism. History shows that sexism and stereotypical gender roles developed perfectly well in the presence of generations of visibly transgendered people who were helpless to stop them. While there may be a connection between sexism, gender stereotypes, and the biases of some doctors who evaluate candidates for transsexual treatment, there is no direct connection between transsexualism *per se* and sexism or gender stereotypes. Individuals who undergo this transition are not universally incapable of social analysis. I interpret Raymond's dogmatic insistence that it is impossible to change sex—which, ironically, occurs on page *xx*, a symbol of the female—and that transsexuals never move beyond gender roles, as a blatant reactionary response to what she perceives as a threat to female bodies, feminism and feminist politics, everything upon which she bases her own identity. It is Raymond's particular brand of feminism that cannot survive without rigid gender roles, and especially not without the objectification and vilification of men.

In *Changing Sex: Transsexualism, Technology, and the Idea of Gender,* Bernice Hausman (1995) also takes on the "medicalization" of gender, asserting that transsexuals are expert at the arts of impersonation, producing gender as "the real of sex," though she says that gender does not exist. She claims that transsexuals are unable to accept and accommodate themselves to the sexual meanings of their "natural" bodies (which may well be true), and the demand for treatment is made to accommodate "a cultural fantasy of stable identity" (193). In this latter clause Hausman reveals her bias against granting transpeople the ability to interpret our own experience. Because she postulates that gender really is the euphemism that has replaced sex in the modern lexicon, and therefore it is nothing, she cannot allow gender variance to exist. She even takes gender away from homosexual people by asserting "gender is a concept meaningful only within heterosexuality and in advocacy of heterosexuality" (194), a statement which is also true if gender is nothing more than sex, and sex is only a binary system. Yet, as Judith Halberstam has pointed out, "[L]esbians are also turned on by gendered sexual practices and restricted by the limiting of gender to bio-binarism" (Halberstam, 1994). Halberstam states, "The breakdown of genders and sexualities into identities is in many ways ... an endless project, and it is perhaps preferable therefore to acknowledge that gender is defined by transitivity, that sexuality manifests as multiple sexualities, and that therefore we are all transsexuals" (226). And while I believe this last remark to be nobly intended, I must disagree with it if for no other reason than to acknowledge the specificity of my own transformation. At least Halberstam's position gives us all individual voices, while Hausman's position links us all to only one path of binary sexual expression: no matter who we are or what we do socially or sexually, our unchangeable maleness or femaleness defines us. She renders us all speechless.

Everyone uses gender to communicate, as much as we use our clothing, our posture, our vocabulary, our tone of voice, and our sex and sexuality. The fact that gender is problematic for some theorists as well as some trans-people is no justification for an attempt to mandate it out of existence.

Like Raymond, Hausman uses the reality of gender confirmation surgery as part of her argument against it, citing descriptions of surgery and post-operative pain in transsexual autobiographies. Hausman notes that the admission of pain serves "to undermine the text's primary argument that the subject was really meant to be the sex he or she must be surgically fashioned into" (167). She implies that if there is pain then there is something unnatural about the body's situation. More faulty logic. All transsexual people do not experience excessive pain following their surgeries. All non-transsexual people are not pain-free, whether they have had any surgery or not. What about menstrual cramps or the pain of childbirth? And both athletes and disabled people can attest to the pain that sometimes accompanies self-actualization. The quality of being free of physical pain does not confer a greater veracity on any subject's experience of gender. Further, Hausman ignores the psychic pain of pre-operative transsexual people.

The fact is that the known biological aspects of sex difference—which we call natural and think of as immutable—are no more immune to change than the psychosocial manifestations of sex difference—which we call gender and cultural, and understand to be mutable (Hubbard, 1998). Many gendered and heterosexist social constructs collapse like cardboard seawalls against the ocean of my transsexual reality. People can argue abstractly about the "real-ness" of my life all they want, but it doesn't change the fact that I exist or the qualities of maleness people observe in me.

What makes a man a man? His penis? His beard? His receding hairline? His lack of breasts? His sense of himself as a man? Some men have no beard, some have no penis, some never lose their hair, some have breasts; all have a sense of themselves as men. Transsexual men are also men. Transsexual men are men who have lived in female bodies. Transsexual men may appear feminine, androgynous or masculine. *Any* man may appear feminine, androgynous, or masculine.

My uniqueness is the same difference that each man has from any other man. If transsexual men want to disappear, to not be seen, it is because they are afraid of not being seen as men, of being told they are not men, and of being unable to refute the assertion that they are not men. All men fear this, deep down, just as all women who know they are women would—at some level—be pained by an assertion that they are not women or a refusal to acknowledge their femaleness. In this way, all men—trans and non-trans—are the same. All men would cling tenaciously to their self-concept as men, even if they lost their penis (though the loss of this unique organ would very likely be a serious threat to a man who had not examined his sense of self). One thing all men understand is that they are not women. This is also true for transsexual men, even though they have lived in female bodies. As soon as a transsexual man reveals his trans status, he is examined for vestiges of "woman" that may then be used to invalidate his maleness, his authenticity.

The crux of the matter of gender for *any*one is their own visibility and sufficient external confirmation of their gender identity; thus if a person is comfortable with her or his gender-body congruity or incongruity, and their gender identity is confirmed by the people around them whom they value, they will feel "seen" and validated by others. Until I changed my body I always had to struggle to be visible. That's not the case for every transperson; it was the case for me.

Appearances

From February 1973 through August 1976, when I was employed as a telephone company construction cable splicer, my life was a concentrated study of gender expectations and violations. I was the first female-bodied individual to pass line school, the physical training program for this position, training so rigorous that the majority of pre-screened and otherwise qualified men regularly failed it. I had always had an unusually high degree of upper body strength; I loved climbing trees as a kid. I used to charge the girls in my neighborhood money for tree-climbing lessons. I also spent a couple of winters as an alpine ski instructor, so I knew how to train my body and to communicate about physical activity. The foreman who was our climbing instructor said I was the best climber he had ever seen. But when I passed the training, the administrators were so surprised that a "woman" had successfully completed their program they offered me a position as a building janitor. I told them I didn't know what a splicer was, but I did know what a janitor was, and it was not what I had signed on to do. I signed on to be a splicer, I passed their training, and I refused to accept the janitor job. They shook their heads, told me I was too small and I'd be a safety hazard, but they assigned me to a crew, where I proceeded to carve out a niche for myself among the men. After I'd been splicing for a year, the administration lowered the training standards to enable more women to qualify for jobs and a dozen new women became splicers statewide. I realized how thoroughly I was perceived as belonging to the class of "other than woman" when the men would complain to me over coffee, or beer at the end of the day, about the folly of hiring women to do this kind of work. "What about me?" I would ask, as a gentle reminder to whom they were speaking. They would look startled and say, "I don't mean you! You're different," or even "You're not a woman!" And a year after that, when all but one of the newly hired women had been injured on the job (and that one escaped because her foreman gave her only light work to do), the men pointed to this as proof of their contention, while I suggested that perhaps the issue wasn't that women shouldn't do the work; rather, the issue was that women should receive better training for it.

During this period, when many white American men were letting their hair grow long and my co-workers were frustrated because of a company regulation against long hair for splicers, I decided to let my hair grow longer in an effort to confound the administration, just to see whether they would ask a woman to cut her hair. When the men realized I wasn't being asked to cut my hair, some of them started to let their hair grow, too. The administration was stymied. I never discussed this strategy with my co-workers; it just evolved, and I was pleased with the result. What surprised me, though, was that the longer my hair grew, the more consistently I was perceived by strangers as male. I had assumed that by letting my hair grow, I would have to accept that I would more likely be perceived as female since long hair was stereotypical of women, but that wasn't what happened. Perhaps because I made no effort to style my hair in a feminine way, and perhaps because I wore standard construction worker attire, strangers didn't seem able to connect my rugged appearance with their idea of women and would refer to me more consistently with masculine pronouns and forms of address. I realized that just having long hair, something that only a few years earlier would have resulted in a man being called a girl, was not enough to tell people I was female. When I cut my hair short again, strangers saw something feminine about me and the incidence of interpreting me as female returned to about even. Just as when I was a teenager and hoped ridiculously that wearing the right dress or carrying a purse would make me a girl, I learned once again that there is something about gender—not sex or sexuality—that transcends clothing, hairstyles, body shapes, voices, and even the conscious awareness that a body has a particular sex. There is something else going on, something more deeply embedded in the *gestalt* of expression, the body language, that a person uses, that expresses something both from the surface and from deeper within.

In the mid-1970s, my friends and I also became aware that female-to-male transsexualism was possible. Among most lesbians I knew then, the concept of "women becoming men" was abhorrent, and many women began holding me up as an example of the kind of strong woman those transsexuals could be if they would only let themselves. A friend who was a medical doctor discussed with me a strategy of offering myself to a gender clinic to see whether they would diagnose me as a transsexual because of my masculine character and demeanor. Of course, I could not admit to her, a "fellow" lesbian, that I actually entertained the notion of surgical sex reassignment. Her fantasy was that once diagnosed I would then stand up and shout, "Aha! You fools!! Do you think that just because I am perceived as a male and hold a 'male' occupation, I will automatically want to be classified physically and socially as a male? What is wrong with being a woman with masculine characteristics?" But as soon as we had constructed this scenario I began to question whether this was the proper statement for me to make. I was comfortable with the label of "lesbian," but I was decidedly uncomfortable with the label of "woman," and I confided to my friend that I didn't think I was fit for the assignment of exposing the gender clinics because I feared that if offered the opportunity to change my body, I would actually appreciate doing so. I sheepishly confessed that in fact I perceived myself as more male than female, knowing I was speaking heresy.

"What do you mean?" my friend inquired.

"I mean I would like to have a male body," I replied.

"Well, so would I, in some ways," she said. "But you wouldn't want to really be a man, would you?"

"What do you mean?" I asked.

"I mean it is so much better to be a woman, don't you think?"

"But I don't think I am a woman," I said. "I don't think I was, or ever could or will be." And I realized in that moment that I wanted to be *something*, to be physically congruent with my gender, both for myself and for others. All the theorizing about gender, about male privilege or the moral superiority of women, about the inappropriateness of altering one's body, or the false dichotomy that the dialectic of apparent biological sex and social gender force onto our bodies and souls would never neutralize that need in me. I also knew that whether or not I ever changed my body, I would always be not completely male and not completely female, even though I knew I would fit in the world better as a man. I would always be different than other conventionally gendered beings. And ultimately, by changing my appearance to reflect my masculine gender, I did not narrow my perspective to obliterate the feminine, but in fact I broadened my own understanding of what it can mean socially to be labeled "man" or "woman."

Appearance has nearly everything to do with how we perceive gender and the kind of attributes we assign to people upon first meeting them. The sound of a voice is secondary. Kessler and McKenna (1978) note: "[B]iology provides 'signs' for us. Signs are not gender, but they serve as 'good reasons' for our attributions in a world where biological facts are seen as the ultimate reasons" (77). In this framework, it is reasonable to assume that I am a man and that I enjoy all the customary attributes of the masculine gender within the society in which I live. This is an "incorrigible proposition," part of the set of beliefs we hold that define what is real, that in turn defines the interpretive structure of the onlooker, the one who is analyzing. I believe gender belongs to each individual, to do with as he or she pleases; it is not possible for an "objective" observer to paste gender onto another person by labeling them with a gender that the person does not feel, whether or not that gender is expressed. Any attempt to make another person's gender a solitary object that can be isolated and analyzed is doomed to failure, not because gender is a social construction and so requires more than one person to create it, but because gender, even though it is imposed by society, is also a private matter, aspects of which *may or may not* be publicly expressed, and it cannot be wholly abstracted from the subject's (conscious or unconscious) control.

Gender is a private matter that we share with others; and when we share it, it becomes a social construction, thus it requires, like language, a "speaker" and a "listener." It is between the two of these actors that gender is defined, negotiated, corroborated, or challenged. But to say that without this interaction there is no need for gender is like saying that if a tree falls in the forest and no ear is there to hear the sound, then there was no sound, or perhaps no tree actually fell! We all have the ability to express and interpret gender, regardless of our apparent biology and whether or not anyone is there to hear us. But if we don't speak a language that others understand, then it can be a source of difficulty, even conflict, if we find ourselves in an intolerant environment.

One "incorrigible proposition" concerning gender today is that it depends on biology. Kessler and McKenna state, "Science will soon be able to construct perfectly functioning penises. Because of this we will never know what would have been the long-range repercussions, on concepts about gender, of having a group of men in society who do not have penises" (120). That was written over twenty-five years ago, and those perfectly functioning penises (as they must have been imagining them) have yet to be surgically attached to FTM bodies. And if they were actually available, I question the logic that dictates that all FTMs would want them. In fact, we have right now a group of men in society who do not have those kinds of penises, and some of those men do not want the surgery it would take to get them. Some of the partners of these men might not be so interested in those penises, either. Moreover, many transsexual men feel that they *do* have perfectly functioning penises without surgery, or with modest surgical modification of the native organs. We know that it is not a penis that makes us each a man, regardless of whether we have, want, or would appreciate having a penis. We are a group of men who do not achieve gender membership through our genitals, yet we are still accused of buying into stereotypical gender roles simply because we are transsexual men and have a masculine appearance, because we have beards or a particular musculature. No one asks transsexual men about our politics; very few of us are asked about the ways in which we manifest sexual desire. How would anyone know whether we are "buying into stereotypical gender roles," or whether we simply fit some categorical gender stereotypes and don't fit others, just like anyone else? It is apparently much more satisfying for researchers to take small samples and ask leading questions, to seek out statements that use "typical" transsexual validation language, such as, "I always felt more like a boy than a girl," and to interpret these statements as a conscious effort to create a sense of the naturalness of the transsexual subject's gender, the assumption being that gender is not natural, the body is natural, and an altered body is no longer natural, while an unaltered gender is impossible since gender is socially constructed. This belief structure is used to justify viewing transsexual people as a class of individuals who are incapable of assailing the paradigmatic ramparts. Never mind that transsexual people often learn that certain language is more effective in eliciting sympathy for their condition, thus ensuring their physical and psychic survival in a world that is resolutely hostile to variation or surprise.

I have chosen to change my appearance, something many people do in many ways. From my perspective, my gender has not changed; I have simply made its message clear. That may be a kind of social construction, but it is not the construction of my gender, it is the construction of my social relationships, like planing the edge of a door so it fits within its frame, opens and closes with ease.

Non-transsexual theorists do not always recognize the fact that when transsexual people undertake this type of physical change, we do not know what form our new physical manifestation will take, and that we cannot will ourselves to look like the perfect incarnations of masculinity or femininity we're accused of striving to be. Just like non-transsexual people we must accept ourselves the way we are, (to paraphrase a common prayer) changing the things we can, accepting the things we can't change, and acquiring the wisdom to know the difference. And those of us who do grow up into adult men or women do not need to bear any greater share of the social burden for the dichotomy between the two dominant forms of gender expression than any other person who appears normatively female or male. The theory that if transsexual people had some other culturally constructed option, a place to be socially male (or female) while remaining physically female (or male), then we would categorically refuse body altering technology is pure utopian conjecture, based upon some particular "incorrigible propositions," or perhaps (for those who already appear normatively gendered) rooted in the desire to step outside the limitations of socially constructed gender without changing one's appearance. This is another way of proving that the people who appear different or non-normative (read transgendered) are deluded for wanting to appear "normal," while the "normal" people can feel at least normal, or possibly even superior (if only *au courant*), for wanting to appear different.

Gender, like race, is not a power system in itself; gender, like race, is a physical trait that some people use to gain or distribute power. Like language, another physical trait, one that varies with ability, our gender is both natural and artificial; the ability to have both gender and language reside in the natural or native being-ness of individuals, whether their expressed gender reinforces, contradicts, or is randomly confused by an observer's social concepts of their body, or whether their ability to speak is compromised by physical deformity, or they happen to speak a different language than their listener can comprehend.

Gender is a type of language, and there are some very adept individuals capable of speaking many dialects, as well as derivative languages. Crossdressers, drag kings and queens, androgynous transgendered people, butches and femmes of either sex, and many transsexual people all may draw upon gender interpretation skills that non-transgendered people don't have, or have not cultivated, or for whom they are unnatural. Granted, some transsexual people are very rigid about their own gender identification, but there may be various reasons for this, such as that they have had to fight very hard to assert it or that they've learned a certain kind of behavior is expected of them. Most non-transsexual people are rigid in their gender identity, too. For many people—not just transsexual people—gender expression is an important survival mechanism. Thus I contend that while sex can be and *is* assigned, gender *cannot* be assigned by others, but only interpreted or misinterpreted. I propose that gender is the interface between our psyche and our cognitive mind/body/sex. I conceive of gender as an aspect of personality, of the way we manifest who we are in the world. When we express negative judgment about another person's gender expression, whether that judgment comes from our own conservatism (supporting a rigid gender dichotomy that disdains fluidity), or liberalism (supporting a wide variety or fluidity of gender expression that disdains rigidity), we are expressing a lack of tolerance for diversity, a lack of appreciation for individuality.

Influencing the Course of Treatment

The fact remains that most transsexual people require medical treatment, treatment that, even in the U.S., can be difficult to access. When I found out in 1989 through Sullivan's *FTM Newsletter* that there was an international association of medical professionals who treat transsexual patients, and that they had developed Standards of Care for our treatment, I was both surprised and wary. Why hadn't I heard of this group before? Why hadn't my own doctors told me about it, when they were members of the association? And when I finally obtained a copy of the then-current Standards, I knew why: they had hardly any bearing on FTM experience, and the association itself existed, it seemed, to serve the doctors, not transpeople.

The Harry Benjamin International Gender Dysphoria Association (HBIGDA, *www.hbigda.org*) has long held a position of power over transsexual people that many transsexual people deeply resent because it has functioned as a barrier to treatment for people its members have felt were unqualified to transition. Founded in 1978 and named in honor of the pioneering endocrinologist Dr. Harry Benjamin, the association now has roughly four hundred members worldwide, mostly surgeons, endocrinologists, psychologists, psychiatrists, other medical doctors, legal specialists, and other social scientists, all of whom work to some extent with transgendered and transsexual people.

I found out in 1995 that a small number of HBIGDA members were medical doctors, psychologists, and sexologists who were also transsexual people, and I thought it might be a good idea for me to join, too, because I wanted to be able to communicate as a peer with the professionals who treat us and help them develop a more substantive comprehension of FTM issues. I wanted to encourage them to take a more proactive role in ensuring that we're able to live the quality lives that we're hoping for when we transition. I wasn't a physician, but with my medical and legal writing background, I did have an ability to understand where they were coming from. I arranged to present a paper on bisexuality at the 1997 HBIGDA meeting in Vancouver, B.C. that had I co-authored with Dallas Denny. I was also invited to co-present on a panel with Dr. Barbara Warren and Rosalyne Blumenstein of New York City's Gender Identity Project. People from many disciplines seemed to be interested in what I had to say. They broke into applause when I challenged a Canadian psychologist for his reductive remarks that stereotyped transsexual men. Dr. Bean Robinson,

HBIGDA's executive director, Dr. Walter Bockting, the membership chairman, and Dr. Lin Fraser, a San Francisco psychologist, took me to dinner and encouraged me to join the association. Because I wasn't a professional, though, I would not be eligible for full, voting membership; I told them I'd think about it.

The next day during the general membership session, Dr. Steven Levine, chair of the Standards of Care Committee presented the latest draft of the Standards for ratification. A dissenting roar filled the auditorium as community members and professionals began to voice their objection to the version of the Standards he offered. The Standards were not sufficiently comprehensive; there was virtually no recognition in them that FTM treatment and experience was different from that of MTF transsexual people; there was no acknowledgement that all people did not follow the same path. Attorney Michael Hernandez stood up and called for an FTM representative on the Standards Committee. Dr. Levine agreed to take on a consultant; I was nominated, and I accepted. The twelve-page paper I wrote critiquing the existing draft of the Standards of Care contained some very progressive, yet absolutely logical changes. To be certain I had covered everything, I ran the paper past a team of eight knowledgeable transsexual men, including Michael Hernandez, Jason Cromwell, Jude Patton, Ben Singer, and Jacob Hale. I also joined HBIGDA as an associate member. I knew HBIGDA would only be able to absorb these changes in incremental stages, still I was very disappointed when the Committee accepted virtually none of my substantive suggestions. Out of the blue, about a year later, Dr. Bockting sent me my certificate of full membership. Another year after that, at the meeting in London, Dr. Anne Lawrence and Dr. Holly Devor, then members of the Standards Committee, resurrected my paper and drove through a number of the changes I had proposed. Not the least of these changes was the recognition that breasts are not genitals or reproductive organs, and transsexual men should be able to have their breasts removed prior to starting hormones if necessary, rather than having to wait up to two years living as men with breasts, possibly putting themselves in mortal danger by pretending not to have them just because the procedure was equated with genital reconstruction. Another critical notion that I advanced was that the Standards "as written purport to be guidelines, when in fact they set forth requirements that in some cases are more like mandates." I offered several proposed changes intended to modify the language so that the Standards might become the "flexible directions" they professed to be. At the 2001 meeting in Galveston, I presented papers on various topics, including respectful language (co-authored with Dallas Denny and Jason Cromwell), healthcare access for FTMs (with Dr. Katherine Rachlin), and training law enforcement personnel (with Stephan Thorne). All of these efforts have had significant effects upon the progressive evolution of HBIGDA, an organization that plays a crucial role in validating sex and gender variance. In 2003 I was nominated for and elected to a four-year term on the board of directors and invited to chair the board's Advocacy and Liaison Committee.

Outside of HBIGDA, I've given trainings about FTM experience and gender issues to groups of attorneys, public health professionals, nurses, doctors, police departments, teachers, psychotherapists, psychiatrists, legislators, governmental officials, and journalists. I've traveled to cities all over the U.S. and to Tokyo, Paris, Stockholm, Copenhagen, Malmö, London, Oxford, Toronto, Sydney, and Perth to speak at conferences, on television and radio, and to journalists in order to raise the issues of transsexual lives, and to help local people find the courage and strength to advocate for themselves. Drawing on my decade of corporate management experience, I've also conducted corporate trainings, as well as trainings for nonprofit agencies and for clergy of many denominations. I never expected any of this to happen, but it's gratifying to see so many people taking an interest and being willing to learn. Everywhere I go I invite people to give up their fear and anger about difference and to work for real equality for all, including gender-variant people.

Rather than trying to control gender expression, or to enforce conformity between gender identities and bodies, opening up to acknowledge and accept the variety of gender/body combinations that exist allows more people to fully experience their gendered and sexual selves. Every person's experience of their own gender is a vital component of their humanity, whether people are gender-variant or gender-congruent, and whether or not they need to change their bodies to become visible—or invisible.

For now, though, transsexual people still must come to grips with the ironies of visibility and invisibility. We still have to choose who and when to tell about our transitions. We still have to live with some amount of uncertainty about who knows and who doesn't know about what our bodies were like as children. We still have to decide how "out" to be about our past. We still have to manage the differences in social treatment as and after we transition, depending on how much we resemble the acceptable standards of masculinity or femininity. We may have things to learn about being gender-conforming if we used to be gender-variant, about how to negotiate being gender-variant if we used to be perceived as gender-conforming, or about being gender-variant as a member of one sex as opposed to of the opposite sex we were living as previously. Those lessons are often the most difficult ones we have to manage as they are carried with us into the future and become part of our internal adjustment. It's difficult to imagine in advance how these factors will affect us; often we don't know how we will react to something until it is happening. As we throw off the yoke of early oppressions and remove the barriers to being ourselves, we are left with—ourselves.

8

Willful Destiny

For the first two years of my transition I did not communicate with my out-of-state relatives. To avoid embarrassing my mother, I would arrive at my childhood home on fortnightly visits in the evening when neighbors would be busy having dinner, not looking out their windows. I hurried in from the driveway hoping no one would see me and wonder, "Who is that teenage boy going into the Greens' house?" In many ways I had it easy: no one in my family tried to kill me. But I still got to experience shame in a visceral way. My mother stopped making eye contact with me. She stopped making conversation about books, about ideas she gleaned from her reading or television, or about people we knew, long-time family friends. She stopped telling me about her communication with the out-of-state relatives. She would refer to my sex reassignment process as "it" or "this" as in, "What does your employer think about this?" or, "How does Samantha feel about it?" She criticized me and warned me about failure with statements like, "You're too small to be a man." She was always disappointed to learn I was receiving support for "it" from anyone.

I was motivated to tell the rest of the relatives when my mother's oldest sister had emergency heart surgery. I reasoned that someday someone's going to die, and my mother will want me to take her to the funeral, and if my relatives haven't been told everyone's interest will turn away from the deceased; suddenly everything would be about me and not about them, and that wouldn't be right. I didn't tell her I was writing a letter to each of my aunts (my three uncles had already passed away). I didn't want her to try to stop me.

The same day my father's sister received my letter, she called to say how proud she was of me, that she had read my letter to her two daughters, and that they were proud of me, too. My mother's sisters wrote letters with similar content. All my cousins assured me of their continued affection. I told my mother, "Now you don't have to worry about what they think anymore. You can talk to them about your feelings. They'll give you some emotional support."

"I'm not going to talk to anyone about this," she said.

On October 20, 1991, Morgan, Marcy, and I were visiting at my mother's home when firefighters lost control of the blaze that was to be known as the Oakland Hills Firestorm. As the sky grew gray with smoke and burning embers drifted into our patio, as helicopters were flying overhead, and loudspeakers announced, "This neighborhood must be evacuated" over and over into the distance, someone from the family that lived across the street came to our front door. Dianne and her younger sister, Barbara, had been my favorite babysitters when I was growing up, and I had played with them and their younger siblings since we'd been old enough to cross the street. Outside our family, no one had known me longer than Dianne and her family. When I opened the door, she said my brother's name with a question, wondering who I was.

"Nope; it's Jamie. I've been through a few changes."

"Yes, I see you have," she smiled. "We're taking my dad over to my brother's house; he's got congestive heart failure and we need to get him out of this smoke. We thought your mom might want to come with us."

"Thanks, but I'll take her to my place. She's packing now. Is there anything I can do to help you?"

"You know, there just might be something. Come on!"

Dianne and I ran through my yard and into hers, with the embers flying and the noise of choppers, and me telling her I'd been through surgical sex reassignment over the last few years, and that it was really a good thing for me, but my mom was not too keen on it.

"Well, you look fine," Dianne said. And as we went in her front door, her mother, Mary, came into the hallway and looked surprised to see a stranger. "Mom, it's Jamie Green," Dianne explained. "Alice is going to go with him, but he's come over to help us get Dad out of here."

"Well, isn't that kind of you," Mary said, sizing me up.

"No trouble at all," I said. "What can I do to help?"

"Great! Go in the kitchen and pack up that food that's on the counter while we move Dad into the car."

A few minutes later we rendezvoused in the hall again, and Mary looked me in the eye and said, "Isn't it a blessing when the Lord shows us the path to who we really are?" I thanked her, and she gave me a hug. We said good-bye and good luck, and I ran back to my mother's house. As they rounded the corner in their car, we all waved, not knowing if we'd ever see our homes again.

The fire stopped three blocks away from the corner where our family homes still stand. A few days later the police let residents back into the area, and Barbara and I had a chance to talk as we helped our parents settle back in. She said she and her mother had had a good laugh as they were driving away earlier, when her dad asked, "Is that Jamie Green with a mustache?" "Yes," they told him, "that's right." But they never told him that I'd changed my sex. He died a few months later. I never saw him again, and he didn't really need to know. But the support I've felt from Mary and her children has meant a great deal to me. Unfortunately, my own mother still refused to let her guard down, even with them.

One day in 1993 I ran into my mom in a local shopping area, and she exclaimed, "What are you doing here?"

"I'm shopping, Mom. What are you doing?" I replied. I thought we might sit in a café together as we had when I was very young.

"I'm not doing anything. I have to go now," she said. She had already turned her back to me and was nearly running away from me as she spoke, leaving me standing alone on the busy sidewalk. "Nice to see you, too, Mom," I said to no one.

Loneliness is the mark of difference. Breaking gender boundaries can make us into proud rebels, defiant contraries, or rugged individualists for whom loneliness is an emblem of courage and determination. Trying to find ways to bridge gender boundaries, to form the connections and communities that are so important to social beings, transpeople often strain the sensibilities of those around us. But once people can look beyond surfaces, once they learn to see the qualities that make us who we are—both positive and negative, as all of us possess—not just the qualities they've learned to judge, which may be an incomplete complement of qualities, it's possible to let go of preconceptions and see valuable human beings.

When we change our sex, we may confuse, confound, frighten, disgust, and disappoint others, but we can also inspire. We live the dreams others are afraid to live, or perhaps even to dream. We carve out our willful destiny from the imprisonment of roles and bodies that are foreign or intolerable, or at best challenging to us. We may also be prisoners of war—the war between the sexes or the war over sexuality. Where others are praised for self-determination, we are subject to ridicule, even vilification. Are we supposed to feel guilty? Many of us do struggle with terrible guilt over just the act of saying who we are. How dare we take up so much social space by making ourselves a confrontation for others whose lives were just fine before we came along?

Physical Proof

Nothing gets media attention like genitals and gender mix-ups. When John Colapinto's book *As Nature Made Him: The Boy Who Was Raised as a Girl* was released, the entire hour of NBC's February 8, 2000, *Dateline*, where stories normally receive about one-third that time, was devoted to the story of David Reimer.

Reimer was one of identical twin boys whose penis was irreparably damaged when he was eight months old (in 1966) by a doctor's attempt to correct a problem with his foreskin. Faced with the appalling circumstance of genital mutilation, his parents were told there was nothing that could be done to restore their son's penis; that he couldn't possibly live a satisfying life as a man, but he could be made into a girl, in which case he would be able to live a normal life, though he would not be able to bear children. When a doctor gave them a sense of hope for their child's future, they trusted in that doctor's authority.

Reimer's case, long known in the medical literature as the "John/Joan" case (before Colapinto's story revealed Reimer's identity), is often conflated with intersex issues and experience. This is because Dr. John Money, a sexologist and one of the experts the Reimer family sought out, had long been consulting on intersex cases at Johns Hopkins Hospital, and had observed that in the majority of cases intersexed patients adapted well to the gender of assignment. As Colapinto's book describes, because it involved twin boys the Reimer case presented an irresistible opportunity to Money to prove something about the social construction of gender.

Here were the perfect test subject and control subject; here was a chance to demonstrate the pliability of gender identity in a child who was *not* intersexed. According to Money's reports on the case, treatment was proceeding with positive results until the patient was "lost to follow-up." "Lost to follow-up" meant that Money's theory of gender as a social and medical construction—that gender identity is consistent with the "sex of rearing"—had not been challenged. This is the theory that provides the psychomedical rationale for the surgical sex assignment of children born with ambiguous genitalia, and also for challenging transpeople's sense of themselves as belonging to the gender opposite their anatomic sex at birth. Money himself has written prolifically on sex and gender, and much of his work has been supportive of and helpful to transsexual people. He is a pioneer in the field of sexology, and like many pioneers, his body of work contains bold strides down paths that ultimately do not lead to desirable destinations. This should not invalidate everything he's ever written, but only time will tell how much of his work survives. His book *The Adam Principle* (1993) is representative of the scope of his work, though it is not his last publication. It was one of Money's own graduate students, Milton Diamond, now a professor of sexology at the University of Hawaii, who questioned Money's theory in the John/Joan case and pursued the quest that Colapinto records.

Readers of Money's reports in the 1980s were left to presume that all was well, but the truth was that at age fourteen Reimer had become suicidal and his parents were shaken to the core. Encouraged by some helping professionals who were close to the situation, the child's father finally, tearfully, explained to Brenda (the name they had chosen to raise him with) everything that had happened. After quietly listening to what must have been a stunning revelation, Brenda's one question—"What was my name?"—is indicative of the drive to be seen, to know that one is recognized by others, that one has an identity to which he or she can relate. He immediately renamed himself David in another act of self-determination. It was a statement that he was neither the girl they raised him to be, nor was he the same boy he had been at birth.

Clearly, David Reimer was not intersexed, but there are parallels between his story and the issues intersexed people face. Those issues are the right to be fully informed about their medical status and history, the right to be free of sexual surgeries imposed by others, and the right to be treated as a human being, rather than a set of unusual or "inadequate" reproductive organs to which the person is secondary. Reimer's story is not a story about intersex or transsexual experience directly, but it is a story that offers a pathway into understanding some of what intersex and transsexual people endure. Our diverse experiences have in common the issue of who has control over our bodies, and whether our sense of ourselves can prevail over what others want for or fear about us. Further, we share the issue of whether different (i.e., gender-variant, sex-variant, or ambiguous at birth or by choice) bodies can have social validity.

Because of what was done to David Reimer, he had a family dynamic and medical experience as a child that is emotionally and physically similar to that of many intersexed people and their families. Ironically, he also had a social experience that is closely parallel to that of many FTM transsexual people. As children, many future transmen are not capable of behaving the way other little girls do. We are teased and tormented by our classmates (and sometimes by our own families) because the masculine gender signals we express conflict with the feminine clothing we are forced to wear. Try as we might to please the adults around us or to be accepted by our peers, we are constantly aware of our inability to be who they want us to be. Eventually some of us find that we can live as men and come to feel at home in our bodies, though we are continually aware that our bodies are, in varying ways, different from those of other men. Reimer went through this and a lot more because he was also forced to go to annual evaluation sessions with Dr. Money, sessions he dreaded and despised. He had terrible problems in school. He had to deal with the collective family stress of the slowly unraveling social experiment of which they were all victims.

Once Reimer was allowed to express his own gender, more similarities arose between his treatment and that of FTMs. For example, testosterone would assist in masculinizing his body since doctors removed his testicles during infancy, eliminating his ability to produce testosterone. Surgeons could only offer him the same phalloplasty surgeries that are available for FTM penis construction. Since his glans and erectile tissues were ablated, metoidioplasty was not an option for him, as it is also not a viable option for some FTMs who do not experience sufficient clitoral growth with testosterone therapy. In Reimer's FTM-related odyssey, though, his one good fortune was that he had tangible proof of his maleness. His own parents and his medical records contained the memory of his genitally defined natal sex that could justify his feeling that he had been living a lie as a girl.

Colapinto and Reimer landed on the February 9, 2000 *Oprah* to promote the book. Producers arranged for transsexual people to appear as well, presumably because there were genital and gender issues in common, though the oversimplification of the correlations the show drew contribute to the invisibility of the harm caused by medical and social treatment of intersexed people, and the invisibility of FTM people. The transsexual people *Oprah*'s producers invited were Dana Rivers, a Sacramento, California high school teacher who lost her job because of her transition from male to female, and another accomplished transsexual woman, university professor Deirdre McCloskey, author of *Crossing. A Memoir,* who appeared in taped footage. Rivers pointed out that the childhood feeling of being in the wrong body was common to both her and Reimer's experience. The show's point was that you can't make somebody be what they're not, which is what transsexual people say, too. But why use MTFs to tell an FTM story? Certainly MTF people are easier to find, but I suspect it's also because non-trans people don't see Reimer's experience as a social, female-to-male transition story: they see it as a penis story. He lost his penis and had to get it back. Rivers and McCloskey had penises and chose to give them up. The crucial factor for most non-trans observers of any gender-variant experience is the body, and their projections about their own corporal wholeness. The story became one of identity and its relationship to a penis, not a story of medical error or arrogance and authority over gender.

Colapinto reinforced the concept that "the inner sense of self as male or female is so overridingly strong that even though people struggle along trying to be [what others tell them], eventually they hit that critical point which they cannot move beyond where they have to make a change somehow or they will kill themselves." That statement helps to tie the result of the Reimer accident and the medical attempt at correction together with the desperation that often accompanies a transsexual person's request for treatment. It's a pretty dramatic statement, and certainly some transsexual people feel they have no reason to live if they cannot transition, but many don't feel that way. It's also a statement that takes away from the issues faced by intersexed people, and avoids the issues of medical authority over the bodies of others who are labeled different.

Any transsexual person can tell you that no matter how much social pressure is applied, one's gender identity can't be changed by forced social performance. Oprah asked Colapinto "What was for you, John, the most disturbing thing you uncovered while doing this?" (That is, while researching his book about Reimer's childhood.) Colapinto replied, "I think the most disturbing thing was the image of a child trying to get the world to hear who he really was, and the effort to try to make psychologists and psychiatrists understand what he was feeling, and his inability to do so. That's extremely disturbing." The same effort to express who they really are is common to transsexual people who don't share Reimer's horrific circumstance. What Colapinto uncovered was his own ability to empathize with someone whose identity is denied.

However, it's still that tangible proof in the body—that particular concrete, visible realness—that people rely on so thoroughly. The fact that he had once had a penis is all the reason needed for the general public to support Reimer's feeling that he should have one now.

It's interesting that it's considered ethical by some physicians to perform genital surgery on infants who can't give informed consent, but unethical to perform genital surgery on adults who are very clear about their gender variance and their need to address it with sex reassignment or gender confirmation surgery. Some people regard intersex surgery as corrective, and transsexual surgery as mutilation.

Mutilation is what happened to David Reimer, and it required some corrective surgery. Mutilation is what happens to some intersexed infants, too, though doctors construe it as necessary. Mutilation can happen to some transsexual people, too, when they are forced to seek unorthodox or economical treatments and fall prey to unethical practitioners. But in the 1990s, intersexed people, who are most dramatically and painfully affected by theories of sexual differentiation and medical decisions about the social viability of different bodies, began to speak out. Now many people rally behind the innocence of the child and the frequently damaging consequences of early surgical intervention when doctors and parents are desperate for a clearly sexed or clearly sex-able child. Is it true that we can envision tolerating ambiguity in infants and allowing, even championing, these children to participate in their own gender/sex definition based upon their own experience and sense of self, but we cannot tolerate this in children, adolescents, or adults who have no recognizable physical anomaly? For that is the difference here: physical proof, something society can see or otherwise connect with the prevailing theories about maleness and femaleness of the body. Without this concreteness, the general public still may not accept the reality of a person's experience of her or his own body or gender difference.

Self-determination

The euphoric state that many transsexual people experience in early transition, and which often lasts or recurs over a period of years, is usually nourished by a multitude of situational factors. Most obvious is that we have found the courage to say how we feel or what we want for ourselves. What psychologists or psychiatrists hope to help their clients determine prior to medical treatment is whether our declaration about our gender identity is survivable through transition, or whether that declaration is a misguided attempt to terminate desperation and confusion brought on by other problems such as organic depression, misogyny or misanthropy, delusional fantasies, low self-esteem, homophobia, or multiple personality or other psychological disorders. Once we have begun hormone treatment, the power of these biochemical substances plunge us into adolescence, creating or recreating all the transitional mood swings, confusion, timidity, and bravado that society expects in teenagers but has no way of interpreting or accommodating in adult behavior. There is also the inevitable fascination with our physical body as it changes right before our eyes into something to which we finally feel connected and of which we want to be proud. We may also share a sense of freedom in wearing clothing of choice, the ability to experience psychologically satisfying sexual interaction for the first time, being recognized at last as a member of the gender category in which we feel most comfortable, and the sense of doing something for ourselves rather than always trying to please others.

It is this euphoria, self-interest, or self-satisfaction that leads others to criticize us for being horribly self-centered. Many of us have spent much of our pre-transition lives trying to please others in order to fit in, or to compensate for our own internalized sense of incompleteness or inappropriateness, so accusations of self-centeredness seem doubly wounding, surrounded as we are in the U.S. with meta-messages about the positive ramifications of self-indulgence. The non-trans general public hears *Be all you can be,* but transpeople hear, "How could you do this to me?" *Indulge yourself.* "You only think about yourself." *Take your time; get away; enjoy; make the most of your life.* "How could you be so selfish?" *Live free or die.* "How could you? How *could* you?" Indignation, disgust, contempt, or disappointment burst through these simple words. They are intended as a slap across the face, a punch to the vital organs.

It is difficult enough to find the fortitude to take on real self-determination when one has the advantages of education and access to various resources. The situation for transpeople who are socially and economically disadvantaged is often severe. Racial and class prejudice and adverse treatment are serious social problems that are exacerbated by transgender or transsexual behavior or characteristics. Well-educated, middle class transpeople are not exempt from anti-trans prejudice, and more than a few middle class, educated transpeople of all races have turned to prostitution for survival when they have been discarded by their families as teenagers or, as adults, lost their jobs and could not find other work in the professions for which they have trained. I am convinced there are thousands of transsexual people living in legal and emotional limbo in the world today simply because they cannot afford to have surgery, no matter the color of their skin or the extent of their education. This limbo creates vulnerability, as transpeople who remain gender-incongruent or who try to survive in criminal environments are easy targets of violence. In fact, known murders of transpeople go across racial and class lines and have averaged over one murder per month in the U.S. throughout the 1990s, occurring in 29 states and the District of Columbia (see the Remembering Our Dead Project website, *www.gender.org/remember/*).

When I was about six months into transition, I saw one of those "help the starving children" ads on television and I was struck by how selfish it seemed that I should be so concerned with something so simultaneously mundane and ethereal, so ubiquitous and so completely private as my gender. When I considered the resources I was applying to changing my body while people were out there dying for lack of simple food and water, while the environment was under siege by corporate greed, while the threat of nuclear annihilation still looms over us all, I was embarrassed. However, even now Colapinto's words come back to me: "I think the most disturbing thing was the image of a child trying to get the world to hear who he really was, . . . and his inability to do so. That's extremely disturbing."

It is also disturbing that to date, in the U.S., we have no reliable, definitive statistics concerning etiology, prognosis, treatment modalities, outcomes, social situations, or any other demographics that we can use to scientifically or morally refute any adverse bias held by policy makers, litigators, journalists, service providers, or those who find us objectionable on religious grounds. All we have is our determination, our willfulness, our intelligence, our compassion, our martyred, and our allies. Certainly we can point to a few professional papers concerning safety in hormone use (Gooren, 1999) and generalizations about treatment outcomes (Carroll, 1999), but when legislators ask us how many people in their jurisdictions will be affected by legislation to protect the employment or housing rights of transsexual people, or when policy-makers ask how many people will be affected by removing exclusions of medical care for transsexual people from insurance policies, we cannot answer them. All we can say is, "Look at me! What about me? What about my rights? Ain't I a taxpayer? Wouldn't I be one if I could?" And even where we have statistics, such as in San Francisco, where only twelve out of roughly twenty-seven thousand city employees (San Francisco Human Rights Commission, 1997) would be affected by the removal of insurance exclusions, the numbers are used against us. When such a small number would logically mitigate the potential expense, we are told instead that there are not enough of us to warrant the effort and expense of offering services when there are many more people affected by other conditions that are either also not covered or deemed more socially acceptable and which therefore should receive priority. In the 2001 legislative session, two bills were headed for the California governor's desk. One expanded the rights of domestic partners; the other extended non-discrimination protections in employment and housing to trans and gender-variant people, providing a mechanism for complaint resolution for those feeling they had been discriminated against due to gender identity or expression. An aide to the governor told us that he would only sign one "gay" bill that year, and he would veto ours if he had to choose between the two. When I related this to an educator friend, she asked me, "Which one would you want him to sign?" I told her, "I don't think civil rights are in such short supply that they have to be meted out a little bit at a time." Governor Gray Davis signed a later version of this measure into law on August 2, 2003.

When facing those who object to transsexual treatments or oppose our efforts to achieve equal access to the benefits of society, this salient question remains: how do we argue with a feeling? (Kaminer, 2000). I think we must start with the feelings inside ourselves.

Self-disparagement is common among transgendered and transsexual people. Granted, there is a certain strength that minorities achieve in creating their own language and a provocative humor that creates an insider mentality from outsider status. Acerbic drag queen humor is a clear example. But in the transsexual world, too often the humor is missing. I'll never forget being on a panel speaking to healthcare outreach workers in 1993 with several transsexual women, and the first woman introduced herself by saying, "Good morning, my name is . . . , and I'm a sex change." Her words were like shattering glass. It stunned me that she would speak of herself, and by extension the rest of us, in that dehumanized way. I don't think she was aware of it in that way, though; she was very beautiful, and the statement may have been intended to shock our audience, but for me it wasn't an effective bridge to our common humanity. In a workshop on relationships at the 1997 FTM conference held in Boston, it pained me greatly to hear man after man from across the U.S. confess his sense of inadequacy and his fear of being compared with "genetic men" or "bio-men." Hearing those phrases over and over, I was compelled to stop the discussion and ask them to listen to their words and realize how much they were taking away from themselves by denying their own reality, their own humanness, and their right to exist with difference from other men. I encouraged them to stop belittling themselves by using this language, and suggested they use "non-transsexual" as the comparative term, placing the lack in the camp of the other, not in ourselves. Because we are real, we are genetic, even though we don't know what causes transsexualism, and even though our bodies are different from those of non-transsexual men. Transmen and transwomen are human beings with needs in relation to other human beings. If we are concerned that others will perceive our physical differences as laughable deficiencies, the answer is not to dehumanize and desensitize ourselves so we can manage rejection, but to sensitize others to appreciate us, and to learn to manage our own self-doubts so that others will be able to see worthy partners in us. It is not that we shouldn't face our differences or pretend we don't have fears or doubts, but that we must not accept the mythology or the rumors that others circulate about us: that we are not real, that we are less than real, or that we are imitation people, trying to be something we are not.

Validity

Who gets to decide who or what anyone is? In modern, Western society, medicine and the law cooperate to validate or invalidate the worth of human beings. That doctors have a lot of authority over gender-variant lives already should be apparent, but people don't often think how important legal procedures and judgments are in confirming identities, trans or non-trans. It seems whenever a transsexual person is party to a lawsuit brought to decide whether that transsexual person has legal standing or entitlement (for instance, the right to inherit property from a spouse, or the right to use a public restroom, or parental rights), the opposing attorney cannot resist using anti-transsexual bias as leverage to discredit them. Cases that are heard in higher courts in Western countries often revolve around the notion that transsexual people, because of their gender variance, are not entitled to equal treatment under the law. Such cases frequently concern employment discrimination, but transsexual and transgendered people also turn up in immigration cases and family law cases. Many disputes turn on the validity of a contracted marriage, and thus lead to the question of who is entitled to enter into marriage contracts. Transsexual men have recently achieved important victories in the area of family law: *Vecchione v. Vecchione*, an unreported California case (see Pfeifer, 1997), validated the marriage of a post-operative transsexual man and went on to disregard his transsexualism in resolving the divorce and child custody matter at bar. *Kantaras v. Kantaras* (Circuit Court of the Sixth Judicial Circuit; Pasco County, Florida; February 19, 2003) was a crucial victory for transsexual people because the judge's conclusions of law recognizes, "Chromosomes are only one factor in the determination of sex and they do not overrule gender or self identity, which is the true test or identifying mark of sex." The decision also notes, "The marriage law of Florida clearly provides that marriage shall take place between one man and one woman. It does not provide when such a status of being a man or a woman shall be determined. The statute does provide that the state has a compelling interest in 'promoting' not only marriage but also responsible parenting. . . . The gender of a person at birth as evidenced by a birth certificate may be relevant, but it is not by law dispositive. There is a presumption of correctness for most purposes, but it is a rebuttable presumption in the face of medical evidence. . . . For the purpose of ascertaining the legal validity of a marriage between two adults of the opposite gender the question whether a person is a man or a woman should be determined as of the date of the application for the license because that is the critical time, and not later than the date of marriage. . . . There is no rule of law or medical basis that requires the circumstances at the time of birth to be the sole factor to determine qualification for a license to marry because there are so many medical variables between birth and a fully grown adult over some 18 years[,] and it [is] on adults the obligation of marriage is placed, particularly, if there are to be children of the marriage." That there were children involved in both the *Vecchione* and *Kantaras* cases, and particularly that the children in both cases were deemed best served by maintaining their relationships with their fathers, distinguishes these cases from those involving fathers becoming women or transsexual people's claims to money such as inheritance or back wages, in which transsexual people are frequently rebuffed due to assumptions concerning legitimacy. Similarly, a marriage in Australia between a transman and his wife was determined to be valid in 2001, and reconfirmed on appeal in 2003. Another important decision for all LGBT people came from the Ontario Court of Appeal, when on June 10, 2003, this Canadian court redefined marriage as the "voluntary union for life of two persons," providing a model of real commitment to equality by eliminating the effects of gender bias from the landscape of marriage. The Bush administration and the Vatican have both reacted strongly against this perceived threat to their understanding of moral order. I am certain we are headed for a showdown between the dogma of civil equality and the dogma of particular forms of faith, a drama in which transpeople will undoubtedly have a part to play. It is my understanding that the U.S. Constitution provides for the separation of church and state, and no citizen should be denied the ability to make an emotional and economic commitment to another person (regardless of sex or gender) or the right to have that relationship treated equally under the law. Certainly churches should have the right to choose not to honor particular marriages, but I believe history will one day find spiritually bereft those churches that deny marriage to some of their faithful.

There have been other favorable court decisions in recent years, many of which flow from the U.S. Supreme Court's 1989 interpretation of the Civil Rights Act of 1964 in *Price Waterhouse v. Hopkins*, holding that harassment directed at a person because that person does not conform to traditional sex stereotypes is covered under Title VII of that act. Since 1999, decisions in the 1st, 2nd, 3rd, 7th, 8th, as well as the expectedly liberal 9th Federal Circuit Courts have been favorable toward plaintiffs who do not conform to stereotypical gender roles, gender norms, or expected sex characteristics. District courts, too, in many states, have reached similar conclusions under Title VII (employment) and Title IX (education) in cases involving gender-variant and transsexual plaintiffs. Additional protections have been found for transgender and transsexual people in state sex discrimination and disability discrimination provisions. See the online resources offered by the Transgender Law and Policy Institute (*www.transgenderlaw.org/*) for documentation of all cases cited, and many more cases that have to do with transwomen, which have not always been as favorable as those concerning transmen, as well as for additional resources on legal topics such as changing identity documents in all fifty U.S. states, various employer policies, texts of hate crime laws, etc.

The concerted effort of many attorneys, legal scholars, politicians, administrators, social scientists, transsexual and transgender activists, and medical professionals to develop and advocate the lines of reasoning and to provide substantiating evidence have led to these favorable rulings, and the establishment of favorable administrative policies in businesses, schools, and governmental institutions. It has been my privilege to work with some of the brightest legal minds in the English-speaking world in helping to develop the scholarship, legislation, policies, litigation strategies, and *amicus* briefs to move these issues forward. Sometimes we win, sometimes we lose, but the scales are slowly tipping in the direction of human equality, and decisions like these matter greatly in the long-range effort to establish the validity of transsexual lives.

Transsexual people are everywhere: in corporate board rooms; in prisons; in academia; on HIV wards in hospitals; on factory floors; preaching from pulpits; litigating in courtrooms; working as nurses, artists, managers, research scientists, sex workers, software engineers, architects; sitting near you on an airplane or in a movie theater; and riding the subway. We are in schools as students and as teachers or administrators. Some of us are very old, some are very young, most are everywhere in between. Some are attractive, beautiful, handsome; some are average; some are unattractive; we are all human beings.

Even if we have all the outward trappings of privilege: gender-normative appearance, a good job, a family that accepts or even loves us, a partner, economic stability, an ordinary life, even though we may rarely think about our transsexual status, it never goes away. It is always with us. As long as the legal system debates our status while relying on the medical system to define us, we do not have the same autonomy as non-transsexual people. Once our transsexual status is known, our health or life insurance may be revoked, our jobs may be terminated, our families may be left without the benefit of our support, we may lose custody of or contact with our children, and we may be subjected to embarrassment, public humiliation, and physical harm. It's no wonder that many transsexual people want to believe that once they've gone through their transition it is all over and done with, that they are now "really" the man or woman they feel they are. And so they are! But only until someone with greater social authority or brute strength takes away their ability to self-define.

How do we argue with our own internalized transphobia and shame? As with any aspect of life that requires change or adjustment, we weigh the alternatives. We think as logically as we can about what is good for us as individuals and as contributors to our immediate social group, family, or extended family, and to our larger social groups such as employers or student bodies. Like athletes visualizing a winning performance, we visualize scenarios in which we have one kind of persona, or wardrobe, or image, or body, or another, one gender presentation or another, or several as the case may be. We agonize over consequences, and eventually we make a decision with which we are willing to live. Over our lifetime, we may make many of these kinds of decisions, whether they are about our career, our relationships, or our gender presentation. We study ourselves in the mirror, and whether we are elated, disappointed, or just introspective, we cannot deny that at some fundamental level we also stare directly into the face of fear, loneliness, and economic or emotional disaster as we debate the potential consequences of our actions.

Why should a gender quest be any less serious or meaningful than a spiritual quest? Is it because it has to do with genitals and sexuality and therefore it is assumed to be base or superficial? Is that why it looks so self-indulgent, like a kind of masturbation? Is that why Oprah presents David Reimer's story as a penis story, to hook an audience that has not yet learned to see beyond the body?

A gender quest is, in fact, a kind of spiritual quest. It is our willful destiny to find that balance, that strength, that peace and logic of the soul that underlies the agony, the frustration, the desperation and anxiety of living on this earthly plane. Naming ourselves is a manifestation of that quest. When David Reimer named himself, he took a step toward that balance. When, at age fifteen, I changed my name to Jamison, and started going by Jamie (because it was cute, safe, and androgynous), it was a way of beginning to define and claim myself. Likewise, twenty-five years later, when I claimed my body and asserted myself as physically male, it was another step along the path toward my own maturity and spiritual peace. It was another few years before I dropped Jamie in favor of the more solid nickname, James. Each step along the way brought me closer to my own center; each candle I lit in the cave of my own fear brought me clarity and stability.

We are living in an era of rapid, astounding change. It is no wonder that some people cling to belief structures and concepts that comfort them: that there are only two sexes; that marriage should only be between a man and a woman; that sexual activity should only occur in a reproductive context, i.e., between a male and a female; that gender identity and expression should align with genital configuration; that we should be able to tell what sex someone is; that transsexualism is never a medical condition, but always a psychotic delusion; that transgender or transsexual identity is nothing more than a sense of cosmetic discomfort equivalent to unhappiness with an ugly nose or cellulite, or a twisted form of sexual attraction that requires the self to become the other, or some such convoluted theory that may indeed fit some unfortunate individuals but does severe injustice to the majority of transpeople. These presumptions are as offensive and ridiculous as beliefs that women are less intelligent or capable than men, or that people of color are less intelligent or capable than whites. Asking the simple question, "Why?" is often enough to expose these presumptions in the face of statements to these effects, but what we get in response is often something on the order of, "Because I said so," or citations of biblical scripture that conflate transness with sodomy, legal precedents from uninformed decisions based on badly argued cases, or medical opinion abstracted from decades-old texts and pop-science clichés. Unfortunately, legislative and judicial bodies are often so stymied by such arguments that they throw up their hands in frustration and let the *status quo* prevail.

Change is inevitable. For me, becoming a visible man has enabled me to find my emotional center and get in touch with my physical body, to establish boundaries that support my values, and to commit myself to creating meaningful social change that will make a positive difference for as many people as possible. Becoming a visible man has meant knowing that the aspects of myself that remain invisible to most people are just as important as the aspects that others see. All people have visible and invisible aspects—we will never see all of a person or know everything he or she has to offer. We project, we imagine, we suspect, we judge constantly. In spite of this, I hold a vision of community that moves toward a world without shame or fear of difference, a world in which people are not afraid of other people's identities or beliefs. That vision of community calls us to be conscious about the way we value human beings.

Just like anyone else, when transsexual people lie down at night and shut our eyes, helpless in sleep and vulnerable as infants, whether we have someone's arms around us or whether we are all alone, we know that all we have to live for is to be the best version of our most authentic self that we can possibly be. Through our introspection and experimentation we can come to realize how very like others we are. We can come to accept the mysterious, the feared and misunderstood aspects of ourselves, to appreciate the whole self, to recognize our differences and similarities, to rid ourselves of anxiety concerning sexuality, to understand the body as a vessel of the spirit in an intrinsic way. For some observers, our journey seems a step outside the boundaries of society; for us, once we have arrived at our own balance point—no matter what that looks like to others—we can recognize our humanity and understand our connections to other people. Though others may persist in excluding or tormenting us, and though we may be driven initially by anger or eventually by compassion, once we find that balance point of self-acceptance we can experience an inner shift toward a kind of peace. The beacon of that inner peace living in each of us enables transpeople to endure, and once we bring it to the forefront of our lives, the resulting self-assurance will eventually speak to and calm the fears of others.

Bibliography

Articles and Books

Allen, M.P. (2003). *The Gender Frontier*. Heidelberg, Kehrer Verlag.

Alter, G.J., and Ehrlich, R. (1999). "A New Technique for Correction of the Hidden Penis in Adults and Children." *Journal of Urology*, 161:455.

Bergstedt, S. (1997). *Translegalities: A Legal Guide for FTMs*. Seattle, Wash.: Spencer Bergstedt, Attorney At Law. *www.spencelaw.com/book/htm*.

Bloom, A. (1994). "The Body Lies." *The New Yorker*. 38–49. July 18.

———. (2002). *Normal: Transsexual CEOs, Crossdressing Cops, and Hermaphrodites with Attitude*. New York: Random House.

Bornstein, K. (1994). *Gender Outlaw: On Men, Women, and the Rest of Us*. New York: Routledge.

Brown, M.L. and Rounsley, C.A. (1996). *True Selves: Understanding Transsexualism for Families, Friends, Coworkers, and Helping Professionals*. San Francisco: Jossey-Bass Publishers.

Burke, P. (1996). *Gender Shock: Exploding the Myths of Male and Female*. New York: Anchor Books.

Butler, J. (1990). *Gender Trouble: Feminism and the Subversion of Identity*. New York: Routledge.

Califia, P. (1994). *Public Sex: The Culture of Radical Sex*. San Francisco: Cleis Press.

———. (1997). *Sex Changes: The Politics of Transgenderism*. San Francisco: Cleis Press.

Cameron, L. (1996). *Body Alchemy: Transsexual Portraits*. San Francisco: Cleis Press.

————. (2001). *Man Tool: The Nuts & Bolts of Female-To-Male Surgery.* E-book: *www.lorencameron.com.*

Carroll, R.A. (1999). "Outcomes of Treatment for Gender Dysphoria" in *Journal of Sex Education and Therapy,* vol. 24, no. 3.128–36.

Colapinto, J. (2000). *As Nature Made Him: The Boy Who Was Raised as a Girl.* New York: HarperCollins.

Cromwell, J. (1999). *Transmen & FTMs: Identities, Bodies, Genders, and Sexualities.* Chicago: University of Illinois Press.

Dekker, R.M, & Van der Pol, L.C. (1989). *The Tradition of Female Transvestism in Early Modern Europe.* London: Macmillan Press.

Denny, D. (1994). *Identity Management in Transsexualism: A Practical Guide to Managing Identity on Paper.* King of Prussia, Pa.: Creative Design Services.

————. (1998). *Current Concepts in Transgender Identity.* New York and London: Garland Publishing, Inc.

Devor, H. (1997). *FTM: Female-to-Male Transsexuals in Society.* Bloomington: Indiana University Press.

Doyle, J.A. and Paludi, M.A. (1998). *Sex & Gender: The Human Experience.* Boston: McGraw-Hill.

Dreger, A.D. (1998). *Hermaphrodites and the Medical Invention of Sex.* Cambridge and London: Harvard University Press.

————. (1999). *Intersex in the Age of Ethics.* Hagerstown, Md.: University Publishing Group.

Ettner, R. (1996). *Confessions of a Gender Defender: A Psychologist's Reflections on Life Among the Transgendered.* Evanston, Ill.: Chicago Spectrum Press.

Ettner, R. (1999). *Gender Loving Care: A Guide to Counseling Gender-Variant Clients.* New York: W.W. Norton.

Evelyn, J. (1998). . . . *Mom, I need to be a girl.* Imperial Beach, CA: Walter Trook Publishing.

Fagan, P.J., Schmidt, C.W., and Wise, T.N. (1994). Letters to the editor. *The New Yorker.* August 22 and 29.

Fausto-Sterling, A. (1985). *Myths of Gender: Biological Theories about Women and Men.* New York: BasicBooks.

Feinberg, L. (1992). *Trans Gender Liberation: A Movement Whose Time Has Come.* New York: World View Publishers.

————. (1993). *Stone Butch Blues.* New York: Firebrand Books.

————. (1996). *Transgender Warriors: Making History from Joan of Arc to RuPaul.* Boston: Beacon Press.

Gamson, J. (1998). *Freaks Talk Back: Tabloid Talk Shows and Sexual Non-conformity.* Chicago and London: University of Chicago Press.

Gillies, H., and Harrison, R.J. (1948). "Congenital absence of the penis with embryological considerations." *British Journal of Plastic Surgery,* vol. 1, no. 8.

Gooren, L.J.G. (1999). "Hormonal Sex Reassignment." *International Journal of Transgenderism,* vol. 3, no. 3. *www.symposion.com/ijt990301.htm.*

Gorney, C. (1994). "A Sex Change Odyssey." *Harper's Bazaar.* 406. September.

Graves, J.A. (2001). "From brain determination to testis determination: evolution of the mammalian sex-determining gene." *Reproduction, Fertility and Development,* 13(7–8). 665–72.

Green, J. (1994). *Report on Discrimination Against Transgendered People.* San Francisco Human Rights Commission.

Green, R. (1974). *Sexual Identity Conflict in Children and Adults.* New York: Basic Books, Inc.

Greenberg, J.A. (1999). *Defining Male and Female: Intersexuality and the Collision Between Law and Biology.* Tucson: Arizona Law Review, v01.41, n0.2.

Groopman, J. (2002). "Hormones for Men: Is male menopause a question of medicine or marketing?" *The New Yorker.* 34–38. July 29.

Hage, J.J. (1992). *From Peniplastica Totalis to Reassignment Surgery of the External Genitalia in Female-to-Male Transsexuals.* Amsterdam: VU University Press.

Hage, J.J., Bloem, J.J.A.M., and Suliman, H.M. (1993). "Review of the Literature on Techniques for Phalloplasty with Emphasis on the Applicability in Female-to-Male Transsexuals." *The Journal of Urology,* vol. 150. 1093–98.

Halberstam, J. (1994). "F2M: The Making of Female Masculinity," in *The Lesbian Postmodern,* ed. Laura Doan. New York: Columbia University Press. Revised and updated in 1998 as "Transgender Butch: Butch/FTM Border Wars and the Masculine Continuum," in *GLQ: A Journal of Lesbian and Gay Studies:* vol. 4, no. 2. Durham, N.C.: Duke University Press.

Hausman, B.L. (1995). *Changing Sex: Transsexualism, Technology, and the Idea of Gender.* Durham, N.C., and London: Duke University Press.

Haynes, F. and McKenna, T. (2001). *Unseen Genders: Beyond the Binaries.* New York: Peter Lang.

Hernandez, M. (1994). "Packing, Passing & Pissing" in *Dagger: On Butch Women*, ed. Roxxie, et al. Pittsburgh: Cleis Press.

————. (1996). "Sex and the New Man: The Taboos" in *FTM Newsletter*. San Francisco: FTM International, Inc. Autumn.

————. (1997). "Sex and the New Man: Part II" in *FTM Newsletter*, Issue #38.San Francisco: FTM International, Inc. August.

Howey, N. and Samuels, E. (2000). *Out of the Ordinary: Essays on Growing Up with Gay, Lesbian, and Transgender Parents*. New York: St. Martin's Press.

Hubbard, R. (1998). "Gender and Genitals: Constructs of Sex and Gender" in *Current Concepts in Transgender Identity*, ed. D. Denny. New York and London: Garland Publishing, Inc.

Jennings, K. (2003). *Always My Child: A Parent's Guide to Understanding Your Gay, Lesbian, Bisexual, Transgendered or Questioning Son or Daughter*. New York: Simon & Schuster.

Kaminer, W. (2000). "Gay Rites." *The American Prospect*, vol. 11, no. 8. February 28. *www.prospect.org/print/V11/8/kaminer.w.html*.

Kessler, S.J. (1998). *Lessons from the Intersexed*. New Brunswick, N.J.: Rutgers University Press.

Kessler, S.J., and McKenna, W. (1978). *Gender: An Ethnomethodological Approach*. Chicago: University of Chicago Press.

Koskovich, G. (2002), ed. *OutWord Online*, monthy e-mail newsletter of the Lesbian and Gay Aging Issues Network. May 2002 issue: *www.asaging.org/lgain* from the American Society on Aging.

Kotula, D. (2002). *The Phallus Palace: Female to Male Transsexuals*. Los Angeles: Alyson Publications.

Kupers, T.A. (1993). *Revisioning Men's Lives*. New York: The Guilford Press.

Lothstein, L.M. (1983). *Female-to-Male Transsexualism: Historical, Clinical and Theoretical Issues*. Boston, London, Melbourne and Henley: Routledge & Kegan Paul.

Marini, R.A. (2003). "New, Improved You: Plastic surgery is no longer the domain of the girls' club." *American Way Magazine*. 38–43. January.

Meyer III, W. (Chairperson), Bockting, W., Cohen-Kettenis, P., Coleman, E., DiCeglie, D., Devor, H. Gooren, L. Hage, J.J., Kirk, S., Kuiper, B., Laub, D., Lawrence, A., Menard, Y., Patton, J., Schaefer, L., Webb, A., and Wheeler, C. (2001). Harry Benjamin International Gender Dsyphoria Association Standards of Care, 6th Version. Düsseldorf: Symposion Publishing.

Meyerowitz, J. (2002). *How Sex Changed: A History of Transsexualism in the United States*. Cambridge and London: Harvard University Press.

Middlebrook, D.W. (1997). *Suits Me: The Double Life of Billy Tipton*. New York: Houghton-Mifflin.

Money, J. (1993). *The Adam Principle. Genes, Genitals, Hormones, & Gender Identity: Selected Readings in Sexology*. Buffalo, N.Y.: Prometheus Books.

More, K., and Whittle, S. (1999). *Reclaiming Genders: Transsexual Grammars at the Fin de Siècle*. London and New York: Cassell.

Morton, S. (1997). "Kweer Korner" in *FTM Newsletter*, Issue #36. San Francisco, FTM International, Inc. March.

Munt, S.R. (1998). *Heroic Desire: Lesbian Identity and Cultural Space*. New York: New York University Press.

Namaste, V.K. (2000). *Invisible Lives: The Erasure of Transsexual and Transgendered People*. Chicago and London: University of Chicago Press.

Nataf, Z.I. (1996). *Lesbians Talk Transgender*. London: Scarlet Press.

Pfeifer, S. (1997). "Transsexual Can Sue for Custody" in the *Orange County Register*. B1. November 26, 1997.

PFLAG, T-Net. *Our Trans Children. www.pflag.org*.

Prosser, J. (1998). *Second Skins: The Body Narratives of Transsexuality*. New York: Columbia University Press.

Raymond, J.G. (1994). *The Transsexual Empire: The Making of the She-Male*. New York: Teachers College Press.

Roughgarden, J. (2004). *Evolution's Rainbow: Diversity, Gender and Sexuality in Nature and People*. Berkeley: University of California Press.

Roxxie, Burana, L., Due, L. (1994). *Dagger: On Butch Women*. Pittsburgh: Cleis Press.

Rubin, G.S. (1992). "Of Catamites and Kings: Reflections on Butch, Gender, and Boundaries" *Persistent Desire: A Butch-Femme Reader*, ed. J. Nestle. Boston: Alyson.

————. (1993). "Thinking Sex: Notes for a Radical Theory of the Politics of Sexuality" in *The Lesbian and Gay Studies Reader*, ed. Abelove, et al. New York and London: Routledge.

Rahman, S.A. (2003). "Transplant Makes History." Courier Mail, Queensland, Australia. World section, page 10. February 25.

San Francisco Human Rights Commission (October 1997). "Insurance Coverage for Transsexual Employees of the City and County of San Francisco."

Scholinski, D. (1997). *The Last Time I Wore a Dress*. New York: Riverhead Books.

Self, W., and Gamble, D. (2000). *Perfidious Man*. London: Viking.

Silver, R.I. (2000). "Micropenis" in *5 Minute Urology Consult*, ed. L. Gomella. Baltimore: Williams and Wilkins.

Stoller, R.J. (1968). *Sex and Gender: On the Development of Masculinity and Femininity*, vol. 1. New York: Science House.

————. (1972). "Etiological Factors in Female Transsexualism: A First Approximation." *Archives of Sexual Behavior*, 2(1). 47–64.

————. (1975). *Sex and Gender: The transsexual experiment*, vol 2. New York: Science House.

————. (1982). Transvestism in Women. *Archives of Sexual Behavior*, 11(2). 99–115.

Stone, S. (1991). "The Empire Strikes Back: A posttranssexual manifesto" in *Body Guards: The cultural politics of gender ambiguity*, ed. J. Epstein and K. Straub. New York: Routledge. 280–304.

Tanagho, E.A. and McAninch, J.W. (1992). *Smith's General Urology: thirteenth edition*. Norwalk, CT and San Mateo, CA: Appleton & Lange. Specific reference is made to Conte, F.A., and Grumbach, M.M., MDs, "Abnormalities of Sexual Differentiation." 629–57.

Thompson, C.J.S. (1974). *The Mysteries of Sex: Women Who Posed as Men and Men Who Impersonated Women*. New York: Causeway Books.

Volcano, D.L.G. and Halberstam, J. (1999). *The Drag King Book*. London: Serpent's Tail.

Von Mahlsdorf, C. (1995). *I Am My Own Woman*, trans. Jean Hollander. San Francisco: Cleis Press.

Westphal, S.P. (2002). "Personal body part grown in a dish." *New Scientist*, vol. 175, issue 2360. September 14.

Wheelright, J. (1989). *Amazons and Military Maids: Women Who Dressed as Men in Pursuit of Life, Liberty and Happiness*. London: Pandora Press.

Whittle, S. (2002). *Respect and Equality: Transsexual and Transgender Rights*. London: Cavendish Publishing Limited.

Young, A. (2000). *Women Who Become Men: Albanian Sworn Virgins*. Oxford: Berg.

Yusefi, M. (2000). "A Mother Takes on the Ayatollah." *The Gully*. *www.thegully.com/essays/iran/001113ayatollah.html*.

Films

The Blank Point: What is Transsexualism? (1991) Xiao-Yen Wang. Beijing-San Francisco Film Company.
Body Chemistry: Hormone Heaven. (1999). BBC documentary, Channel 4.
A Boy Named Sue. (2000). Julie Wyman.
Boys Don't Cry. (1999). Kimberly Peirce.
The Brandon Teena Story. (1997). Susan Muska and Gréta Ólafsdottir.
Changing Sexes–Female-to-Male. (2003). Film Garden Entertainment; Discovery Channel.
I Am My Own Woman. (1992). Rosa Von Praunheim (Germany).
Investigative Reports: Transgender Revolution. (1998). A&E Television Network.
Kate Bornstein: Adventures in the Gender Trade. (1993). Susan Marenco and Jay Mason. Filmmakers Library, Inc., NY.
Linda, Les & Annie. (1989). Annie Sprinkle.
Ma Vie en Rose. (1997). Alain Berliner (Belgium).
Men Like Me. (1994). Silvie Shaw (Australia).
The Opposite Sex: Rene's Story. (2003). Josh Aronson. Hensel-Krasnow Productions.
Transexual Menace. (1996). Rosa Von Praunheim (Germany).
Trappings of Transhood. (1997). Elise Hurwitz and Christopher Lee.
What Sex Am I? (1984). Joseph Fevry Productions. MPI Home Video: Oak Forest, IL.
You Don't Know Dick: Courageous Hearts of Transsexual Men. (1997). Candace Schermerhorn and Bestor Cram. Northern Light Productions: Boston.

Illustrated Books in Spanish

Cameron, L. (2004). *Cameron: Volume 1* (FTM). Santiago, Chile: Cuerpos Pintados.
———. (2004). *Cameron: Volume 2* (MTF). Santiago, Chile: Cuerpos Pintados.
———. (2004). *Cameron: Correspondence (1997-2001).* Santiago, Chile: Cuerpos Pintados.

Index

CPSIA information can be obtained
at www.ICGtesting.com
Printed in the USA
LVHW021623120219
607290LV00002B/221/P